CASEY

The Remarkable, Untold Story of
Frederick Walker "Casey" Baldwin
Gentleman, Genius, and Alexander Graham Bell's Canadian Protegé

John G. Langley
Foreword by Sean Baldwin

NIMBUS
PUBLISHING
— NIMBUS.CA —

Nimbus Publishing Limited
3660 Strawberry Hill Street, Halifax, NS, B3K 5A9
(902) 455-4286 nimbus.ca

Printed and bound in Canada
NB1446

Design: John van der Woude, JVDW Designs
Editor: Marianne Ward
Front cover (top): Casey at controls of White Wing; Front cover (bottom): Casey piloting HD-4 to world water speed record, Baddeck, N.S., September 9, 1919; Back cover (right): Frederick Walker "Casey" Baldwin, c. 1908; Back cover (left): Official opening of Casey's tetrahedral tower atop Red Head, August 31, 1907. All cover images courtesy of Alexander Graham Bell Museum.

Library and Archives Canada Cataloguing in Publication
Title: Casey : the remarkable, untold story of Frederick Walker "Casey" Baldwin : gentleman, genius, and Alexander Graham Bell's Canadian protegé / John G. Langley ; foreword by Sean Baldwin.
Other titles: Remarkable, untold story of Frederick Walker "Casey" Baldwin
Names: Langley, John G., author.
Identifiers: Canadiana (print) 20190139463 | Canadiana (ebook) 20190139501 | ISBN 9781771088039 (softcover) | ISBN 9781771088046 (HTML)
Subjects: LCSH: Baldwin, Frederick Walker, 1882-1948. | LCSH: Aeronautical engineers—Canada—Biography. | LCSH: Flight—History—20th century. | LCGFT: Biographies.
Classification: LCC TL540.B394 L36 2019 | DDC 629.130092—dc23

Nimbus Publishing acknowledges the financial support for its publishing activities from the Government of Canada, the Canada Council for the Arts, and from the Province of Nova Scotia. We are pleased to work in partnership with the Province of Nova Scotia to develop and promote our creative industries for the benefit of all Nova Scotians.

To my sons Adam Craig and Andrew Kyle

Nova Scotians, sailors, gentlemen

Table of Contents

Foreword

My grandfather died before I arrived on the planet. Despite that fact, I spent a substantial part of my childhood in Casey's shadow. My pride in his achievements and my understanding of who he was as a man have been enhanced through photographs, old articles, artifacts, models, and most importantly stories from those who knew him.

Casey's life is truly unique from so many perspectives. I am sure you will enjoy his story.

Sean Baldwin
Baddeck Bay, NS
April 8, 2019

Preface

I, LIKE MANY OTHERS, HAVE HAD AN ABIDING INTEREST IN THE STORY of the Bells and Baddeck. Theirs is a story like none other, and it all happened right here in Cape Breton.

That said, I have always wondered about the red-roofed "bungalow," built on the brow of a hill halfway down the bay on the peninsula Alexander Graham Bell called Beinn Bhreagh and commonly described as "where Casey lived." Bell history seemed to revolve around the inventor and the local boy, J. A. D. (Douglas) McCurdy. Who was this man Casey, and how did he fit into the saga of Bell and Beinn Bhreagh?

I am so thankful that an opportunity led me to seek out the answer. This is *a* biography and not by any means *the* biography of a great Canadian—there is more that can and should be written about Frederick Walker "Casey" Baldwin. This modest effort is an attempt to shed light, long overdue, on an integral character in the history that is uniquely Baddeck's. Casey, however, by the time his life was over, belonged to Nova Scotia, to Canada—and the world.

As a long-time resident of Baddeck I have had the good fortune to befriend many of the Bell descendants. Apart from being good friends, they have provided great insight into the Bell family. It is only more recently that I have become acquainted with anyone from the Baldwin family. The decision by Casey's grandson Sean Baldwin and his wife, Deborah, to build a retirement home on Baddeck Bay changed all that. After learning about my abiding interest in his grandfather, Sean very graciously agreed to share papers from

Casey's estate to aid in my research. The result is this book, which is largely gleaned from literally hundreds of pieces of heretofore unseen Baldwin correspondence, as well as the Bell papers archived at the Alexander Graham Bell National Historic Site in Baddeck.

Here there is a veritable treasure trove of materials—hundreds of volumes of fascinating reading found in Bell's Home Notes, Lab Notes, AEA Bulletins, Beinn Bhreagh Recorder, Letter Books, and the Fairchild Papers. Leaving aside the Fairchild Papers (which represent many volumes of family correspondence), the other sources are recordings that were for internal use, often as a means of keeping Bell and his associates at Beinn Bhreagh aware of what was happening between Baddeck and Washington where the Bells customarily spent winter. Home Notes (1879–1922) were written daily in the form of a diary by Bell, workers, associates, and secretaries and described Bell's experiments and observations. Much the same with Lab Notes, which cover the 1880s to 1910. The AEA Bulletins diarized the eighteen months of experimentation during the lifespan of the Aerial Experiment Association (AEA). The Beinn Bhreagh Recorder noted developments in Bell's scientific research and family events from 1909 to 1923. The Letter Books include 127 binders of letters between Bell and colleagues, family, etc. Finally, Dictated Notes (1899–1904) represent a modest collection of Bell notations and photographs, mostly aviation related.

Inexplicitly, a biography, the story of Frederick Walker "Casey" Baldwin, has never before been written. Perhaps the closest anyone has come to this was J. H. Parkin, an engineer and consultant to the National Research Council of Canada, in his book *Bell and Baldwin: Their Development of Aerodromes and Hydrodromes at Baddeck, Nova Scotia*, published in 1964. Casey was a truly remarkable individual who left an indelible mark in the annals of Canadian aviation and marine history. It is no credit to the country of his birth that his story has been largely unknown for so long. This book is an effort to redress that oversight.

One possible explanation for this shortcoming is the fact that the story of Casey Baldwin cannot be told in isolation. His is really the story of "the Bells, Baldwin, and Baddeck." It represents a heretofore missing link—a central chapter in the Bell saga. It is also a love story. A love that is multifaceted but shares a common thread. It is about the love shared between Alexander Graham Bell and his wife, Mabel; the love between Casey and his wife, Kathleen, and ultimately their children; and finally the undisguised and transparent love of the Bells for the Baldwins. Among it all is a golden thread, a mutual unremitting love for Cape Breton and the Bras d'Or Lakes.

Casey's story is about people and personalities, people whose characters were shaped and defined by circumstance. It is a story of true genius, of epic accomplishment, and of epic failure to seize upon those achievements by a country too complacent about success and too indifferent about going its own way.

For me, the research and writing of this book also became a personal journey, one of pride and remembrance. My family on my father's side has roots in Cape Breton dating back to the mid-1700s. My great-grandmother was an Embree, part of a family of highly skilled shipbuilders, many of whom settled in Port Hawkesbury in the nineteenth century. The venerable Port Hawkesbury firm of H. W. Embree and Sons was well known to Alexander Graham Bell and produced a number of vessels for the Bell family including Alec's favourite hideaway, the houseboat *Mabel of Beinn Bhreagh* and Mabel's motor yacht *Kia Ora*. Many a carefree day in my youth was spent playing in the old abandoned Embree boat shop on the shore of "Ship Harbour."

My wife and two sons will always remember with great fondness the two summers we spent at Driftwood, the cottage at Crescent Grove built by the Bells for Georgina McCurdy, Douglas McCurdy's aunt, early in the twentieth century. The cottage was virtually unchanged from when it was originally built and included a small library containing a reproduction of the AEA Bulletins that kept me up reading many a night in the soft glow from the fireplace. We also enjoyed the company of our landlord, Joseph Jones, widower of Lillian Grosvenor, a granddaughter of Mabel and Alec Bell, who was camped in the boathouse beside Driftwood. Thanks to his efforts the Langley family spent a remarkable summer afternoon having tea with "Doctor Mabel," the Bells' granddaughter, in the Great Hall in the Point house where the Bells' presence is still very palpable.

Casey's story is broad, involving many elements and large subjects in their own right. It is impossible to explore those subjects in any detail within the constraints of a single volume; however, every attempt has been made to interpret the facts gleaned through extensive research. Any errors made and views expressed are entirely those of the author, for whom it has been a privilege and pleasure to compose a biography of a great, unheralded figure in Canadian history.

Honour to whom honour is due. It's about time.

John G. Langley, Q. C.
Baddeck, Nova Scotia
March 8, 2019

Timeline

1847   Alexander Graham Bell (AGB) born in Edinburgh, Scotland

1857   Mabel Gardiner Hubbard born in Cambridge, Massachusetts

1863   Mabel contracts scarlet fever and becomes deaf

1877   AGB and Mabel are wed

1878   Elsie May is born to AGB and Mabel

1880   Marian Hubbard ("Daisy") born to AGB and Mabel

1881   Edward born to AGB and Mabel; dies following premature birth

1882   Frederick Walker "Casey" Baldwin born in Toronto to Robert and Elizabeth Walker Baldwin

1883   Robert is born to AGB and Mabel, dies at birth

1885   Bells discover Baddeck, Cape Breton, after being shipwrecked in Newfoundland

1886   J. A. D. McCurdy born in Baddeck

1900   Elsie Bell weds Gilbert H. Grosvenor

          F. W. Baldwin enrolls at University of Toronto (U of T)

1905   "Casey" Baldwin is captain of U of T football team, which wins the Dominion Championship

1906   Casey graduates with degree in mechanical engineering; is introduced to Bells at Beinn Bhreagh by J. A. D. McCurdy

1907   Formation of Aerial Experiment Association (AEA) by AGB, Baldwin, McCurdy, Thomas Selfridge, and Glenn Curtiss

1908   AEA designs, constructs, and successfully test flies four "dromes" at Hammondsport, New York; Casey is the first Canadian to fly a heavier-than-air machine

Casey weds Kathleen Stewart Parmenter

1909   Silver Dart, with J. A. D. McCurdy as pilot, becomes first heavier-than-air machine to fly in British Empire, at Baddeck, Nova Scotia

Establishment of Canadian Aerodrome Company and Aerodrome Park; birth of Canadian aviation industry

Tests of Silver Dart at Camp Petawawa, Ontario; the first passenger flight in Canada

1910–11 Baldwins accompany Bells on world tour; McCurdy barnstorms in USA

1912   Casey with his sailboat *Scrapper* wins Coronation Cup in Sydney, NS

1913   Casey made manager of Beinn Bhreagh estate

Robert Parmenter Baldwin born to Casey and Kathleen

1915   Elizabeth "Betty" Baldwin born to Casey and Kathleen

1918   Casey made Honorary Commodore of Bras d'Or Yacht Club

1919   Casey sets world speed record for a watercraft at Baddeck, NS, with HD-4; establishment of Bell-Baldwin Hydrodromes Limited

1920   Casey and William Nutting cross Atlantic in ketch *Typhoon*

1921   Patrick Alexander Graham Bell Baldwin born to Casey and Kathleen

1922   AGB's health deteriorates; he dies and is buried at Beinn Bhreagh

1923   Mabel Bell dies at Chevy Chase, Maryland; buried alongside AGB at Beinn Bhreagh

1932   Betty Baldwin passes away from tuberculosis; brother Patrick recovers from TB

1933   Casey runs as a Conservative and is victorious in provincial election

1935   Casey crosses Atlantic aboard *Bluenose* with sons Robert and Patrick

1937   Casey elected president of Nova Scotia Conservative Association

1942   Robert Baldwin marries Maureen Mahoney; Casey Robert "Casey Bob" is born to them the following year

1946   Casey and J. A. D. McCurdy receive honorary degrees from Nova Scotia Technical College

1948   Frederick Walker "Casey" Baldwin dies at Beinn Bhreagh
1951   Patrick Sean is born to Maureen and Robert Baldwin
1955   Kathleen Deneen born to Maureen and Robert Baldwin
1959   Golden anniversary flight of Silver Dart at Baddeck, NS
1965   Kathleen Baldwin dies at Bedford, NS
1966   Robert Parmenter Baldwin dies at Halifax, NS
1974   Casey Baldwin inducted posthumously into Canadian Aviation
        Hall of Fame
1981   Maureen Baldwin dies at Beinn Bhreagh
1984   Patrick A. G. B. Baldwin dies at Halifax, NS
2009   Centenary of flight of Silver Dart at Baddeck; flight on Baddeck
        Bay by Silver Dart replica built by Aerial Experiment
        Association (2005); replica donated to Bell Museum in 2013
2019   Centenary of Casey Baldwin's world water speed record with HD-4
        celebrated at Baddeck, NS

CHAPTER 1

Paradise Found

A Book, a Boat, the Bells, and Baddeck

I have travelled around the globe. I have seen the Canadian and
American Rockies, the Andes, the Alps, and the Highlands of
Scotland, but for simple beauty, Cape Breton outrivals them all.
—Alexander Graham Bell

B Y THE SUMMER OF 1885, THE INVENTOR ALEXANDER GRAHAM
Bell and his wife, Mabel, were ready for a rest.

The past few years had been exceedingly busy for them both. The
seemingly endless patent litigation over the invention of the telephone continued unabated. In spite of that and with Mabel's backing, Bell had pressed
on with other inventions. The audiometer, devised as a means of measuring
hearing ability, gave birth to a word that incorporates Bell's name, *decibel*,
representing a unit of measuring sound and electric signals. His photophone
produced a wireless transmission, the precursor of modern fibre optics.

The Bells had purchased an expensive new home in Washington, and
money from the Volta Prize, some 50,000 francs awarded to Bell by the

French government for the invention of the telephone, had been used to finance a laboratory in Washington, the Volta Bureau, to promote research and invention to benefit the deaf.

Through it all the family had been beset with tragedy. On August 15, 1881, Mabel gave birth to a son, Edward, who was premature and died at childbirth. Undaunted, Alec and Mabel tried again and were rewarded with the birth of another son, Robert, on November 17, 1883. Tragically he too died at birth. Alec pressed on, focusing his energies on medical research, which resulted in the development of a vacuum jacket, an early version of the iron lung. Bell's metal detector, similar to today's ultrasound, attracted considerable attention when Bell employed it in an unsuccessful attempt to save the life of President James Abram Garfield, victim of an assassin's bullet.

Mabel's sister Berta, who had suffered from TB most of her life, passed away July 4, 1885, in childbirth. The Bells' plans for a European tour for their own rest and relaxation had been shelved due to the anxiety and uncertainty surrounding Berta's health. A European tour was a major proposition and not in the cards at this time. A compromise offered by Alec was accepted by Mabel. They decided on a much shorter cruise, accompanied by Alec's father Melville, to the colony of Newfoundland, where Melville had lived from 1838 to 1842 in an effort to improve his health. When Alec's father-in-law Gardiner Hubbard heard of the new plan, he asked Alec if he might consider a side trip to Nova Scotia en route. Gardiner was invested in the Caledonia mine at Glace Bay on Cape Breton Island, and Alec agreed to divert and inspect the mining operation there for Mabel's father. It was decided. Late in August, Alec, his father Melville, Mabel, daughters Elsie and Daisy, aged seven and five, and their nursemaid Nellie set off from Boston.

The routing was radically different now that a side trip to Nova Scotia was agreed upon. Rather than take an ocean steamer from New York or Halifax direct to Newfoundland, the troupe found themselves on a train from Halifax to the Strait of Canso, which separates mainland Nova Scotia from Cape Breton Island, and ultimately by the paddle steamer SS *Marion,* which transported them across the Bras d'Or Lakes to the quaint village of Baddeck, Cape Breton.

Alec had some inkling of what to expect, as he had read the book *Baddeck and That Sort of Thing,* written ten years earlier by Charles Dudley Warner, an American travel writer. Bell was already looking forward to meeting the proprietress of the Telegraph House Hotel and her daughter, Maud, whom

Warner had affectionately described in his travelogue. Soon after the steamer *Marion* was secured alongside the wharf in Baddeck, Alec and the others made their way up the hill for the short walk to the Telegraph House. Here Alec was greeted by Mrs. Dunlop, who represents the first of five generations of Dunlops who continue to run this historic establishment to this day. A fine meal, during which he made the acquaintance of the charming Maud, concluded what for Alec had been a most pleasant day and his introduction to the charm of the little village of Baddeck nestled away on the shore of the Bras d'Or. It was a moment that would change his life.

The entourage, after visiting the mines at Glace Bay, did eventually make their way to Newfoundland aboard the Allan Line steamer ss *Hanoverian*. It landed them in rather dramatic fashion when it ran ashore and became a total wreck near Trespassey Bay on the southeast coast. Fortunately there were no lives lost, but all the passengers, including the Bells, had to endure considerable hardship before their eventual "rescue" and transport to St. John's. After a week during which Alec spent most of this time looking after the shipwrecked passengers, they had had enough of Newfoundland. For Daisy and Elsie it was all a great adventure, but Alec and Mabel had seen enough; both harboured thoughts of Baddeck and yearned to return to Cape Breton.

By September 17 Mabel was writing in her journal from the cozy confines of the Telegraph House in Baddeck, while Alec and the girls were down on the Baddeck wharf fishing perch. Daisy and Elsie were having a grand time. Mabel wrote, "They both have enjoyed their travel immensely."

Alec was in his element and perfectly happy. Despite the challenges and hardships of the past two weeks he seemed to thrive. "He never looked so well, had such a fine, healthy sunburnt colouring or so good a figure since I have known him," Mabel wrote.

Both Alec and Mabel were fast becoming caught up in the charm and gentle ways of Baddeck, a peacefulness Mabel hoped it would never lose. She wrote, "Baddeck is certainly possessed of a gentle, restful beauty and I think we would be content to stay here many weeks just enjoying the lights and shades on the hills and isles and lakes....May it be long before fashionable people with their big hotels, big trunks, and high charges find their way here." And so they would stay there, not just for weeks, but for the rest of their natural lives.

One of the first Baddeckers to make Bell's acquaintance was Arthur McCurdy, editor of the local newspaper, the *Island Reporter*. The McCurdys were a well-established Baddeck family. When Arthur was nine years old, they had moved to Baddeck to take over the general store established by Arthur's uncle. By the time the Bells first arrived on the scene, Arthur had acquired his father's share in the store and was running the business along with his brother William.

Interestingly it was the telephone that brought Alexander Graham Bell and Arthur McCurdy together. Soon after first arriving in Baddeck, Alec found his way to the office of the *Island Reporter* where he was interested to see that there was a telephone. Apparently William McCurdy had seen the device at an exhibition in the USA and had bought a few sets to link the store with the family home and newspaper office. Arthur McCurdy, the editor, was at work here when Bell entered the premises and found McCurdy fidgeting with the telephone, which was not working. As the story goes, upon request, Arthur handed the receiver to Bell who found and removed a fly after unscrewing the end of the earpiece and removing the diaphragm. One can only imagine McCurdy's surprise when he learned that his guest was none other than the inventor of the telephone.

This proved to be a defining moment for both men. When Alec and the others returned to Baddeck from the ill-fated Newfoundland expedition, the friendship between Alec and Arthur McCurdy was renewed and nurtured, frequently over a game of chess and inspired by their common interest in invention. Before leaving Baddeck in the early fall of 1885, Mabel and Alec had determined to return and put down summer roots in Cape Breton. Arthur agreed to act as a go-between or agent in finding and negotiating the acquisition of property in the area for the inventor and his young family.

Soon after the Bells departed Baddeck, McCurdy set about finding a place to accommodate the family for their much anticipated return the next summer. He didn't have to look too long nor too far before locating a house "down the bay," a short distance outside the village of Baddeck at Crescent Grove, beside property owned by the McCurdy family.

The Bell family enjoyed a few wonderful, and for the young girls, adventuresome summers at Crescent Grove. The property was nicely situated on a rise overlooking Baddeck Bay and the wooded peninsula known as Red Head, which lay opposite. Alec and Mabel spent many a soft summer evening sitting out on their veranda looking over the water of the bay to the opposite shore. They were drawn to it and soon found their way over by horse and carriage for a closer look. What they saw was breathtaking views at every turn.

Alec and Mabel were completely captivated by Red Head, so much so that for the next number of years, and with the help of Arthur McCurdy, they went about purchasing virtually the entire peninsula. They would call it Beinn Bhreagh, Gaelic for "beautiful mountain."

While acquiring title to the various properties comprising Red Head, the Bells erected a building, designed by Arthur McCurdy, above the inlet off Baddeck Bay on Beinn Bhreagh, which they appropriately called "The Lodge." The Bells henceforth would have a name for everything relating or connected to their new mountain paradise. The Lodge was intended to provide temporary accommodation only while they consolidated lands and made plans for their ultimate home, which would soon rise from the promontory at the end of the peninsula.

The Bells' new home when finally completed in 1893 was described by the Halifax press as the finest mansion in eastern Canada (indeed, in 2018 it was designated a Provincial Heritage Property by the Province of Nova Scotia). Perched as it was at the very tip of Red Head, it had commanding views across the water to Baddeck and the Washabuck Peninsula. Here at last the Bells could escape the summer heat of their home in Washington in serene surroundings that reminded Alec so much of his native Scotland. It had been a busy few years, which had seen Mabel and Alec move from their renovated house in Crescent Grove to the newly built "Lodge" on Beinn Bhreagh, and finally taking occupancy of their new dream home on "The Point." It was now time for Alec to get back to his own work.

Arthur McCurdy and his family had quickly become very near and dear to the Bell family. Arthur, as the Bells soon learned, was a man of extraordinary talents and interests. Within two years of first meeting Alec and shortly after the McCurdy family business went into bankruptcy due to economic decline, Arthur McCurdy became Bell's private secretary, a position he held for fifteen years. He took daily dictation of Bell's thoughts in Lab Notes and Home Notes, designations that indicated where each book was kept. He worked regularly with Bell on experiments and became one of two assistants to Bell when he reopened his laboratory in Washington in 1889. Arthur and Bell shared a common interest in photography, and McCurdy became the first employee to visually record the inventor's experiments and activities. Arthur's passion for photography peaked when in 1899 he invented a small portable tank for developing film in daytime called Ebedek (the

Mi'kmaw name for Baddeck), popularly used by photographers for generations. Spurred on by encouragement and financial assistance from Bell, McCurdy obtained a patent for his invention in 1902, following which he sold the rights to Eastman Kodak.

Arthur and his wife, Lucy, had four children: a daughter, Susie, and three sons—George, John Alexander Douglas, and Lucien, who was but a week old when on March 25, 1888, Lucy passed away. Arthur now found himself sole caregiver and provider for four children, the oldest of whom, Susie, was just seven years of age; Douglas was not yet two at the time. Fortunately, Arthur had an unmarried sister, Georgina, who stepped in and raised the children. By this time the Bells' association with the McCurdy family had become very close. In fact, Mabel and Alec wished to adopt young Douglas, a plan that was thwarted by Aunt Georgina who made it quite clear that "Arthur's children were born McCurdys and would die McCurdys." Nonetheless, the McCurdy children spent much of their youth growing up in and around the Bells' Baddeck home, Beinn Bhreagh.

Although adoption had been ruled out, Alec and Mabel treated Douglas as a son. When he was seven, the Bells took Douglas with them to Washington for the year. Long afterwards, as he neared the end of his life, Douglas McCurdy would relate that, as a trial placement, things worked out very well; however, back in Baddeck Aunt Georgina prevailed, and the Arthur McCurdy family remained intact under her care. She proved to be a good mother to them, but in spite of her best efforts to raise her brother's children "as McCurdys," they spent virtually all of their time at Beinn Bhreagh. There they helped out with Bell's experiments, in the process becoming nearer and dearer to Alec and Mabel, effectively becoming part of their extended family.

In an odd twist of fate, it was Douglas McCurdy who would become responsible for introducing Frederick Walker "Casey" Baldwin to the Bells and Baddeck.

MABEL WAS AN ASTUTE, HIGHLY ORGANIZED BUSINESSWOMAN WHO single-handedly managed what became the Bell Estate—a working farm and enclave with various "departments" employing dozens of locals from Baddeck and the surrounding countryside. She took care of business and was largely responsible for the care and upbringing of Daisy and Elsie. This in turn freed up Alec and allowed him to devote his time almost exclusively to inventiveness, always with Mabel's support and encouragement.

For some time now Bell had been infatuated with the concept of flight. He was first introduced to this subject by his good friend Samuel Pierpont Langley (no relation of mine, at least that I know of), pioneer of American aviation, who was secretary of the Smithsonian Institution and a regular visitor to the Bell home in Washington. Langley's experiments with unmanned "aerodromes" launched from houseboats in the Potomac River in Virginia were an inspiration to Alec. After watching a sixteen-foot-long unmanned biplane launched by catapult from atop a houseboat in 1895, Bell wrote to his friend, "I shall count this day as one of the most memorable in my life." And so it was. From that moment on, Bell became preoccupied with the potential for manned fight.

It wasn't long before Baddeckers bore witness to the sights and sounds emanating from the Bell laboratories at Beinn Bhreagh. Bell was a firm believer that tetrahedral cells—four-sided cells in which each side is an equilateral triangle—could be employed in the construction of kites that were strong, light, and could ultimately be manned and powered by an engine. He was consumed by his belief that kites, if they could be "flown" and landed on water, were far safer and more stable than biplanes, which he felt exposed their pilots to far greater risk in test flights. Bell was predisposed to safety consciousness. In his way of thinking, kites permitted him to experiment in flight without risk to human life. To quote Bell, "the great difficulty in developing an art of aerial locomotion lies…in the difficulty of profiting by past experience. A dead man tells no tales."

His decision to proceed with powered kites convinced Bell of his need of engineering knowledge for their design and construction. The Bells therefore decided that they would underwrite the costs of educating young Douglas McCurdy and his brother Lucien at St. Andrew's College, a private school that first opened its doors in 1899 at Chestnut Park in Toronto.

Laboratories were built on the Beinn Bhreagh estate and staffed by men and women from Baddeck and the surrounding area. For everyone it was a case of learning on the job, as no one had any prior experience in this kind of work. Those Bell employed proved very much up to the assigned tasks. They were a very talented and devoted workforce. Bell became one of the biggest employers in the area.

By 1905 the Bells had become integrated into the Baddeck community, and local residents had become accustomed to the sights and sounds of Beinn Bhreagh. At that point there were more than forty people working in Alec's laboratories. Each day most would be picked up in Baddeck and taken across the bay to Red Head by water taxi—Bell's motorboat, *Gauldrie*. When Bell's experimentation with tetrahedral kites was at its peak, the men typically were engaged in construction while the women were responsible for cutting and sewing the imported red silk over the kite frames.

With his sixtieth birthday nearing, a visibly aging Alec Bell confided to his wife that some new and younger blood was necessary to encourage and assist in further experimentation. Mabel, ever watchful of both the mental and physical demands upon her husband, was of the same mind. Douglas McCurdy, whose education they continued to finance, was now at the University of Toronto. Mabel wrote to Douglas early in 1906 asking if he could possibly recruit any of his fellow engineering students to come to Baddeck and help Alec with tetrahedral constructions. Her intervention on behalf of her husband would have profound results and change the course of history.

CHAPTER 2

Frederick Walker "Casey" Baldwin

Blueblood

T HE NAME BALDWIN IS SYNONYMOUS WITH POLITICS IN CANADA—not what became the Dominion of Canada in 1867 but rather what prior to then was somewhat confusingly referred to as the Province of Canada, which was created by the Act of Union in 1841 of Upper Canada (Canada West) and Lower Canada (Canada East).

The politician who gave fame to the surname was Robert Baldwin, born May 12, 1804, in York, which became Toronto. Robert's parents—Margaret Phoebe Willcocks and William Baldwin, an Irish-born doctor turned lawyer, judge, and politician—had high expectations for him, and his character was shaped by their continual exhortation to "goodness and correct conduct." In 1827 he married his first cousin, Augusta Elizabeth Sullivan. The marriage, however, was short-lived; Augusta died in 1836, shortly after giving birth by caesarian section to their fourth child, a son also named Robert.

The senior Robert Baldwin's resolve and sense of duty, ingrained in him from birth, remained steadfast. He entered politics despite the fact that he disliked and was seldom comfortable in the political arena. It seems, however, that he was destined to succeed. Soon Robert and his father, William, were playing leading roles in the move toward responsible government. After joining the executive council of Upper Canada in 1836, Robert was appointed Solicitor General in 1840 and became a political ally with his counterpart in Lower Canada, a French Canadian by the name of Louis-Hippolyte LaFontaine. Their friendship, conceived amid a harsh political battlefield, was enduring and personal. Robert Baldwin was convinced that bilingualism was the only way that bringing French and English Canada together would work in practice as well as theory. His belief was soon put to the test. Soon after the 1841 Act of Union, Baldwin introduced resolutions on responsible government in the House of Assembly. Over the next few years, the "great experiment" proved to be more difficult to take root than had been hoped.

In 1848 LaFontaine was called upon to form a new government by Lord Elgin, the Governor General, thus for the first time acknowledging the principle of responsible government. He agreed to do so on the condition that Robert Baldwin be appointed with him to serve as co-premier of the United Province of Canada. Baldwin agreed and served in this capacity with LaFontaine until 1851 when he was defeated in North York and resigned from office. Upon his death in 1858, Robert Baldwin left a political legacy that would shape the fortunes of an emerging country. A decade later, the nation of Canada was created by Confederation.

Baldwin's son Robert, born in 1834, lacked his father's high sense of moral duty. After completing studies at the seminary in Quebec City, Robert was sent with his brother Wilcocks to Toronto's Upper Canada College. He survived his education to please his father but had no interest in politics or profession. Instead, he went to sea and thus earned the differentiating nickname of "Robert the Sailor." He took up navigation at a school in Glasgow and by 1856 was sailing between Quebec City and Liverpool as captain of the *Bramley Moore*.

Sadly Robert the Sailor's career at sea was ended almost as soon as it had begun. In 1858 he returned home suffering from polio and became bedridden at the same time as his father's health was in serious decline. Now home from sea permanently, Robert found time to take a wife and in 1859 married Jemima MacDougall. This union produced six children, four boys and two girls. Jemima died in 1873, and in 1877 "Bob" remarried. He and Elizabeth Mary Walker had four children. The third, Frederick Walker Baldwin—who became known as Casey—was born January 2, 1882, in the year between the births and deaths of Alec and Mabel Bell's only sons, Edward (1881) and Robert (1883). Bob was never the role model that Casey's famous grandfather had been. He had found religion and became a familiar figure preaching on Toronto street corners until his death in 1885, when Casey was just three years old.

Little is known of Casey's early life. He was raised by his mother, who made sure that her son received a good education. He was educated at Ridley College, one of Canada's oldest and most prestigious boarding schools, located in St. Catharines, Ontario. The school was founded in 1889 by a group of Anglican clergymen seeking to provide boys in Ontario with an education that emphasized strong academic and religious values. Casey began his secondary education there in 1893 under the supervision of the school's first headmaster, the Reverend Dr. John Ormsby Miller, a highly regarded scholar and administrator.

The school's overall curriculum, then and now, emphasizes a balanced and disciplined combination of academics, athletics, school involvement, and community service—the school motto is *Terar dum prosim,* "May I be consumed in service." While a student there, Casey more than achieved the objectives of the curriculum as well as the lofty motto. He held prominent student leadership roles, won the Blake Gold Medal, and was captain of the school cricket team. It was at Ridley that the nickname Casey was given to him. In the June 10, 1933, edition of the *Halifax Herald,* the renowned Canadian author and historian Dr. Archibald MacMechan explained how Casey acquired this moniker.

> One man is known all over Canada by his nickname. Though he was christened Frederick Walker, few of his friends and acquaintances know what the initials F. W. stand for. To friends and acquaintances (and they are many) and to his enemies (if he has any) he is simply "Casey" Baldwin, perhaps the most popular man in the Dominion. His nickname goes back to an "eminent baseball virtuoso" of the city of Boston in the last century and to the once famous song "Casey at the Bat." It is a compliment to his prowess in all manly games and was acquired while he was a schoolboy at Ridley. The Irish soubriquet is not unfitting, for the first Baldwin in Canada came from Ireland.

Casey's next stop was the University of Toronto, Canada's largest university. The Baldwin family, notably Robert Baldwin "the reformer," has left its mark on the evolution of this venerable institution. It was originally founded as King's College by royal charter in 1827 by the colonial establishment and the Church of England. Reforms advanced during the Baldwin–LaFontaine ministry in the Province of Canada included a scheme to secularize the Anglican King's College as the University of Toronto, which came into being January 1, 1850.

Casey entered U of T at the turn of the century, in 1900, with a challenge—to carry on his brilliant academic and athletic achievements. He didn't disappoint. First enrolled as an Arts student, the following year Casey transferred to the School of Practical Science. In the spring of 1906 he graduated with a degree in Mechanical-Electrical Engineering. Sadly Casey's mother didn't survive to see him graduate; she passed away in 1903.

As an alumnus of U of T Casey was best remembered for his unmatched athletic skills. During his time there he became the consummate all round athlete. He played cricket and baseball and was a member of the University Gymnastic Club. He played golf and fenced. He was vice-president of the University Athletic Directorate from 1904 to 1906.

Undoubtedly Casey's greatest contribution to athletics at U of T was as a football player. While there he became a legend in that sport. As a freshman in 1901 he played on the Junior School team, while at the same time was a halfback on the Senior University Team, which went through that season undefeated and won the 1901 intercollegiate championship. During the next few years, the school team with Casey on it continued to win intercollegiate and city championships. During that time the team was described as having the "best back division" in Canada, led by Casey.

The pinnacle of Casey's football career occurred in 1905 when, captained by Casey, the U of T football team won everything—all the intercollegiate games as well as the Dominion Championship, when it defeated the Ottawa Rough Riders. It was a classic finish to the Dominion final, the forerunner to Canada's Grey Cup, when with the score 9–6 in favour of Ottawa and with only minutes left in the game, Casey used a ruse to score the final touchdown, giving his team an 11–9 victory and the national title.

Casey became the inaugural recipient of the University of Toronto's "First Colour" when the award was instituted in 1905. His fame on the gridiron was also immortalized in song at the university.

'Twas Casey Baldwin; 'twas Casey Baldwin,
The finest half Toronto'll ever see,
'Twas Casey Baldwin; 'twas Casey Baldwin,
'Twas Mister Casey Baldwin, U of T.

It was a fitting way to end his time at U of T. In addition to his athletic prowess, the other thing that set Casey apart was his consummate sportsmanship. Casey always played to win but not at any cost. He was always modest in victory. In the Ridley College archives is this undated description of Casey by one of his contemporaries:

Casey was a superior athlete. He often won. He is considered to this day one of Canada's top ten football players. He was captain of football, hockey, and rugby throughout Ridley and all through U of T. But it was how he built a team and lost or won a match that made him remarkable. He was competitive, mostly against himself. When he won he was modest; he never boasted of his achievements. This, in part, explains why you have never heard of him! He was modest, self-effacing, and shared all accolades, which is why he was a great team builder. It was no surprise he was captain of most teams he played. He was always the first, whether he won or lost, over the line, across the field or the gym floor to congratulate the opposing challenger with a warm handshake. He was always and in all ways, fair and honest. So, it does matter how you treat others, no matter if you win or lose the game.

Casey Baldwin was inducted into the University of Toronto Sports Hall of Fame in 1989.

This kind of person, although quiet and unassuming, does attract attention. It was now spring of 1906 and Casey was graduating from his studies in mechanical-electrical engineering. During his final years at U of T Casey had developed an interest in manned flight. On December 17, 1903, the Wright brothers had successfully flown a heavier-than-air machine (i.e., an aircraft weighing more than the air it displaces, requiring lift by aerodynamic means) near Kitty Hawk in North Carolina, and the world was riveted on the concept of man taking to the air.

Recently published papers by two American pioneers in flight—Octave Chanute and Samuel Pierpont Langley—had attracted Casey's attention, so much so that he and another student spent some time in the university drafting room designing Casey's own idea of a flying machine. In an ironic twist, Casey was reprimanded by his instructor in the engineering department "for wasting class time on such foolishness." Undaunted, Casey persisted with his new-found passion. And within a few short months he would become the first Canadian to fly.

Although he was far removed from Nova Scotia, Casey was well-read enough to have heard about experiments in manned flight being carried on in Cape Breton by the now world-famous inventor of the telephone, Alexander Graham Bell. Casey had also learned more about Bell and his work from a school chum from Baddeck by the name of Douglas McCurdy, also an engineering student at U of T.

The course of history was about to change, although neither McCurdy nor Casey knew it at the time. Douglas, who had virtually grown up on Beinn Bhreagh as the next thing to a son to the Bells, had received a letter from Mabel in which she asked him to keep a lookout for anyone he knew at U of T who might like an opportunity to work with her inventor husband. That spring of 1906 McCurdy casually posed this question to Casey as he was preparing to leave the university after graduation. No one knows what other plans Casey may have had for himself post-university. He was, however, sufficiently intrigued with this offer that within days he and McCurdy were on the train heading east to Nova Scotia, which heretofore Casey had only known as a place on the map of the Dominion of Canada. Little did he know then that it was there he would spend the rest of his life.

CHAPTER 3

Homecoming at Baddeck

I T WAS LATE SPRING OF 1906 AS CASEY BALDWIN AND HIS COLLEGE chum Douglas McCurdy made their way east by train. McCurdy was heading home. Casey was leaving home and heading off into the unknown, to a far distant place in Cape Breton at the invitation of a man he only knew by name—the world-renowned inventor Alexander Graham Bell.

It was an awesome time for Casey, just twenty-four years old and fresh out of college with his degree in engineering. Douglas would have been considerable comfort to him and able to allay any of his misgivings due to his lifelong relationship to the Bells. Still, Casey was leaving family and friends behind, none the least of which was a young lady by the name of Kathleen Stewart Parmenter.

McCurdy was going home for the summer. He still had one more year at U OF T before obtaining his engineering degree. Casey, having now secured his, was moving ahead with his life. His interest in aeronautics, developed in his latter years at university, was piqued by the invitation to visit Bell at Beinn Bhreagh near the village of Baddeck. Casey knew from conversations with Douglas that the great inventor had been experimenting there in an endeavour to produce a powered kite employing tetrahedral cell construction.

Casey's interest in flight was more than theoretical. Anxious to expand his knowledge, he had already enrolled in a summer session at Cornell University in Ithaca, New York, where he was planning to take four shop courses in the Mechanic Arts Department. In the meantime the opportunity now given to him to meet the man who was pioneering flight in Canada was almost too good to be true, and Casey was no doubt both nervous and excited.

McCurdy and Baldwin arrived in Baddeck that spring in much the same fashion as the Bells first had back in 1885. After leaving the train at Iona, the steamer *Marion* carried them down the Bras d'Or Lakes, rounded Washabuck Peninsula, and with the Bell mansion atop Red Head looming to starboard, tied up at the government wharf on the Baddeck waterfront. It would turn out to be a homecoming for both McCurdy and Baldwin.

Mabel Bell was not at Beinn Bhreagh when Casey arrived. She was home in Washington preparing to look after her new grandson, Alexander Graham Bell "Sandy" Fairchild, born to David and Daisy Fairchild on August 17, 1906. Alec was on his own at Beinn Bhreagh. It was clearly a frustrating time for Mabel who had to rely on sporadic correspondence from her husband to learn what he thought and how he was getting along with the new engineering graduate from Toronto. On June 22, 1906, she wrote to Alec, "I hope you will like Mr. Baldwin and will get to work nicely. I am so mad I couldn't be there to help things along. Oh dear, it is so hard to have to stay here doing nothing when there is such lots for me to do in Beinn Bhreagh. Please, please get up early and go to bed early." The following day, June 23, she wrote again. "I am going to spend the night with Daisy so goodbye. I hope you like Mr. Baldwin." Clearly Mabel was waiting each day for word from Alec. Her impatience was showing when she wrote yet again on June 27: "No letters yet and no telegrams even from you directly. Can't you tell me how you like Douglas's friend and how things are going? I am anxious to know."

In fact Alec had written. A letter to Mabel dated June 25 probably crossed hers in the mail. Mabel would have been heartened by the news and Bell's first observations of Casey Baldwin. "I am very much pleased with the appearance of Mr. Baldwin and think it very likely I may make some arrangements with him. I have had no conversation with him yet upon the subject, but should I find him capable of taking up the question of reinforced concrete I think it might be worthwhile having him conduct experiments with steel structures."

Casey was thoroughly taken in by Bell, Beinn Bhreagh, and Baddeck. Casey's honest, down-to-earth manner, as well as his avowed intention to work along with Mr. Bell, is readily apparent from a personal letter dated July 17, 1906, that he sent to Mabel during the course of his studies at Cornell.

Dear Mrs. Bell,

I hope it is not altogether too late to thank you both for your hospitality and the privilege of meeting Dr. Bell. The gratitude that I feel is very hard to express, and I hope you will understand it without my telling.

It is indeed a rare opportunity for me to be in any way associated with a man like Dr. Bell, but I fear that if I tried to tell you just how much I appreciated that opportunity and how grateful I am to you for it, you might think that I am a boy inclined to gush. This is an impression I would hate to give so will not attempt to even at the risk of being considered ungrateful.

I was particularly sorry to leave Baddeck without meeting you but look forward with great pleasure to the time when I may thank you in person for all your kindness. Beinn Bhreagh in itself would be delightful anywhere, but situated as it is, with all its beautiful surroundings and facilities for sailing, etc., I think it is ideal.

There was not a dull moment during my very pleasant visit, not even when Douglas was in his usual morning stupor, and the only anxious one (which must have been much more so for the rest of the party) was when Dr. Bell almost got me to sing.

The authorities at Cornell were very obliging in giving me just the work I wanted. My time between eight and five is divided between the foundry, forge, and machine shops, with one lecture on machine shop practice. This is delivered by the superintendent as tersely and ungrammatically as it is practical. However, the instruction is very good and I hope to pick up a few things that may be of use to me before returning about the middle of August to the interesting work that Dr. Bell contemplates carrying out and to which I look forward keenly.

Remember me to everybody at Beinn Bhreagh where I enjoyed myself very much indeed and look back longingly.

Allow me to thank you again, Mrs. Bell, and believe me to be very sincerely

Yours
F. W. Baldwin

This letter is provided in its entirety for a number of reasons. Of all the reams of correspondence emanating from the Bell estate, this piece, as it relates to Casey Baldwin, is of particular significance. He wrote it to Mrs. Bell, not to Alec, and in doing so immediately established a connection, the kernel of a bond that would grow between him and the Bells. It is also clear from his carefully chosen words that Casey was committing himself to work alongside Mabel's husband at Beinn Bhreagh where Casey had already established roots. In the simplest of terms, this letter is tantamount to a blueprint for Casey Baldwin's future.

It must have been considerable comfort to Mabel, as were endorsements of Casey by other family members. Letters she wrote to Alec late in August after Casey had returned to work at Beinn Bhreagh speak to this. "Charlie [Charles Bell, Alec's cousin, married to Mabel's sister Grace] thinks very highly of Mr. Baldwin," she wrote. "He says he certainly has ability and thinks that he could help you more than Mr. Bedwin [superintendent at Beinn Bhreagh]."

Mabel, the businesswoman, suggests to Alec they should be prepared to pay good money for good help, and so it should be with Mr. Baldwin. "If you like him I'd be generous and make him feel it's worth his while to stay with you. We have the money to spend. There is no need to live on just our income. The children have enough and you've given away enough. Don't count dollars and cents but get what you want." On August 26 she wrote again, clearly of the mind that Casey was their man. "I hope you will press Mr. Baldwin into service. I think your commonest workman should all be graduates of mechanical schools. Charlie was very favourably impressed by him; he thinks that he has ability and that he is an all round fine fellow who could help you. Don't be afraid to pay him well if on trial you like him. I am sure you need someone."

Mabel wasn't letting up on the subject. A few days later she wrote Alec again, this time talking about potentially utilizing Baldwin's engineering skills in tetrahedral cell construction. Once again she quotes Charles Bell. "He

[Casey] impressed him as a gentleman, a college graduate, a man of energy and intelligence, and he [Charles] would be glad to introduce him to his friends and people who would be likely to take hold of it."

On September 2 Mabel wrote to Alec to say that her sister Grace had just arrived back in Washington from Beinn Bhreagh, where she too had met and was favourably impressed by Casey. "Grace spoke of Mr. Baldwin's admiration for you; he thinks you something tremendous. You see this is sincere, for he has evidently been expressing himself in strong terms."

Alec by this time had already made up his mind and needed no further convincing. Casey was taken on. On September 29, 1906, Alec wrote in Home Notes that Douglas McCurdy had left that morning for Toronto to begin his final year at U of T. "Mr. Baldwin remains with me as a general assistant for a year, salary to be $50 per month and board for the present."

Mabel wrote to her daughter Daisy at this time describing the close friendship between Casey and Douglas. "Father seems well and happy. Douglas goes Saturday and I will mourn, but Mr. Baldwin remains one year—whatever shall I do with him without his *Fides Archates* Douglas? The affection between the two is wonderful—never imagined two fellows could be so fond of one another. Please write him; he will be lonely in Toronto." Mabel needn't have worried about Casey. He soon became part of their lives as neither the Bells nor Casey could have imagined.

Throughout the fall of 1906 Casey was constantly at Bell's side working on different concepts for the use of tetrahedral design in water-borne craft. Bell enjoyed the exchange of ideas and banter back and forth with his young protegé. They shared a common enthusiasm for their work, and there were no set hours. Casey soon got used to the idea that Bell was a night owl, preferring to work through the night and take his rest during daytime. On October 20 Alec and Casey spent an all-nighter together aboard the *Mabel of Beinn Bhreagh*, Bell's hideaway houseboat where he often took refuge for his work. There, between midnight and 6:00 A.M., "some important ideas concerning boat construction were developed as a result of discussion with Mr. Baldwin," wrote Bell, "and it may be well therefore while the matter is fresh in my mind to note the progression of thoughts as they took place, for I am inclined to think that improved form of boat construction may result."

Multi-tasking was something that Casey quickly learned was commonplace in work around the Bell laboratories at Beinn Bhreagh. It often seemed that no sooner was an idea conceived than a model was built, followed in very short order by the working structure. Typical was the project involving boat design that kept Alec and Casey up all night in mid-October aboard Bell's houseboat. By the next day they had built a scale model, and as Alec wrote in Home Notes, "On November 9 a tetrahedral boat was launched when Mabel poured water over her bow while she said, 'I name thee Bedwin's Baldwin.' The large motorboat to be named the 'Baldwin' could not be made in time for me to experiment with her, so Bedwin rushed a 7.5 motorboat through, of strong material substantially on the lines of the proposed Baldwin but made of small tetrahedral cells. We have therefore called her 'Bedwin's Baldwin.'"

As an indication of the respect he had for the young engineer's talents, Alec proposed that Casey design and construct a tower atop Beinn Bhreagh as a means of demonstrating the inherent strength and viability of tetrahedral construction. Plans began in earnest for the design of "Outlook Tower." On November 1, 1906, Alec wrote in Home Notes, "This evening gave Mr. Baldwin a cheque for one thousand dollars to build a lookout tower at his own expense on Beinn Bhreagh to illustrate tetrahedral construction. His wooden model is almost completed—it is now in the Kite House. The structure will be about eighty feet high, and there will be a magnificent view from the top."

Mabel wrote to her mother on November 11, 1906, obviously very pleased with how Casey was fitting in.

We are quite swell these days with the grandson of one of Canada's great statesmen working in our forge…and another of the shining lights of Toronto University [McCurdy] on the way here. It is such a lovely thing for me to see my husband at last, before it is too late, working in company with a capable young man who so thoroughly believes in him and his latest invention that he is staking his whole future on it and is bringing his friends in also. This young fellow Mr. Baldwin is building a lookout tower for Alec on top of the mountain. It would be a great piece of extravagance, but Alec must have his system worked out practically so as to learn by practical experience its weak points and remedy them, that we may go before the commercial world ready to begin with the assurance of success. This young man is coming in with his friends, and he is as enthusiastic and confident as Alec and has inspired his friends with the like enthusiasm. Isn't this nice?

Outlook Tower was quite a test of Casey's engineering skills. Just fresh out of college and lacking any practical experience, he was now contracted by the world's foremost inventor to design and construct a novel structure in a harsh environment, employing a radical tetrahedral fabrication process. Bell had already demonstrated the utility of the tetrahedral cell as a structural unit in the construction of kites, observation huts, and most recently, boats. Now he wished to take advantage of the opportunity presented by Casey's arrival to demonstrate in a spectacular way the utility of the cell in stationary structures. It would also be a test of Casey's own ability and Bell's faith in him as an assistant. Bell left the entire matter, including completion date and formal opening of the tower, in Casey's hands.

The tower was quite a feat of engineering and like all things happening at Beinn Bhreagh was made entirely on-site by local workmen and women, in this case with oversight by Casey Baldwin. The tower was composed of three seventy-two-foot legs arising from a triangular base. Each leg was constructed of four-foot tetrahedral cells made of half-inch galvanized wrought iron pipe threaded into tapped corner connectors of cast iron. Some 260 of these cells were used in construction of the three legs and top, an observation platform. One leg carried a wooden stair up to the platform, with the whole structure weighing less than five tons.

Casey chose not to be rushed into completion, and the tower ultimately was formally opened by Dr. Bell before a considerable gathering on August 31, 1907. The tower stood six hundred feet above the water, giving a commanding view of the surrounding Bras d'Or Lakes, as Bell had predicted. It was a complete success, everything Bell had hoped for, and stood for more than a decade with little if any maintenance before it was dismantled, having served its purpose.

While working on the tower and other projects during the winter and spring of 1907, Casey boarded at the Point house, the Bell mansion at Beinn Bhreagh. The Bells typically spent this period at their home in Washington, returning to Cape Breton for the summer. Casey had his own room, the use of common areas in the house, as well as meals prepared by a cook and a housekeeper provided by the Bells.

During this time Casey maintained a long-distance relationship with his lady friend Kathleen Stewart Parmenter. It does not appear that Casey returned to his home province of Ontario in the months immediately after assuming the role of assistant to Bell. Alec was, however, aware of this relationship and in fact made every effort to arrange a time for the official opening of the tower that might accommodate Kathleen.

Early evidence of her appearance on the scene is a letter in Kathleen's distinctive handwriting, addressed to Mabel and dated August 8, 1907, in which she acknowledges a letter recently received from Mrs. Bell. "It was awfully good of Mr. Bell to want to postpone the opening of the tower till I could come, but I couldn't possibly have left immediately so thought it better to tell you not to wait." Seizing the moment and not wishing to miss out on an opportunity to meet the Bells, Kathleen wrote, "I don't know whether you would care to have me later on, and perhaps I shouldn't suggest it as it may not be convenient for you, but I could go after the 17th. Please don't hesitate to tell me if it doesn't suit you, as I should hate to think I was putting you out in any way."

The opening was postponed until August 31, and Kathleen did attend and came into the lives of the Bells at Beinn Bhreagh as had Casey just a year earlier. In choosing to follow her man, her life, like his, would be changed forever at a place far removed from home.

CHAPTER 4

The Aerial Experiment Association

"A Brilliant Coterie"

SINCE THE TURN OF THE CENTURY, ALEC AND MABEL BELL HAD discussed ways in which Alec's passion for the concept of flight could best be pursued. The 1903 success of the Wright brothers in Kitty Hawk as first to get an aeroplane off the ground further whetted Bell's appetite for the subject.

What Alec had in mind was to form a small group much like he had done years previously with the Volta Association through which younger minds would be invited to participate in the inventive process. This was an admission on Bell's part that advancing years were catching up to him. Mabel described the work that he was trying to do now with the concept of flight as "essentially young people's work. He is now in the prime of life, but it is not more than this, and he has nothing more to look forward to."

In January 1906 Alec attended an aero-automobile show in New York in which he exhibited one of his tetrahedral kites. There he made the acquaintance of a young man by the name of Glenn H. Curtiss, a motorcycle and engine manufacturer from Hammondsport, New York. There, in that small village situated on the shores of Keuka Lake and not unlike Baddeck in size, Curtiss just the year previously had incorporated his small motorcycle plant into G. H. Curtiss Manufacturing Company. Although motorcycles and cycle engines were his mainstay, he had become interested in engine-powered flight, which was still at the very formative stages of development in America. He had recently acquired a client by the name of "Captain" Thomas Scott Baldwin, a balloonist and parachute jumper who had learned of Curtiss and contracted him to build an engine for his dirigible. There in Hammondsport, Curtiss built a 5 h.p. engine that Captain Baldwin (not to be confused with Casey Baldwin) had installed in his California Arrow, which in 1904 made the first circuitous flight in America.

Alec was looking for the best means to motorize his "aerodromes," this being the name his good friend Samuel P. Langley had given as a substitute for the word *aeroplane*. Glenn Curtiss was both young and talented, and early correspondence that followed between the two suggested to Alec that he may have another recruit to his "team."

Curtiss was quick to take the cue. On April 18, 1906, he wrote to Bell at his home in Washington.

I had the pleasure of meeting you at the New York Automobile Show where you were inquiring about a light motor for use on some experimental craft in which you were interested. Since that time your Mr. Bedwin has been here and purchased a single cylinder motor for a similar purpose. I am very much interested in aerial navigation. Have built quite a number of engines for such purposes and have become acquainted with most of the men who have been in the air with a dirigible balloon. In fact, a Captain Baldwin now has one of his airships here and I expect will carry on considerable experimenting at our place.

Clearly, Curtiss was hoping to enhance their recently made acquaintance over matters of mutual interest. "I take the liberty of addressing you in the hope that a slight acquaintance may at some time become a benefit to us both, and I wish to assure you that I will be glad of an opportunity to be of assistance to you in getting out special motors, or in any other way that comes in my line."

Curtiss, demonstrating a certain business acumen of his own, also took the opportunity to commend and encourage Alec on the continued use and potential for his tetrahedral design. "The kites at the Automobile Show, those constructed of small triangular cells, which I believe you were instrumental in placing on exhibition, interested me very much, and I believe that this construction could be used successfully in a motor propelled aeroplane. Would be glad to here [sic] from you at your convenience."

In a postscript to this letter Curtiss made mention, perhaps as an afterthought and perhaps by design, of a common medical condition shared by both the Bell and the Curtiss families. "P. S. Your interest in the deaf mute regarding which Mr. Bedwin spoke is mutual. My sister having the misfortune to lose her hearing, she is now a teacher in the Deaf Mute Institution at Rochester." Familiarity with this condition would help later to create a bond between Curtiss and Mabel Bell, who also was deaf. J. H. Parkin in his book *Bell and Baldwin* suggests that perhaps the habit Curtiss acquired in speaking to his sister after she became deaf, of forming the words carefully, made it easy for Mrs. Bell to read his lips and created a sort of kinship between them.

During the summer and fall of 1906 Curtiss and Bell exchanged correspondence that led to Bell placing an order for an air-cooled, 100 h.p., four-cylinder engine that Curtiss thought would be "crack-a-jack." As it turned out, it was much delayed in construction as Curtiss's small plant was inundated with orders for motorcycles during this time. So, in the spring of 1907, while Casey still laboured with construction of Outlook Tower at Beinn Bhreagh, Bell left Washington and travelled to Hammondsport to see Curtiss and have a firsthand look at his plant. He was impressed with what he saw and invited Curtiss to come to Baddeck. Initially Curtiss balked at this invitation, but in July, after the failure of a motor he had previously sent to Cape Breton, Curtiss agreed to deliver a replacement motor in person on Bell's undertaking to pay him $25 per day plus expenses. Curtiss was after all a businessman, and for him time was money. An expanded working relationship as originally sought by Curtiss had now developed between him and the inventor.

As both Mabel and Alec continued to ponder creating some sort of a working group, Mabel's thoughts, given Alec's unwavering belief in the merits of tetrahedral construction, were that they form a Tetrahedral Association, on the same model as the Volta Association. In her journal she wrote, "My idea was not the production of a flying machine but the reducing to commercial use...of the tetrahedral system of construction in any way. Its use in the manufacture of flying machines was to my mind and purpose but one of many possible ways."

Alec and Mabel were getting closer to coming up with a plan and acquiring the additional expertise to enable Alec to re-energize and kick-start his enthusiasm for the challenge that lay ahead in the new field of aviation. By this time a close affinity had been established between Alec and Casey Baldwin, a fact that was not lost on Mabel. In a letter to Alec dated March 26, 1907, on the topic of honourary degrees, she opined, "Doesn't Casey's love and devotion and belief in YOU touch you? He is the first to come forward in a practical way to help you to carry on your present work, and it is his generation that is offering you these honours. It is his fellows that are doing what they can, all they can for you. It is they whose confidence and whose help you need and must have to carry on your own new work."

Also in the spring of 1907 another young face was added to the mix. Lieutenant Thomas E. Selfridge was a twenty-five-year-old American army officer who had graduated from West Point in 1903. He had an intense interest in aviation, convinced as he was of the practicability of mechanical flight and that aircraft would prove an important weapon in future warfare. In that regard he would prove to be well ahead of his time and the thinking of those in both the American and Canadian military establishments.

Selfridge was well researched on heavier-than-air machines and through his research had learned of Alexander Graham Bell's experimentation in that field. Selfridge was very anxious to obtain practical experience and saw Bell's work as offering him that opportunity. That spring, before Bell moved back to Baddeck for the summer months, Selfridge visited him in Washington to introduce himself. He must have made a good impression; at that meeting Bell extended an invitation for Selfridge to visit Baddeck and observe his ongoing kite experiments. Selfridge was quick to accept. He, like Casey before him, was very taken with Beinn Bhreagh and the Bells. Mabel in particular developed an instant liking for this affable young man and was charmed by his quiet, courteous, good-humoured manner. Alec wanted him to be part of his team and, using his influence, immediately wrote to President Roosevelt requesting that Selfridge be sent to observe his experiments in Canada. By early August 1907, First Lieutenant Thomas Selfridge was detailed to Baddeck as an observer in the interest of the US Army.

At this time Glenn Curtiss was also at Beinn Bhreagh. True to his word, he had arrived in July, staying long enough to ensure that his latest engine met with Bell's satisfaction. More importantly, it was an opportunity to meet Alec in his own backyard and witness some of his kite experiments, which to this point he had only been told about. Curtiss was impressed by the whole scene and in particular with Mabel Bell, with whom he seemed to hit it off, perhaps due in part to the special bond he had developed with his deaf hostess.

This was a pivotal moment for organizing a group to work with the aging inventor and his quest for flight. The four "youngsters"—McCurdy, Baldwin, Selfridge, and now Curtiss—were all willing to move forward with the group concept. Alec, sensing that the time was now opportune, shortly after one o'clock on July 19 met with the four of them in his study for the purpose of talking over plans for continued co-operation in solving the flying-machine problem. With Casey acting as stenographer, Bell later dictated the ideas as well as his thoughts on how he perceived they might form a working group. It was a long session, interrupted during the afternoon when visitors from aboard the vessel *Canada* arrived, and resumed again later that evening, running into the wee hours of the next day. Although Bell may never have had the time for or interest in business, it is clear from this account that he certainly had a head for business as well as a fair and reasonable approach to protecting the interests of those about to engage in a joint venture. An excerpt, in Bell's own words, from what became the blueprint for the association that emerged later is quoted at length here.

The experiments at Beinn Bhreagh point to an early conclusion of the problem of aerial flight.

In carrying on these experiments I have called to my assistance two young men who have graduated from Toronto University as Mechanical Engineers, J. A. D. McCurdy and F. W. Baldwin, as it seemed to me that, as engineers, they could be of great assistance in the engineering problems involved in the construction of a flying machine. I have also called to my assistance Mr. G. H. Curtiss of Hammondsport, New York, as a well-known expert in the construction of light gasoline motors, as I felt that his knowledge and experience with such motors would be invaluable, and indeed necessary to the successful conclusions of these experiments.

I have also invited the co-operation of First Lieutenant Selfridge, Fifth Regiment F. A. and assistant instructor in Ordinance and Gunnery at the United States Military Academy, West Point, New York, because Lieutenant Selfridge is making a special study of the whole subject of aerial locomotion in its application to warfare. He expressed the desire of making himself familiar with what we are doing here in the hope that he might be able to glean ideas that might be of advantage to the United States Army.

I also was pleased that an officer of the United States Army should take an interest in our experiments and desire to make himself familiar with the work going on here; and specially so because none of the people associated with me here in the capacity of workmen or assistants are American citizens. Mr. Curtiss, who is now here on his first visit to Beinn Bhreagh, is the only American among my assistants. Lieutenant Selfridge appears as an onlooker and advisor.

Now it appears to me that in the above personnel we have an ideal combination for pursuing aerial researches.

For many years I have been a close student of what is being accomplished in relation to aerial flight and for many years my laboratory experiments have been directed mainly along lines leading up to aerial flight as a logical conclusion. I now have associated with me gentlemen who supplement by their technical knowledge my deficiencies; and in this combination I now feel that we are strong where before we were weak.

I think therefore that the progress of the experiments will be greatly promoted and the world benefited if these young men who are now temporarily associated with me can be given some personal inducement to continue co-operation together in accomplishing the great object we have in common—to get into the air.

One is left to wonder what must have been going through Casey's mind as he sat with his mentor taking this dictation. It was just a year since he had left the classroom at u of t. In that time he had settled into Beinn Bhreagh, where he had been taken in by the Bells; had demonstrated to Alec his engineering skills in the construction of a unique tetrahedral tower; and now was on the cusp of joining a small group to pursue the concept of flight in Canada. What would his naysaying professor at university have thought of "this foolishness"?

In considering what inducements could be proffered to the associates, Bell was of the view that firstly each man should have the opportunity, while carrying on experiments in common, of making a name and reputation for himself as a promoter of aviation or mechanical flight, and that they should share in any profits that might accrue from their efforts. The devil was, as always, in the details.

This dictation, which ran into a number of pages, was a compendium of Bell's thoughts; he now gave it to the associates for their consideration.

Alec's overriding view of the group initiative was that commercial purpose and monetary gain was secondary to their avowed purpose of "achievement" and the personal satisfaction to be derived from succeeding in "getting into the air." In Bell's own words, "The chief inducement that can urge us to keep together is the actual accomplishment of aerial flight and the honour and glory that will attach to those who succeed."

This was not to say that financial success was not possible. On the contrary, Bell noted that "there may be nothing in it from a financial standpoint and yet there are possibilities of enormous returns." This after all was the man who had gone through a similar scenario as inventor of the telephone.

Maybe Bell was a bit naive in his belief that altruism would be the mainstay of the association. He was "convinced that none of us have any mercenary idea in working together but are simply actuated by a desire to do what we can to help the world to solve the problem of aerial flight." This was the inventor musing. These words would come back to haunt him years later, after "the honour and glory."

Shortly after this dictation was distributed among the associates then gathered at Beinn Bhreagh, Thomas Selfridge returned briefly to West Point while Glen Curtiss returned to his home and plant in Hammondsport. He was a bit of a wild card in the group. He was neither well-to-do nor university educated and certainly had nothing of a "silver spoon" background. He had made his own way in life and was both an inventor and highly respected and successful machinery manufacturer. He was his own man and not surprisingly would have regarded his involvement in this sort of joint venture with a greater bias toward business and reward than the others. Alec probably had a sense of this but was prepared just the same to take Curtiss on, given the importance of his particular expertise.

Correspondence exchanged between Bell and Curtiss that August adds credence to the notion that the latter had a more business-like approach to the association. Bell quickly reached a consensus with Baldwin, McCurdy, and Selfridge, who had returned to Beinn Bhreagh, as to how the association would be configured, including a form of remuneration for the associates. He outlined much of this in a lengthy letter to Curtiss dated August 21, 1907. In it Alec mentioned one of his concerns being how, with a new association, the services of all the past employees at Beinn Bhreagh could be recognized.

> This difficulty has been overcome by accepting the principle that the past belongs to the past workers exclusively and that the future associates should only share in what is developed in the future during the time that they are associated together…the same thing would apply to you. Any inventions relating to Aerial Locomotion made by you before the organization of the proposed association belong to you personally and not to the association.
>
> The past being provided for in this way, the exact nature of the new organization is immaterial to me and may take any form that may be agreeable to us when we meet, provided the principle is recognized that we only share in inventions relating to Aerial Locomotion, made by the Associates, conjointly or individually, during the period we are associated together.

These words would take on more meaning years later, following the dissolution of the association. It appears that Curtiss was agreeable to what was being proposed for an association, although he was at some disadvantage; it was somewhat more difficult to reach a consensus with Curtiss now separated from the group. Bell concludes this letter with some other details, including suggested remuneration, all of which he notes "are satisfactory to us" and concludes saying, "Everything now rests with you. Come up as soon as possible and let us organize our association and GET TO WORK."

As August wore on, Beinn Bhreagh was the scene of great activity. With Casey busy putting finishing touches on Outlook Tower, Alec and McCurdy were consumed with kite experiments with everyone working toward completion of Bell's first priority—developing a tetrahedral, man-carrying kite. Much of their attention had been to devise a means whereby the kite could be safely launched and landed on the water. Alec was consumed by the desire to ensure that danger to life and limb of test pilots be reduced to a minimum.

By August 23 they had conducted various experiments with "The Selfridge Kite" by launching it off a large float on pontoons called the *Ugly Duckling*.

On August 30 the Bells hosted a dinner party for thirteen at The Point on the eve of the official opening of Outlook Tower. As was custom, Alec was part of the entertainment for the guests, who were treated to a talk on "superstitions" before Alec slipped away "to give my thoughts to the Tower and my speech upon the occasion."

The following day, Saturday, August 31, Outlook Tower was formally opened promptly at three o'clock. A short account of the event appeared in the *Sydney Herald* on September 4 and reflected the curious attitude of the public toward the structure. "The tower was opened for sightseers on Saturday afternoon by Professor Bell in the presence of about 300 invited guests. Professor Bell and A. C. Ross, MP, delivered addresses. The tower is constructed of metal, and the account of the opening proceedings does not state whether the tower is to be used in connection with the inventor's flying machine or to enable him to find out what is going on in Mars."

Prior to the opening ceremony atop the mountain, Bell gave a lecture on the principle of the tower illustrated with magic lantern views (i.e., glass slides) in the boathouse. The newspaper correspondent noted that the only reference to a flying machine, which was what everyone wanted to hear about, was that he was starting the construction of one.

By September, Mabel, who had been observing the interaction between these young men and her husband, had determined that they were the perfect mix to form an association for the purpose of "getting into the air." More than that, she was prepared to finance the venture with $20,000 she had recently come into from the sale of property in Washington inherited through her father's estate. Alec was overjoyed with Mabel's generous proposal and placed his laboratory with its splendid equipment and trained staff at the disposal of the proposed association.

In September 1907 four men stood poised to help Mr. Bell move forward in the field of aviation. With the exception of Alec, they were a young bunch—the oldest, at twenty-nine, was Glenn Curtiss. It was now time to formalize their working relationship. The question remained as to what form the group would take. Alec's thinking differed somewhat from Mabel's view of an association focused solely on tetrahedral construction. He was insistent that the object of the group be to develop a practical flying machine without any restrictions as to its design, a much more broad-based approach than Mabel's. His only caveat was that his tetrahedral man-carrying kite be finished first, after which, each associate in turn, with the help of the others, should build a flying machine of his own design.

Mabel well knew that her husband had no time for business. His focus was on the idea, the invention, and not the bringing of it into practical use. Mabel called this his "attitude of mind," which she feared "soon will be his attitude toward the kites and flying machine that is now engaging his thoughts." She continued,

> And it is this attitude of his mind that is at the bottom of the purpose for which I offered my own small fortune. To take these inventions whose practicability has been demonstrated by Mr. Bell and make them practical. To take inventions made by Mr. Bell, inventions of which he and no one else is the inventor, and prepare them for actual commercial use.
>
> Now of all these inventions, I am especially interested just now in Mr. Bell's Tetrahedral Construction System, on which he has obtained letters patent and which is adapted for use in a variety of ways, all of which require development. The use for which it was especially invented and which engages Mr. Bell's attention now is its applicability to the construction of flying machines.
>
> But Mr. Bell will never probably fuss with it, certainly not alone, and I am seeking to induce someone else to take up and carry on this work of Mr. Bell's.

What an amazing woman. Mabel has been described as "Alec's silent partner." That is very much an understatement. What Mabel may have lacked with her diminished speaking ability she more than made up with the quill. She wrote magnificently and often, always in a clear, precise, and frequently affectionate manner. She was very insightful and demonstrated a great grasp of facts, always considering them with logic and precision before rendering her opinion. She was a tremendous support and confidante for her husband.

Final discussions with all in the group took place September 9 and 10, during which various aspects of the proposed association were discussed and tentative understandings set down in writing. One of the key decisions was to define the duties assigned to each associate and their remuneration, described by Bell in Home Notes.

> Lieutenant Selfridge: As Secretary of the association should keep the records of the meetings and preserve the gist of discussion. I think he should also have charge of the library of the association and make it his duty to see that the literature of the world relating to aerial locomotion is rendered accessible to the members so that all may have the opportunity of studying what has been done elsewhere, what is being done, and what plans are in contemplation....He should also attend to the correspondence of the association....If, as seems probable, Lieutenant Selfridge should be willing to give his services to the association without remuneration it would be a very proper thing for the association to provide him with an assistant....
>
> Douglas McCurdy: In addition to acting as Treasurer of the association and rendering financial reports from time to time might be assigned the special duty of keeping photographic records of apparatus and experiments, photographing such apparatus and experiments as he may be directed to photograph by the Director of Experiments. It should also be his special duty to make calculations for the associates and generally to verify weights and measures and calculations and act as assistant engineer. Remuneration of $1,000.
>
> Mr. Baldwin: Should be recognized as Engineer in Chief in charge of theoretical construction to see that all structures made should be designed on sound engineering lines. He should also have special charge of drawings, plans, and designs for structures, and the engineering drawings made by him should be preserved and placed on file in the Engineer's office. Remuneration of $1,000.
>
> Mr. Curtiss: Should be recognized as Chief Executive Officer of the association having as his special duty the direction of experiments under the direction of the council and also have special charge of motive power, the designing of engines, propellers, and their accessories, consulting with the Engineer in Chief regarding structures to support the strains produced by their operation. He too will have exclusive control of the laboratory staff as stated above, acting through the Superintendent. Remuneration of $5,000.

A. G. Bell: To act as General Advisor without remuneration to the association without specific duties assigned. To preside at meetings of the association as permanent Chairman and in his absence the members present to appoint a temporary chairman.

During the latter part of September, as steps were being taken by Bell to reduce an agreement to writing, all members of the group were working together in harmony. On September 21 Bell wrote in Home Notes that "man-carrying part of flying machine was suspended today by three ropes in the new Aerodrome House at the Lab with engine and propeller and man (Mr. Curtiss) in it. The structure supported the weight perfectly, not a sag in it anywhere, excepting at the sides of the man…Curtiss number 2 engine was worked while the whole was suspended by the ropes following median line of kite with Bell noting that there were about 20 persons present to witness the experiment."

The following day Bell wrote again from the quiet confines of his houseboat about the enthusiasm, and particularly that shown by Casey for their work. Bell could be quite dramatic in his prose and this was one such occasion. As one can see in this excerpt, Bell was a stickler, often hounding the associates to diarize all advancements in their experimental work.

Sparks are flying around ready to be fanned into a blaze by the breath of encouragement. Baldwin is in a state of eruption and he does not know it—throwing out sparks all the time which are not being preserved so far as I know. He thinks, but does not note. Must get him to use his scribbling book. He got out something else the other day which he noted in Kite House book at my request, but I forget what it was. He jotted down only a few words, but they will be sufficient to record the thought. The influence of association is already being felt by a general stimulation of ideas all round. Douglas and Lucien McCurdy have made a number of supportive points, but I do not think they have been noted, and I forget now exactly what they are. Curtiss is deep in engine problems. Selfridge has evolved a mathematical formula for calculating the number of cells in a tetrahedral structure. All are giving signs of original thinking on the common subject of study.

"Bell's boys" were already impressing their mentor in just the short time they had been together. Already they projected both enthusiasm as well as an ability to work together toward attaining the common goal of getting into the air. As the day approached for executing a collective agreement, Bell was heartened by what he had observed to date. He wrote:

> Think I should make a special study of the men and what they are doing and try to steer their attentions into what seem to me to be advancing directions. I find they are very easily affected by appreciation and encouragement. Douglas McCurdy has evidently been stimulated by my appreciation of his bent for calculation and is already looking upon weights and measurements and calculations as belonging to his realm. I can also see the effect upon Selfridge of former remarks concerning his special functions. He has taken to arranging and cataloguing my old photos so that we may have the advantage of knowing what we have done in the laboratory.... Baldwin is thinking of structures and strains. Curtiss of engines, so that all are taking to different parts of the problem as individual specialties, while freely talking and exchanging ideas. My special function is, I think, the co-ordination of the whole—the appreciation of steps and progress and the encouragement of efforts in what seem to me to be advancing directions. I am myself greatly encouraged by observing that the mechanism for research is moving without friction.

During the latter part of September, Bell and his young associates packed up and headed off to Halifax. The purpose of the trip was twofold: to execute the agreement creating the AEA, and to take in an air show in which the balloonist, Captain Thomas Scott Baldwin, was to perform in his dirigible.

The air show fit in well with the business at hand and gave everyone in the group an opportunity to meet up with "the captain" and witness first-hand the performance of both dirigible and pilot. The event, and their experience while passengers aboard the train to Halifax, was described in a letter to Mabel that Casey hastened to write from the hotel on September 27.

> The train was packed full of people all in a great state of excitement over the airship. Everyone was talking about it and it took very little jockeying to get the smoking room experts to deliver themselves "in

extenso" on the subject. One local wiseacre from Sydney with inside information bulging out all over him told us all about Bell's machine as he familiarly termed it. Then he went on to tell us about some gasoline motorman they had up there, but from his personal experience he knew it as a matter of actual fact that not one motor in a thousand was any good. Not satisfied with this, another armchair critic announced with authority that if there was a motorcycle made in America of which anything good could be said; that machine was an "Indian."

About the only people on the train who weren't busily engaged pulling airships to pieces and giving us a life-sized idea of ourselves as others see us were some fifteen or twenty newly married couples. It seems to be the proper caper to get married before going to the fair....

Curtiss doesn't think it is altogether the fair but is inclined to think it is an epidemic, so you had better be careful of our John [McCurdy] as I fear he is very susceptible.

It would seem that McCurdy, known to his contemporaries as John, had an eye for the ladies. Whether the same was true of Casey is not well known, but there was that young lady in Ontario by the name of Kathleen.

Then it was on to the air show, which from Casey's account was a great success. Casey by now knew Mabel well enough to appreciate her appetite for detail, as is evident here.

We had an interesting time watching them get the airship ready. Mr. Baldwin seems a very good sort. He doesn't know why but he does know how and strikes me as a man who takes pains and is cautious but absolutely without fear.

It blew too hard all yesterday until the sun went down when it moderated a good deal and he made a very successful flight.

The wind, while very light on the ground, however, was blowing about twelve miles an hour about one hundred feet up and at about two hundred was twenty miles an hour so he kept very low. He had perfect control of his machine all the time, and the thing was so fascinating that it was all I could do to let go when he went up.

He made two flights, the second time he simply let her go without steering to show us the effect of the wind and propeller. It simply went around in right-handed circles, drifting off with the wind at about ten miles an hour.

Alec had chosen the capital of Nova Scotia as the venue where the formal agreement incorporating the Aerial Experiment Association would be signed. This was intentional on his part. He wanted to recognize the international flavour of the group: three Americans—Bell, Curtiss, and Selfridge—and the two Canadians, Baldwin and McCurdy. To this end he sought and received the participation of the Consul General of the United States at Halifax, David F. Wilber, at a meeting held at the Halifax Hotel on Monday, September 30, 1907. Wilber provided a certificate in which he certified the bona fides of William L. Payzant as a notary public for the County of Halifax, duly authorized to act as witness to the signatories to the agreement. For this service Payzant was paid the princely sum of $5.00, which he acknowledged with a receipt to "Alex G. Bell et al."

The document incorporated all the terms discussed and agreed upon earlier by the associates. The following day, October 1, everyone, now members of the Aerial Experiment Association, met briefly again at the Halifax Hotel to ratify the agreement, elect officers, and to adjourn to meet at the call of the chairman at Beinn Bhreagh.

Alec, as chairman, was not long in calling the next meeting, which took place at Beinn Bhreagh at 8:30 P.M. the following day, immediately after returning from Halifax. At this meeting, Selfridge as secretary read the following note from Mrs. A. Graham Bell: "I am very happy to hear of the organization of the Association upon the success of which my heart is set. I shall be glad to advance it funds from time to time as may be requested by the proper officers for the purpose of enabling the Association to carry on experiments relating to aerial locomotion, providing the total amount advanced does not exceed, in the aggregate, the sum of twenty thousand dollars."

In business that followed, the secretary was directed to express thanks to Mrs. Bell for her offer, which was accepted, and that she be given a 1 percent interest in all proceeds resulting from the work of the Association for every $1,000 she contributed. Dr. Bell's offer for the use of his laboratory was also accepted, and finally the secretary "was instructed by note to notify Mrs. Bell, as funds are desired, to send a cheque of amount to Treasurer." On October 14, Selfridge, as directed, wrote to Mrs. Bell, "I have been accorded the privilege of thanking you on behalf of the Aerial Experiment Association for your munificent offer made to the Association in your communication of October 2nd, which the Association voted unanimously to accept. All communication will be addressed to you by the Secretary and all monies donated to the Association should be by check in the Treasurer's name and forwarded to him through the Secretary."

The Aerial Experiment Association was now a reality. The agreement provided for a term of one year from October 1, 1907, "unless otherwise determined by the unanimous vote of the members." The short term took into account the uncertainty of success as well as the underwriting commitment by Mabel Bell. It was a formidable challenge, which the group immediately embraced.

Over the course of the ensuing eighteen months (including a six-month extension in the term), until dissolved on March 31, 1909, the AEA was a force that contributed materially to the advancement of manned flight. As acclaimed by the press, it was a "brilliant coterie" of four young men who, with their mentor and chairman, Alexander Graham Bell, succeeded beyond their wildest dreams in attaining their avowed purpose, at no material gain for themselves, of "getting into the air."

Perhaps J. H. Parkin best summed up the AEA when in his 1964 book *Bell and Baldwin* he wrote, "In the history of man's conquest of the air, the Association was unique in many ways. Founded, financed, and inspired by a woman, organized for the specific purpose of achieving practical powered human flight, proceeding systematically step by step, each of its machines embodying lessons derived from its predecessor, it had achieved its objective and bequeathed to the future practical flying machines, the equal of any. Never before perhaps had such a group, with such slender resources achieved so much and made such important contributions in so short a time."

CHAPTER 5

Getting Into the Air

"Those Magnificent Men in Their Flying Machines"

T HE INK WAS HARDLY DRY UPON THE AEA AGREEMENT WHEN TRUE to script, the associates honoured their commitment to the inventor by completing the construction of a man-carrying tetrahedral kite—Bell's tetrahedral cell aerodrome. The Cygnet I was massive—so large in fact that a new building was constructed to house the structure. The "aerodrome shed" was built on piles at the head of Beinn Bhreagh harbour and had a floor area of thirty by sixty feet with the entire wall facing the water made removable to enable the kite to be moved directly onto the *Ugly Duckling* as launch raft. Earlier that summer Casey had found the motorboat that provided the tow, *Gauldrie*, in Sydney. It was named after a village in Fife, Scotland, that was the home of Bell's great-grandfather, Andrew Colville. The boat, after being fitted out with a marine motor driving a propeller, provided yeoman service as a tug and a launch.

The Cygnet I was test flown successfully in unmanned flight off the deck of the *Ugly Duckling,* but further tweaking was required before attempting manned flight. The group agreed that this honour would be given to Thomas Selfridge.

The kite was completed November 13, 1907, and an initial unmanned trial was made in Baddeck Harbour on December 3. The local steamer *Blue Hill* was secured as towboat. *Gauldrie* towed the Cygnet 1, lashed to the launching arms on the *Ugly Ducking,* to a rendezvous point in the outer harbour. With the *Blue Hill* pulling the raft into the wind, the Cygnet 1 gently rose from the deck of the *Ugly Duckling* and remained, poised aloft, flying steadily in what Bell described as "really a most imposing sight."

Heartened by the success of this trial run, a decision was made to attempt a manned flight three days later on December 6. Once again the *Gauldrie* delivered the *Ugly Duckling* to the steamer *Blue Hill,* this time with Thomas Selfridge "bundled up in rugs and lying in the manhole" made to accommodate the pilot. Bell had taken pains to record the event, arranging for two photographers to be present. Ever concerned for the safety of the test pilot,he had also arranged for a Baddeck physician, Dr. MacDonald, to be on hand. Baldwin and McCurdy watched from the *Blue Hill* along with Mabel Bell and her two-year-old granddaughter, Mabel Grosvenor. (Young Mabel eventually became a pediatrician, whom Baddeckers affectionately referred to as "Dr. Mabel.")

An initial attempt was aborted due to the centre of gravity, Selfridge's weight being too far forward. With that addressed—Selfridge simply moved further aft—on a second pull the Cygnet 1 rose gracefully into the air and flew steadily for some seven minutes at a height of 168 feet.

As the kite descended, Selfridge's view was obstructed by the projecting bow of the kite so that he felt rather than saw the kite gently alight on the water. Meanwhile the coal smoke belching from the stack of *Blue Hill* momentarily obscured Cygnet 1, and before the tow rope could be detached at either end, the forward motion at full speed through the water tore the lightly built kite apart and unceremoniously threw Selfridge into the water. After a few anxious moments he was retrieved and taken aboard the *Blue Hill* where, under doctor's supervision, he was warmed up and as Bell said, given "appropriate stimulants internally of a nature which seemed to give great satisfaction to the Lieutenant."

The first effort by the fledgling AEA was a resounding success. Thomas Selfridge, an American, had made history in what was the first manned flight of an unmechanized, heavier-than-air craft in Canada. The Cygnet 1 was beyond repair, but as the group gathered round the fireplace in the Great

Hall that evening Bell expressed his satisfaction that "she had fulfilled her function" and "demonstrated the important fact that the tetrahedral system can be utilized in structures intended for aerial locomotion."

As it turned out, this was as far as Bell would go in his attempts to apply his tetrahedral principle into practice. The youngsters in the group, already well read on the success of others like the Wright brothers in the aeronautical field, were anxious to experiment with gliders. The AEA had hardly been in existence for three months and was already at a turning point. As provided for in the agreement, with winter fast closing in at Baddeck, the decision was made to move their operations to Hammondsport, NY, where the weather conditions were deemed to be more favourable and they could avail themselves of the Curtiss shop facilities. This would prove to be an ideal location; work would begin immediately on a glider in the Curtiss cycle shop.

Hammondsport is a small village not unlike Baddeck in size and geography. Founded in 1827 by Lazarus Hammond, it was here that Glenn Hammond Curtiss was born in 1878. The visitor approaching from the south would unsuspectingly drive by the meadow just outside the village where Curtiss and the other members of the AEA would test-fly their aerodromes. Hammondsport would later become known in the United States as "the cradle of aviation." One enters the village almost before you know it, making a sudden transition from countryside to the lovely cluster of homes and shops that, much like Baddeck, are built around the water—in this case the shore of Keuka Lake in the Finger Lake District of New York State. It is quiet and peaceful, being far removed from any other major centre or interstate highway.

Curtiss was at Hammondsport to greet the group when they arrived at the end of the year. Alec had chosen to bring Mabel along, and they were welcomed into the modest Curtiss home on Castle Hill. The boys—Baldwin, Selfridge, and McCurdy—found accommodation in a local rooming house. Casey was already familiar with the area, having taken summer courses a year earlier at Cornell University in Ithaca, NY, about forty-five miles to the east of Hammondsport.

Hammondsport proved to be an excellent venue for both construction and test flying of the AEA aerodromes. As promised, the Curtiss machine shops were well equipped for construction, and the hangars built down on the lakefront for Captain Thomas Baldwin's dirigibles provided adequate storage facilities.

In winter the frozen surface of Keuka Lake made a perfect, unobstructed runway. On land, the racetrack at Stoney Brook Farm in the meadow at Pleasant Valley, just outside Hammondsport, proved to be an excellent airfield.

Alec and Mabel did not stay long. Unfortunately Mabel came down with an illness necessitating that she return to Washington accompanied by Alec who thereafter kept in touch with his associates through regular correspondence with Casey.

Throughout January of 1908 the foursome was busily engaged in building a biplane type of glider, made of bamboo with double arched wings spanning twenty-five feet in diameter. It was very light, weighing only seventy-five pounds, which helped them become accustomed to a contraption in which none had any prior experience. A hillside (opposite the present-day Glenn Curtiss Museum), just down the road from the meadow and racetrack that would be the venue for later aerial experiments, provided an excellent jumping-off point for the glider. Starting January 13 Casey and Selfridge took turns and soon mastered the art of gliding and most importantly, "getting a feel for flight."

The stage was now set. Unfettered by any oversight by Bell, the men were now working on their own and anxious to get on with their primary objective of getting into the air with a man-carrying, powered aerodrome. They were about to make the quantum leap from glider to mechanized aircraft, again lacking any prior experience other than what they had read on the subject. They knew that experimentation would likely necessitate the production of more than one machine and resolved that each associate would be in charge of building his machine. That associate would have final approval of its plan, but all associates would partake and contribute their combined knowledge toward the final product.

Considerable collective thought went into the design of the first machine. They were beginning from scratch, attempting to apply the experience of others like Octave Chanute into a practical flying machine of their own making. Harkening back to their own recent experience with gliders, they decided upon a lightly built rigid biplane capable of supporting an engine and pilot. Casey was deemed most experienced of the group given his academic studies of Chanute and immediately assumed the role as lead structural engineer in the group. This was also in keeping with his stated role as chief engineer within the association. It was agreed that Thomas Selfridge, who had so recently "flown" the Cygnet 1, would be the sponsor of "Drome No. 1," a.k.a. Red Wing, so named as it was covered with the red silk used on the Bell kites.

As was the case with all the prototypes, the materials used were all made and the machine constructed entirely on-site. Although it was a collective effort, Casey's influence, particularly with some unique features like the bow-string truss, was strong. He was already demonstrating a grasp of the technology exceeding anything learned from a textbook, which quickly earned him the admiration of his associates.

Curtiss, as one would expect, focused his attention on engines and oversaw the fitting of an eight-cylinder air-cooled motor for Red Wing. It was first tested in trials made from a motorized iceboat on nearby Keuka Lake where, only seven weeks from inception, Red Wing was ready for trial. The drome was fitted out with runners for takeoff from the ice-covered waters of the lake. It was mid-March and already the ice was melting in the southern part of the lake. Selfridge, whose drome it was, happened to be away in Washington at this time. The associates felt they could wait no longer and took Red Wing by barge farther up the lake to where there remained solid ice. There it was assembled, the engine checked over by Curtiss, and in Selfridge's absence, Casey was chosen as test pilot. With a number of curious onlookers present, Casey gave the thumbs-up, and after a short run over the ice, Red Wing lifted off and flew for some three hundred feet before being forced down due to a buckled tail strut.

It was March 12, 1908, and Casey Baldwin had just made the first public flight in a heavier-than-air machine in America, the first Canadian to fly a heavier-than-air aircraft. It was a flight of historic proportions. When accurately measured it was found that Red Wing had been in the air for 319 feet, making it the longest first flight of any such aircraft. An amazing achievement when one considers that this was the associates' first machine and flown for the first time by Casey, who until that time had only managed to get his feet off the ground in a glider.

Selfridge never would get to fly his plane. A few days later, on March 17, after making some adjustments Casey once again flew Red Wing off the frozen surface of Keuka Lake. It was not perhaps a good idea. It was raining and windy—the rain added considerably to the weight of the fragile drome. He succeeded in getting lift and levelling off, but then Red Wing dropped one wing tip and side-slipped onto the ice. Neither Casey nor the engine was hurt, but the drome was a write-off. The cause was attributed to lack of lateral stability and control. The group would make this the focus of their attention as they regrouped and immediately started work on Drome No. 2.

The supply of red silk had been exhausted in the construction of Red Wing. New material was sourced, the choice being white cotton (nainsook), which provided the name White Wing. The sponsor of Drome No. 2 was Casey Baldwin. From all outward appearances White Wing looked identical to its predecessor; however, there were differences in keeping with the group philosophy that they would learn from prior experience and make adjustments, incorporating better and sometimes new efficiencies into each succeeding craft. The most important difference with White Wing was the introduction of hinged wing tips as "lateral rudder" for lateral control. Designed by Casey following Bell's suggestion, this innovation in White Wing would represent the first appearance in North America of this type of lateral control, more commonly known as ailerons, in an aeroplane.

It was spring and henceforth the AEA would use the racetrack in the meadow as their testing ground. To this end, White Wing was fitted with a tricycle undercarriage running on unsprung pneumatic-tired bicycle wheels. This was the first wheeled undercarriage in America. The same size of engine was used but now controlled by a foot throttle much like in a motor vehicle.

Although White Wing was Casey's drome, he shared the test-flying with all his partners. The first to fly it was Thomas Selfridge—he had some catching up to do. Unfortunately in his first few attempts starting May 14, 1908, he encountered problems with rough terrain, and it was not until Casey gave it a try on May 18 that White Wing got airborne. On that occasion he flew a distance of some 279 feet at an altitude of 10 feet.

Selfridge was successful the following day when he managed to make a number of short "jumps," the second being the longest at 240 feet at an altitude of 20 feet. His efforts were nonetheless of historical significance as they represented the first flights in a heavier-than-air aircraft by an officer of the United States Army.

Not to be outdone, Glenn Curtiss took the opportunity for his first attempt at powered flight when on May 21 he flew White Wing a distance of 1,017 feet at the astounding speed of 37 mph. Speed after all was his forte.

The last to fly White Wing was Douglas McCurdy. On May 23 he managed to fly for 519 feet at about 20 feet before the wind tipped the machine and the right wing tip struck the ground, followed by the nose, and White Wing came to rest upside down. Fortunately all McCurdy hurt was his pride. This may not have been his day, but it did represent his first flight; he would soon master the art and later become the most accomplished aviator in the group.

It was over for Casey's White Wing. A short life perhaps, but by sharing his drome with all the fellows each had been given a chance to experience what it was to get into the air. The engine was salvaged—now it was on with construction of Drome No. 3.

Mabel and Alec had travelled back to Hammondsport to take in the flights of White Wing while on their way to Beinn Bhreagh. Bell was very impressed by what he witnessed, as well he should have been. In a few short months his boys had designed, built, and flown not one but two aircraft. It might have been enough for them to stop then and there and bask in the afterglow of their recent successes; however, their appetites for the challenge were just whetted—it was a case of moving onward and upward.

Drome No. 3 was assigned to Curtiss. As with the first two dromes, Casey oversaw various modifications and further improvements in the design of the third aircraft, which otherwise appeared identical to both Red Wing and White Wing.

Casey could have been excused if he appeared somewhat distracted during this time. Somehow during all these months he had managed to maintain a romantic liaison with Kathleen Parmenter to whom he was by now engaged to be married. Despite the best efforts of the group to complete Drome No. 3 before the nuptials, they were not successful. Construction was held in abeyance for a few days to allow for the wedding, a pretty affair that took place at St. Catharines, Ontario, on June 12, 1908.

Honeymoon deferred, Casey was back to work in Hammondsport a few days later. Once again the Bells appeared on the scene to take in the first flights made by Curtiss and his drome on June 21, 1908. They were respectively 456, 417, and 1,266 feet in length. After watching this performance Alec stated that he thought the drome reminded him of a June bug, and so that name was adopted for Drome No. 3.

In subsequent flights Curtiss continued to extend the distance flown, and after some modifications, including treating the wing covering with a new varnish that sealed the covering and was pigmented with yellow ochre to improve photography, he had accomplished flights of more than 3,400 feet.

These "long-distance" flights brought the group closer to yet another possible milestone. The Scientific American Trophy was put forth to anyone who was first to fly a distance of one kilometre, or 3,281 feet, in a straight line. Although they were supposed to be exclusively an experimental association, the associates were hooked. It was game on. The association took immediate steps for a trial with the Aero Club of America, a social club formed in 1905 to promote aviation in the US.

On July 4, 1908, flying June Bug from the meadow grounds just outside Hammondsport, Glenn Curtiss gave America a birthday present and the AEA a trophy. A second attempt that day resulted in a flight of nearly one mile—well in excess of the targeted one kilometre. For the third time in succession an AEA drome had made the history books. In addition to attracting the attention of Americans to what was happening in Hammondsport, June Bug represented the first official test of an aeroplane made in America.

This success was not without some unsavoury repercussions. The spectre of patent infringement reared its ugly head when the Wright brothers claimed that the lateral rudders of the June Bug infringed the Wright patent 821,393. The Wright brothers let it be known that they would initiate legal action if any attempt was made by the AEA to exploit their machines commercially. Curtiss was the focus of their displeasure. He replied to the Wrights stating that he did not intend to enter the exhibition business (though it must already have been at the back of his mind) and that he had referred the patent matter to the secretary of the AEA.

In one fleeting moment, one flight, the AEA lost its innocence and found itself in a world confounded by accusation and litigation, just exactly what their mentor had endured following the invention of the telephone. Alexander Graham Bell was very unhappy with this turn of events, something that he had taken pains to address and hopefully avoid in the careful wording of the articles incorporating the AEA. This marked an early turning point in the relationship between the associates; preoccupation with patents would become more pronounced in the ensuing months.

Following the accidents with Red Wing and White Wing it was decided that just Curtiss would fly June Bug, both for the experience gained in repeated flights and to avoid damaging the machine, which had been their unhappy experience when all had taken turns as pilot. Curtiss flew his June Bug successfully and consecutively nineteen times. By August this flight restriction had been relaxed, and with Curtiss in Washington attending an airship trial with Captain Thomas Baldwin, both Selfridge and McCurdy made a number of flights in June Bug. Both had satisfactory trials and the machine performed well, but it seemed to both that air-cooled engines had their limitations and suffered from inadequate cooling after running at full power for ninety seconds. McCurdy was anxious to get started on his Drome No. 4. This mechanical shortcoming would be addressed with his plane.

Meanwhile there was a move afoot for the AEA to move back to Baddeck for the summer months as originally contemplated. In thinking it over Bell concluded that the move back to Baddeck should be deferred until his tetrahedral aerodrome, Drome No. 5, could be made ready for experiments. The Hammondsport work would continue without interruption until his aerodrome was completed. So it was that Alec asked Casey to return to Beinn Bhreagh with his new bride in order that he could assist in completing Drome No. 5. Casey and Kathleen left Hammondsport on July 11, heading for Baddeck via New York where Casey arranged for the purchase of a boat destined for Cape Breton.

The AEA workforce was thus now divided, with Baldwin and Bell at Beinn Bhreagh and Selfridge, Curtiss, and McCurdy at Hammondsport. This was effectively the end of the close-knit working relationship among the associates. Their work continued but had now been impacted by a number of circumstances: Casey's marriage, the Curtiss–Wright brothers tiff over threatened patent violation, and now Bell's decision to withdraw Casey from Hammondsport and construction of Drome No. 4 to focus on Bell's baby, the arcane tetrahedral drome. In hindsight Alec may have wished that he had reconsidered this decision to split the workforce and slow the momentum the AEA had built up with their first three aircraft.

Time was a factor—the AEA had been created with a finite lifespan of one year, perhaps an overly ambitious term that did not take into account contingencies of life. Work proceeded in haste at Hammondsport on the next aircraft, McCurdy's Drome No. 4. Lessons gained from June Bug gave rise to yet more innovations in the newest craft, which was ready for assembly in mid-August. It would have a new engine—a 50 h.p., water-cooled engine as proposed by Curtiss. Another of the design changes was the body covering. A lightweight, tear-resistant, rubberized balloon silk was chosen. It had a silver finish on one side, which prompted McCurdy to name his machine Silver Dart.

Selfridge did not have much to do with the construction of Drome No. 4. His American political masters had other plans for him at this time, during which the Wright brothers had been contracted to build aeroplanes for the US Army Signal Corps. In early August Selfridge was ordered to Washington, transferred to the Signal Corps, and appointed to an aeronautical board tied in with the forthcoming trials of the Wright planes, as well as a Thomas Baldwin airship. On August 20, 1908, Selfridge wrote to Mr. Bell on letterhead of the Army and Navy Club, Washington.

I arrived here on the 10th and have been pretty busy ever since. Up till Saturday we were working hard helping Baldwin get his balloon accepted. On Monday we started our lessons. I made four trips that evening, one as a pilot and three as engineer, and two last evening, one as pilot and one at the engine. It's great sport but can't compare with the June Bug. It seems slow and sluggish after the aeroplane. This evening it was too windy to try, but we expect to get up tomorrow. The balloon will be deflated in a few days so as to make room in the tent for the Wrights' machine, which has arrived. Their two assistants, Taylor and Furness, will start assembling tomorrow in the balloon house. The work here so far has been intensely interesting and promises to grow more so. I had the pleasure of dining and spending the night with the Fairchilds [the Bells' daughter and her husband] on the 10th. David and Daisy came out to see the flight on the 12th.

I can't tell you how much I appreciate all you have done for me nor how deeply I realize the fact that my present status is due entirely to you. I'll not bore you with expressions of my gratitude but do hope you'll always consider me wholly at your and Mrs. Bell's service. I received a very sweet letter from her the other day, which gave me a great deal of pleasure.

With love to all,
Tom

Glenn Curtiss was on hand when the trials began and for the first public flight of the Wright machine on September 3. Things proceeded well until September 17. One of the stipulations of the US Army was that the Wright machine demonstrate capability to carry two persons at an airspeed of 40 mph. New propellers of larger diameters were installed and Lieutenant Thomas Selfridge volunteered to fly with pilot Orville Wright. It was a fateful decision. While they were flying at a height of fifty feet, one of the propellers broke after fouling a rudder wire and the plane nosedived into the ground. Both Wright and Selfridge sustained serious injuries, with Selfridge succumbing to his later that night.

In typical military efficiency Selfridge was buried just two days later at Arlington National Cemetery with full military honours. In life and now in death Selfridge made history. He was the first officer of the United States Army to die in an aeroplane accident and the first man killed in the crash of a powered, heavier-than-air machine.

Mabel and all the surviving members of the AEA were devastated. While the others were in Washington to attend Selfridge's funeral, Mabel wrote the following to Alec from Beinn Bhreagh:

> I can't get over Tom's being taken. I am so sorry for you, dear, in this breaking of your beautiful association. But it was beautiful and the memory of it will endure. Bell, Curtiss, Baldwin, Selfridge, and McCurdy—it was indeed a "brilliant coterie" as one paper said. Do anything you think best but let the AEA be only these to the end and take some other name. Give my love to them all and let's hold tight together, all the tighter for the one that's gone. Casey called me "the little mother of us all" and so I want to be. I love all our boys and there can't be any others just the same. Come back to me as soon as you can and bring them all.

Mabel's grief over the loss of one of "her boys" was still very much evident in a letter written to her mother postmarked September 22.

> I don't think any of you ever realized how near and dear Tom and the other boys were to me. For the others including Alec my relation was more or less of caring for them; he cared for me, looked after me in a hundred little ways I have never been looked after before. I know he loved me very much, not more and perhaps not as much as the others, but he was a different kind of a man, the man who takes care of women and children. He was so very gentle and thoughtful. You see, he lived with us in the closest possible intimacy, entered into my life as only these boys who were living with us could.

They did not have the luxury of time for mourning. Alec and the others gathered in Washington after the funeral and had a formal meeting of the association on September 26. There it was decided to extend the term of the association for an additional six months until March 31, 1909. This decision was considerably facilitated by the grand gesture by Mabel Bell to infuse an additional $10,000 into the association. Douglas McCurdy became the new secretary, and it was agreed that the headquarters of the association would be moved back to Baddeck on October 1, 1908, exactly one year to the day since conception. A lot had been achieved by the group in that short time, and now, ironically, their number had been reduced by one at the hands of a competitor.

The ever safety-conscious Bell made a great study of the apparent causes of the Wright disaster. Two things came out of that: McCurdy's plans for installing two propellers in Silver Dart were nixed, and Bell, asserting himself as chairman, dictated that the associates would not carry a passenger in any future flights of AEA machines, a restriction that was not strictly adhered to in the months following.

Bell also wrote to President Roosevelt offering to make the AEA machines and knowledge available to the US army. The Assistant Secretary of War replied to say that "observers" would be made available to "witness flights upon being informed of the dates of the flights." Clearly the passion, expertise, and input to the AEA by Selfridge as an associate would not be replicated. Casey, McCurdy, and Curtiss were left to complete the mandate of the association in the few months remaining in its term.

On October 1, 1908, Casey returned to Baddeck while Curtiss and McCurdy settled back in at Hammondsport and work on Silver Dart. While the new engine was being made, both McCurdy and Curtiss spent considerable time modifying June Bug with the installation of floats or pontoons in an effort to achieve water takeoff. Repeated tests with flat-bottomed floats as well as floats with foils proved unsuccessful, and June Bug was dismantled for the winter. Meanwhile, by early November the new engine had been installed in Silver Dart. Testing proceeded well into December with considerable tweaking required before Curtiss and McCurdy were satisfied with its performance.

McCurdy began test-flying Silver Dart in the meadow outside Hammondsport on December 6, 1908. There were early problems encountered in getting lift. Despite the larger and more powerful engine, the Dart was also heavier than the earlier machines. Bell himself visited Hammondsport

December 20–21 and while impressed with Silver Dart was denied an opportunity to see it fly due to inclement weather. Following his departure steps were taken to dismantle, crate, and ship Silver Dart to Baddeck; final components, including the engine, arrived there by February 11, 1909.

Up until now all three AEA dromes—Red Wing, White Wing, and June Bug—had been built and flown in the United States. Bell wanted to make history with Drome No. 4 by flying it in Canada, where up until now there had never been a flight by a manned, heavier-than-air machine (i.e., a powered craft). This honour would fall by process of elimination, and Bell's methodical planning, to his "boy from Baddeck," Douglas McCurdy.

The flight took place on a cold winter day, February 23, 1909, from the frozen surface of Baddeck Bay. Scores of people from Baddeck and the surrounding countryside showed up for the event. Bell was careful to take the names of more than one hundred, as witnesses to the historic occasion. After a first attempt was aborted due to a broken gas line, McCurdy roared down the bay and flew for half a mile before alighting on the ice again. McCurdy was by this time already well versed in flying Silver Dart—this was his fifteenth flight—but, according to script, it was a flight of historic proportions, the first in Canada and the first flight of a British subject in a heavier-than-air machine in the British Empire. Lost in the excitement of that day, and largely forgotten with the passage of time, was an equally important aviation milestone: eleven months previously Casey Baldwin became the first Canadian, and the first born in the British Empire, to fly anywhere when he flew Red Wing at Hammondsport on March 12, 1908.

In the days that followed, McCurdy made many more flights in Silver Dart, which was becoming a common spectacle in the skies over Baddeck. McCurdy was the talk of the village and the subject of considerable interest by the local press.

Interestingly, neither Casey nor Curtiss was present to witness McCurdy's historic first flight on February 23. Casey and Kathleen had set off for New York on February 18 where Casey took in an automobile and motorboat show. They then proceeded to St. Catharines and Toronto where Casey was engaged in a speaking tour. He first gave an address to the boys at Ridley College in St. Catharines followed by an address on aviation at his alma mater, the University of Toronto, which was greeted with near wild enthusiasm. His concluding remarks were prophetic: "The usefulness of flying machines in war ensures the continuous development of the art of aviation. The great military powers are afraid of the flying machine, and the struggle to improve it must therefore go on. Self-protection demands more practical, more airworthy, and more efficient machines. Flight has been accomplished. The flying machine is actually here and no great nation can afford to neglect it." The overwhelming response to Casey's talks precipitated more invitations, including the Canadian Club of Toronto.

Casey sent a telegram to Bell following his speech at U of T, delivered to eleven hundred students and a "prostrated faculty completely collapsed." This prompted Bell to write the following in Home Notes:

> Evidently the publicity given to Douglas's flight served as an introduction to Baldwin's lecture. What a scene it must have been. What volumes are expressed by the statement that the faculty collapsed. Hooting, yelling, singing, cheering by 1,100 students must have constituted a perfect ovation, and I have no doubt the whole student body joined in the chorus of the old student song "Casey Baldwin, Casey Baldwin." I am glad Casey has accepted the invitation of the Canadian Club. That is quite an honor for a Canadian, a resident of Toronto. As a rule, Canadian Clubs invite distinguished foreigners or people from a distance to address them. "A prophet is without honor in his own country," and it is very rarely that a local club makes much of a fuss over people from its own locality.

Following his address to the Canadian Club, Casey returned to Beinn Bhreagh and wrote to Kathleen, who was still in Toronto. She wrote a letter back in which she made mention of his future plans.

> Everyone said how well you had done at the Canadian Club that night and I only wish I could have been behind the scenes to have heard.
>
> I am overjoyed to know of John's grand flight—I hope you will go up the next time. Isn't it perfectly great! Flying certainly is no longer a dream. I am aching to know what decision you come to as to the future. I imagine you and John will decide to go out on the road and make some money. No doubt you and John have been pow-wowing your d___ed heads off, and by the time I get back I may possibly be able to get you to bed at a reasonable hour.

Mabel, who had an innate ability to look beyond the success of the invention to the commercial viability of the product, encouraged Alec to "strike while the iron was hot" in taking advantage of their success with Silver Dart. On March 17 she wrote,

> I look upon it that the success of the Silver Dart means everything to us in the prestige it gives all our work. I have spent all the money and more than I can hope to get from my little property; still I do want you to go on and put more of your money into the venture so as to assure the success of the Silver Dart and its purchase by the government. I'd a hundred times rather have Mr. Curtiss's motor succeed than any other, but still the first thing is the success of our aerodrome. Nothing succeeds like success, you know. We'll win out of course—it's only a question of time, and though it seems so long to us, yet how short a time it is in the world's history, and your work is to endure so long as the world shall last. Because it is great, it cannot be done in a hurry.

The final days of the AEA were spent by Bell, Baldwin, and McCurdy in Baddeck attempting to get Bell's Drome No. 5, which by now he had named Cygnet 2, into the air. It was the final element, the fifth machine, in the AEA mandate, and there were only days left before the association was due to be dissolved. Bell was persistent in adhering to his decision to construct a man-carrying powered tetrahedral cell aerodrome despite the fact that his young associates clearly favoured and were committed to the more popular and now proven biplane configuration. This clear differentiation in philosophy between the patriarch chairman and his young associates was a distraction to the latter, and yet, to appease their mentor, Casey and McCurdy pressed on with completion of Dr. Bell's machine.

It proved to be the only unsuccessful, non-record-setting machine of the five. During March of 1909 first McCurdy and then Casey made several attempts to fly Cygnet 2, which had been fitted out with the motor from Silver Dart. They were never successful in getting the craft into the air.

Time ran out. On March 31, 1909, a somber group met around the fireplace in the Great Hall at Beinn Bhreagh. Three members of the AEA, Bell, Casey, and McCurdy, were joined at the fireside by Mrs. Bell's secretary, Mabel McCurdy, Kathleen Baldwin, and Bell's personal secretary, Charles R.

Cox. Despite being aware of the importance of this meeting and strenuous efforts by Bell to encourage his attendance, Glenn Curtiss was absent. He had become quite distant from the group once Silver Dart had been removed from Hammondsport and the AEA headquarters relocated back to Baddeck. He was then, and always, the odd man out in the group.

Some preliminary discussions that included Curtiss as to the future prospects of the associates after dissolution of the AEA were shelved. There had been nothing hard and fast arrived at, and it was clear that Curtiss had his own, more self-interested thoughts on that subject. There were some important business matters to attend to, including disposition of association assets. That could wait. For now it was a case of recognizing the contribution of the Bells toward the success of the AEA. Both Casey and McCurdy submitted resolutions in appreciation of Dr. Bell's labour in preserving information and accurate records of their work in the AEA Bulletin as well as the financial and emotional support of "their little mother," Mabel Bell.

Alec described the dissolution of the AEA in a letter to Mabel immediately after the event.

We had quite a pathetic little meeting on Wednesday, March 31, 1909 when the remains of the Aerial Experiment Association—Douglas, Casey and I, with Kathleen, Mabel McCurdy and Mr. Cox watched the hands of the clock go round towards the hour that marked the expiration of the Association. We could not allow it to expire by itself so one minute before midnight Casey moved the final adjournment, Douglas seconded it and I put it formally to a vote. We had hardly received the response "Aye" when the first stroke of midnight began. I do not know how the others felt but to me it was really a dramatic moment. All that remains of the A.E.A. now is the trustee.

The AEA had experienced an amazing run. In eighteen months, beginning with a rudimentary glider, it had produced four flying machines for an outlay of just $38,000. The associates Baldwin, Selfridge, Curtiss, and McCurdy truly were "magnificent men," as were their "flying machines."

TOP: *Alexander Graham Bell and Mabel with daughters Elsie (left) and Daisy in 1885.* BOTTOM: *Houseboat* Mabel of Beinn Bhreagh.

TOP: *Casey and workmen constructing tetrahedral tower atop Red Head.*
BOTTOM: *Aerial Experiment Association members (from left): Curtiss, Baldwin, Bell, Selfridge, and McCurdy.*

TOP: *Casey making practice flights with glider at Hammondsport, NY.*
BOTTOM: *Casey (centre) and others with Red Wing on Keuka Lake, NY, in 1908.*

TOP: *Author at Pleasant Valley Racetrack/airfield outside Hammondsport,* NY.
BOTTOM: *Casey preparing Baddeck No. 1 for trials at Petawawa,* ON.

TOP: *Pontiac Hotel at Fort William,* PQ, *on Ottawa River opposite Camp Petawawa.* BOTTOM: *Captain Daniel Mazurek hosting author at Cavalry Field, Camp Petawawa,* ON.

CHAPTER 6

Canadian Aerodrome Company

The Birth of the Canadian Aerospace Industry

PRIL 1, 1909, REPRESENTED A NEW BEGINNING FOR CASEY
Baldwin and Douglas McCurdy. The magnificent experiment with the
AEA was behind them. Of the original group of four only Casey and
Douglas remained. Selfridge was dead and Curtiss, to use Mabel's words, had
"defected."

Alec and Mabel wanted very much to ensure a good future for "their boys,"
Baldwin and McCurdy. Alec had ensured that the historic first flight of Silver
Dart was well publicized in Canada and knew that this feat could be a launch
pad for Casey and Douglas into the commercial production of aircraft.

In the waning days of the AEA after February 23, 1909, Bell took to the
speaker's circuit, ostensibly to talk about aviation but also indirectly to campaign for employment opportunities for his two young protegés.

Bell, given the outstanding achievements of the AEA, had every reason to
be optimistic about the future for aviation in Canada; however, he was soon

to confront the reality that it was the politician, not the businessman, who determined and directed public policy in Canada. He may not have seen it, but from the very outset there were storm clouds on the horizon for the inventor and his two young aviators.

After the flight of Silver Dart and the publicity it garnered at both local and national levels, the question of whether the Canadian government was intending to now take steps to encourage the science of aviation was raised in the House of Commons in Ottawa by Sam Hughes, an Opposition member who later became Minister of Militia early in the First World War. J. H. Parkin's book *Bell and Baldwin* provides the following response by the then Minister of Finance, which set the tone for all future deliberations on that subject: "The Government had the highest appreciation of the work accomplished by Dr. Bell, McCurdy, and Baldwin *but* there was no branch of the public service which could conveniently utilize the discoveries of these scientific gentlemen. However, they [the government] felt that they should take some notice of their achievements and so had drawn them to the attention of the Imperial Government in the hope that the War Office or Admiralty might be able to utilize the service of these young Canadians and thus retain them for the benefit of the Empire."

It was a decisive moment for aviation in Canada. Baldwin and McCurdy had a hard-earned new reputation, gained from employing their engineering skills as designers, builders, and flyers of the most advanced aeroplanes in America. They were the country's first "aeronauts," equivalent of today's astronauts, akin to the first men to step foot on the moon. Despite that, they would have to deal in the future with a disinterested government and "brush-offs" much like the one above.

Shortly after the flight of Silver Dart at Baddeck, Bell received an invitation to address the Canadian Club of Ottawa about the AEA and its experiments. It was awkward timing with the final work on his drome and the pending windup of the association but too good an opportunity to pass up. The possibility of meeting with Governor General Earl Grey and Prime Minister Sir Wilfrid Laurier and some of his cabinet would afford Bell a unique forum to share his account of the work of the AEA.

In preparing for his address, Alec and Casey met aboard the houseboat on March 21, where Bell dictated his thoughts on the future of aviation and potential roles the AEA associates might play in this new field. His observations recorded in Home Notes, presented below, give insight into how and why the relationship between the AEA associates Curtiss, Baldwin, and McCurdy would be impacted upon dissolution of the association. It is apparent that Bell's primary interest was the future well-being of Casey and Douglas, while at the same time he addressed the role Curtiss might have in the manufacturing of aeroplanes. He mused about how any future efforts in manufacturing aircraft would be impacted by the interests each had in aeroplane technology arising out of their joint association in the AEA. Bell felt that having patents would have simplified this matter, but they had none at this point. He was concerned about how to separate the rights of the AEA from those of a proposed new Aerodrome Company.

> I cannot go to Ottawa without some definite idea or proposition in my mind....
>
> It seems to me therefore that an understanding should be arrived at that during a certain period, say two years, Douglas and Casey on the one hand in Canada and Curtiss on the other hand in the United States should agree to pay the Aerodrome Company some definite royalty on every aerodrome they sell with the understanding that if within two years the Aerodrome Company should succeed in obtaining patents in the United States, Canada, and Great Britain, that then the Aerodrome Company should licence Curtiss to manufacture aerodromes in the United States under a US patent and should licence McCurdy and Baldwin to manufacture in Canada under the Canadian patents or in Great Britain under the British patent....
>
> With such an understanding Curtiss in the US and Baldwin and McCurdy in Canada would be free to go ahead and make what they could by the manufacture of aerodromes. Any such understanding, however, would be a matter between them and all the interests concerned in the Aerial Experiment Association....
>
> In approaching the Canadian Government we could point out that the AEA will be dissolved March 31st and that Curtiss desires to enter the commercial field in the US and that Messrs. Baldwin and McCurdy in Canada. Curtiss has already secured the backing of capital in the US but that Baldwin and McCurdy have not in Canada. Would it not then be a proper thing for the Canadian Government to

do something to assist them in founding a new industry in Canada by placing an order with them for one or more aerodromes of the Silver Dart pattern?…

It would be to the advantage of Canada to have this industry established and maintained here rather than in Great Britain as Canadian subjects would be supported by it.…

In a word—ask the Canadian Government for an appropriation to encourage the establishment of a new industry within the Dominion of Canada to be carried on exclusively by British subjects.

This summary of Bell's thoughts was profound and so typical of the man. Bell, the inveterate thinker, was considering the big picture and how this might all eventually play out with the three young men who otherwise were too involved with their day-to-day work to contemplate the potential for future conflict. Now that the AEA had been dissolved, Bell believed that it would be "equitable" for Curtiss, Douglas, and Casey, in manufacturing aeroplanes incorporating the inventions (i.e., patents) belonging to the Association, to pay a 10 percent royalty to the trustee. He described this as a "voluntary arrangement" that "should be made at once in the case of Curtiss because he is now entering on the manufacture of aerodromes without any agreement or understanding as to his relation to the old A.E.A." His reflections became a blueprint for events that later transpired.

On March 27, 1909, Bell gave a stirring address to the Canadian Club at the Château Laurier in Ottawa in which he described the work of the AEA and emphasized that in the case of Canada, or any nation, control of the air for tomorrow was as important as control of the sea today. A keynote of his speech, described in Parkin's book *Bell and Baldwin*, was when he implored the Government, "To take steps to secure for the nation the services of the two brilliant young Canadians who had been working with him for the last two years and who were then branching out for themselves with their inventions for aviation."

Bell underlined the fact that both Baldwin and McCurdy were Canadians who "wanted to do something for the Canadian Government, if not for the British Government," and failing that, they would go in business for themselves, prepared to deal with any government as being the most likely market for their machines.

It was an august audience, which included Bell's friend Governor General Earl Grey. Lord Grey gave clear evidence of his support by stating that Canada, which had given the world the telephone and wireless telegraphy, could "complete her services to the British Empire and to civilization by giving to the world the best aerodrome, the possession of which will make the nation that is fortunate enough to own it, to quote Dr. Graham Bell, the foremost nation of the world."

Mr. Fielding, the finance minister, was present as well. He noted that he had already drawn the attention of the Imperial Government to the impressive accomplishments of both Baldwin and McCurdy through the Governor General. No one, he intoned, "would be more pleased if the names and fame and services of these two devoted young Canadians could be kept for the Empire."

These were pretty heady words, but they were just that—words. Bell had given it his best shot. The rest would be up to the Canadian government.

Mabel was enthused over Alec's "perfectly grand" address in Ottawa. She wrote on April 9 both to commend him as well as to give advice, which, had it been taken, might have improved the prospects of McCurdy and Baldwin in the months ahead. "We want to go on striking while the iron is hot," she wrote. "Don't you think it would be well for Douglas and Casey to associate themselves with someone more experienced in the business end? I think Casey would always much rather go on with his engineering work and Douglas with the demonstrating. Douglas might do more office work if he had the business training, but it seems to me that there is plenty of work for three, and it's time to hustle or we'll get left. Machines that have never been tried are selling for thousands." Time would prove Mabel to be correct.

Returning home to Beinn Bhreagh, Bell gathered Casey and Douglas and outlined a proposition for their future career path. They would continue to work as his assistants but would form a company to build aircraft using Silver Dart as a prototype for sale to the Canadian, British, or any other government. Bell would allow them the use of the Kite House, the former headquarters of the now defunct AEA, for an aerodrome factory. He was also prepared to advance them sufficient funds to build two aerodromes, which they could reimburse to him from sales. It was too generous an offer to refuse. Baddeck, Nova Scotia, was now home to the Canadian Aerodrome Company, the establishment of which gave birth to the Canadian aviation industry.

Bell as promoter and benefactor to the new company allowed the young and now independent aerodrome manufacturers full access to the tools, apparatus, and materials of his Beinn Bhreagh laboratory. His only stipulation was that Baldwin and McCurdy, as Canada's first aircraft designers and builders, keep separate records for their company from that of the Laboratory.

The aviators, now turned aviation entrepreneurs, immediately took to their new vocation. By May a number of staff had been hired, including shop foreman Ken Ingraham who had overseen the building of Silver Dart in Hammondsport. Work began almost immediately on their first aerodrome with a decision made to fabricate materials for two machines at the same time, thus allowing for the construction of the second while the first was being test-flown. As planned, Silver Dart was used as the prototype, with modifications. Casey and Douglas were in effect picking up from where they had left off with the construction of Silver Dart, the AEA's Drome No. 4.

These were exciting times. The Bells had embarked on a trip to the UK aboard SS *Cedric* shortly after consummating the new working arrangement with Casey and Douglas. Kathleen and Casey wrote a joint letter to the Bells on May 11, 1909, in which both spoke very positively about life at Beinn Bhreagh. First Kathleen wrote, "We may see you in dear old London—if we go. Of course I'm crazy to, but I must learn not to bank too much on things in the Flying Machine business as it's too uncertain.

"Things are going on swimmingly down here," she continued, "and everybody is very bright and happy about the future prospects of the AEA—oh, excuse me—the Canadian Aerodrome Company. Douglas is getting a fine system working: letter files, time cards, and all sorts of business-like contrivances."

Casey joined with his own account:

The "business contrivances" may be all right and are undeniably imposing, but what is much more important is that the new machines are nicely underway. It is just about as rash to predict when a flying machine will be finished as it is to prophesy what it will do later; still nevertheless and notwithstanding I think that by the end of the month one of them should be about ready for the new motor.

John and Kass and I hatch out schemes ad infinitum every evening, and all of them look good so the future is rather bewildering. The present however is clear cut and A-1 at Lloyd's [of London, insurance company].

The first aeroplane to be built in Canada was appropriately named Baddeck No. 1 in honour of its birthplace. The new innovations were primarily technical in nature and included such things as trussed ribs and replacement of the rubberized silk used on the Dart with a light, rot-resistant cloth fabric similar to what was used for sails on yachts. Their choice of power was interesting. Curtiss was no longer on the scene and rather than approach him for a motor (they had experienced problems with the last Curtiss engine mounted in Silver Dart) they found what was felt to be a more satisfactory engine, which they purchased from the Kirkham Motor Company of Bath, New York, which was just a few miles removed from Hammondsport.

Baddeck No. 1 was completed by early July, and on the ninth residents from Baddeck and the surrounding area were invited to come to Beinn Bhreagh for a first-hand look at the new aircraft. McCurdy acted as host for the occasion, giving all those present a full account of the machine and its history. Afterwards everyone was invited to take tea in the nearby Baldwin bungalow. It would have been an occasion much like today visiting the Kennedy Space Center, albeit on a much smaller scale.

While Baddeck No. 1 was under construction Alec was in the UK. It was during this time that, arising out of Bell's address to the Canadian Club, the Canadian Department of Militia and Defence wrote to Casey and Douglas indicating a desire to assist them but also to say that Parliament "had not provided funds for airship investigation or construction." However, the department was prepared to offer the use of the new military grounds at Petawawa, Ontario, including "such men and equipment as might be available" should they wish to make trials of their new aircraft there. They were also asked whether the two of them might serve as specialists in aviation matters to the department and what appropriation they might seek for next year for their remuneration.

Casey and Douglas immediately sent a telegraph off to Bell who was then, on May 14, 1909, a passenger aboard ss *Cedric* en route to England. "Have been invited to test machine at Petawawa by Military Department, Ottawa. We answered in the affirmative and would like to take Silver Dart with new engine to practice. Are you agreeable? Bon voyage. (John – Casey)."

Bell sent his reply ashore by pilot boat. "Glad to have you do anything you want with Silver Dart in Canada. Good luck."

While in England and after giving the matter more thought, Bell wrote to Casey and Douglas suggesting that they meet with him in Montreal following his return to Canada by the ss *Corsican* so that he might share his views on their best course of action vis-à-vis the government proposition. On June 9, 1909, Bell wrote:

> I presume that you are waiting my return before making any definite proposition to the Canadian government relating to your service, etc. As one or both of you are now in Petawawa or will be shortly there, it seems to me a good plan for us to have a conference upon the subject in Montreal as speedily as possible. We leave Liverpool June 17th by ss *Corsican* and will go on to Montreal instead of leaving the steamer at Quebec. I will then be in position to lend assistance to you in the matter....
>
> I hope you have not and will not commit yourselves until I can be on the scene to help you.
>
> Great things are undoubtedly in store for you...do not allow yourselves to be tempted by [indecipherable] etc., but go steadily ahead and build your machines. The success of your machine will mean your success. Don't worry your heads about your future. Think only of the machine.

In May Casey and Douglas had accepted the offer of the Canadian government without committing themselves regarding the question of remuneration for future services. Steps were taken to ship Silver Dart to Petawawa in late June even though, as it turned out, the military camp there was only in early stages of construction. Baddeck No. 1 would arrive later in July. Things were happening fast and clearly both Casey and Douglas were making their own decisions at this juncture.

Casey was on hand to greet Alec when he arrived in Montreal at the end of June. It perhaps was not the "conference" Bell had hoped for, given what had already transpired in his absence and the fact that McCurdy was not present. Bell and Casey journeyed to Ottawa where they met with Prime Minister Sir Wilfrid Laurier who, not having any personal knowledge on the matter, referred them to Sir Frederick Borden, the Minister of Militia and Defence, who unfortunately was out of town. It proved to be a wasted effort. Bell set out for Baddeck while Casey headed off for Petawawa.

The two young aviators, and now businessmen, were up against it from the time they arrived at the camp. The site was only in the formative stages of construction; only one aircraft could be accommodated inside a single "tar paper and lumber shed," which was still under construction, and the cavalry field offered as a runway was rough, irregular, and little more than a blueberry patch. It proved to be an enormous undertaking to dismantle and ship, then assemble Silver Dart and Baddeck No. 1. This is to say nothing about transportation, moving aeroplanes (a first), plane parts including motors and accessories, and people by boat and train the 1,750 kilometres between Baddeck and Petawawa. Just to accomplish that feat was a testament to the energy and determination of the boys from Baddeck.

Back at Beinn Bhreagh Bell was anxiously awaiting news from Camp Petawawa. On July 30 a letter arrived from McCurdy. He and William MacDonald, an assistant from Baddeck, had arrived at Petawawa on July 23 where it had been raining for the previous two weeks. Casey was not on hand for his arrival. He was staying about two miles away across the river at a small resort that he and Kathleen had found together, the Pontiac Hotel at Fort William on the Quebec side of the Ottawa River opposite the camp. Nonetheless, McCurdy seemed quite upbeat. "The military here are awfully keen, and the Old Colonel casually remarked to me yesterday that he was looking forward with a great deal of pleasure to a ride in the machine. All the officers are interested, and in general things look bright. The Assistant Deputy Minister of Militia is here and is going to stay over for a flight."

Kathleen spent the weeks before the Petawawa tests visiting family and travelling about Toronto and St. Catharines. She kept up regular correspondence with Mabel during this time and finally joined Casey at "the resort" in Fort William in mid-July. It had been quite a while since the two women had seen one another. Kathleen wrote to Mabel on July 19 to say, "Your letters are always so full of love that we long to be with you, where you have made us feel we belong. Casey and I so often say that you and Mr. Bell couldn't have done more for us had we been your own children, and if loving appreciation is the compliment of that love, no adoption was ever more complete—and though it is impossible to express one's deeper feelings, we both know that you and Mr. Bell understand."

Kathleen found the time long. She stayed at the hotel while each day Casey was ferried back and forth across the Ottawa River, to and from Camp Petawawa. Then it rained steadily for a week. Kathleen described the work at

Petawawa: "Things are so beastly slow. Only now, after one whole month, is the shed nearing completion. John arrived back just at the tail end of almost a week's continuous rain—he was just about sick of things generally, the Army in particular, and the rain was most inopportune as things always appear so much worse in wet weather, and it certainly was rotten.... I often wish the government had never written, although really and truly it is a fine chance for the boys."

The weather turned hot and on July 25 they assembled the Dart and installed the engine out of doors in anticipation of a trial run the following week. Evidently the military personnel on-site shared McCurdy's enthusiasm.

It was decided to conduct initial flights using Silver Dart to obtain a feel for the site and terrain before employing the untested Baddeck No. 1. Early in the morning on August 2, before dawn and before the pesky media could interfere, McCurdy and Casey took up the Silver Dart together, in contravention of the express prohibition Bell had made earlier about never flying with a passenger; it seems they must have taken their mentor literally when he said that they could "do anything they wanted with the Silver Dart in Canada." In any event, they found the plane worked perfectly well with both onboard. Another Canadian aviation milestone had just been achieved: the first passenger flight in Canada, and it was made by an AEA machine. Before the day was out the Dart made a number of more flights with two aboard.

It was to be the last hurrah for AEA's Drome No. 4. On the fourth flight of that morning, just as the sun poked its head above the horizon, McCurdy was piloting the Dart back toward the shed with Casey aboard at an altitude of ten feet. He was too low and, temporarily blinded by the sun, he miscalculated his altitude. The front wheel struck a small knoll, the Dart dropped her right wing, struck the ground, and splintered to pieces. Casey and McCurdy escaped with a few cuts and bruises, but it was the end of the plane and an ominous start for their "trial" at Petawawa.

Bell learned of the accident by virtue of two letters received from Kathleen and a letter from McCurdy. In describing the injuries sustained in the accident Kathleen noted that "Casey is perfectly well and enjoyed a good breakfast." As for McCurdy, she wrote,

I haven't seen John yet and don't expect to for some days as his face is anything but beautiful to behold, so I imagine he will keep himself in hiding till it looks a little more presentable. In case you are wondering the extent of John's damages, he got his nose and cheeks pretty badly scratched. Casey says he looks as if he had been in a prize fight.

He and Casey of course are not by any chance going to let anyone know just how disappointed they really are—naturally they were both very fond of the Dart and they hated to see her smashed up. Still, she did her work, though not quite enough, and they would so much have liked to get a few more trys out.

Oh dear, I can't get it out of my head—and the part that's really troubling me is the fate of the new machine. Not having had as much practice with the Dart as they should have makes it doubly uncertain.

Her unease would soon prove to have been warranted.

Casey was quite cavalier about their close call in the crash. As he later wrote in the *Beinn Bhreagh Recorder* from Fort William,

The good old Silver Dart is no more. Although she gave a convincing demonstration of the possibilities of the new motor before giving up her aerial ghost, still it is hard to think of the old Dart as gone. Every Tommy in Camp has a souvenir splinter by this time. The wreck was no uncertain one, and besides losing our practice machine, a great deal of official faith probably went by the board.

John scratched his face and will not be cursed by his fatal beauty for a week or two; and I got my leg under something that took some skin off. Otherwise we are intact, which I think is one more example of the fact that you have very good chances of coming out of the worst kind of a wreck with nothing more than scratches.

You have no idea what a satisfaction it is to feel that we have a motor upon which we can rely.

Thank you very much for the portfolio with the notes [the Beinn Bhreagh Recorder about the ongoing work at the Laboratory]. I enjoyed reading them. The discussion especially made me feel quite homesick.

On August 4, just days after the mishap, Casey wrote to Mabel to reassure her that the accident was not due to carelessness.

We have just been reading the accounts in the newspapers and hope that those you have seen were not too lurid. Most of them are over dramatic and might cause you some anxiety. As a matter of fact, John and I are perfectly all right and hope to have Baddeck No. 1 assembled in a few days. John came over last night and brought Mr. Bell's telegram. It really was not carelessness in any way which brought about the mishap to the Dart, but if possible we will feel our way more carefully in the future. Of course, now that it is over we can see many ways by which the accident might have been avoided.

In reference to a reliable motor, Casey and Douglas had installed in Silver Dart the Kirkham motor built and delivered to Petawawa from Bath, New York. It was a heavier but more powerful commercial automobile engine with greater endurance than earlier Curtiss engines had proven to have. This motor appeared to have given the Dart the extra power required for sustained flight as well as the ability to carry two men. Bell acknowledged this when he wrote, "The flights of the Silver Dart at Camp Petawawa August 2nd have shown that it [i.e., a commercial automobile engine] has not only abundant power for this purpose but can also carry the additional load of another man." He was not, however, ready to entirely abandon his previous position that all testing should be done with just one man aboard, and strongly urged both aviators to maintain this position in all future testing of Baddeck numbers 1 and 2.

The catastrophic crash of Silver Dart, before the Canadian military and press had an opportunity to see it fly, would turn out to be a defining moment for Casey and Douglas, the Canadian Aerodrome Company, and the immediate prospects for aviation in Canada.

For the next number of days Casey and Douglas worked to get Baddeck No. 1 ready. Casey sent regular reports to Beinn Bhreagh that suggested quiet optimism. "Everybody is tremendously interested. If we can make good flights with Baddeck No. 1 the Silver Dart episode will be forgotten as an accident and remembered only as an entirely satisfactory test of a new motor."

It was equally clear from what Casey wrote that they were going to take no chances in rushing to get Baddeck No. 1 into the air. The terrain at the cavalry field was treacherous as they had learned with the Dart. Casey emphasized this when he wrote to Mabel on August 7. "Flying over this undulating ground is a very different proposition from the ice or level fields. A landing can be effected anywhere on the ground if necessary, but some parts are much better than others and we cannot afford to take any chances. From our brief experience of making a landing not perfectly judged on uneven ground the danger seems to me to be on the rebound, which is almost certain to be erratic."

The two weeks that followed involved extensive tweaking of Baddeck No. 1 before the aviators were prepared to take it into the air. The press and the military observers naturally became impatient as days went by. In fairness to the media, they had great expectations and many of them had literally camped out for weeks waiting to see Canada's new aviators take to the air. They had not seen the four flights of Silver Dart due to the pains Casey and Douglas had taken to avoid the press, making those flights before dawn.

Many of the military officials, impatient with travelling back and forth to Petawawa while awaiting *the* test flight, spoke negatively about prospects for aviation in Canada. The following account from the *Citizen* newspaper of August 9, 1909, was typical:

> The repeated calling off of flights is a source of great disappointment to many who have come from a distance. The difficult journey to the military camp day after day, only to hear that there will be no flight has caused a lot of grumbling, but of course the aviators know their own business better than spectators.
>
> The consensus of opinion among the military officers seems to be that it will be many years before the aerodrome or aeroplane is of practical use in warfare. Colonel English, Camp Commandant stated that in his opinion the science of aviation was yet in its infancy and the aerodrome would be only of use for scouting purposes. It would not carry any great weight as yet. Other officers interviewed gave the opinion that as an offensive weapon a flying machine would be practically useless for some time.

During this time the headlines in the local press reflected this growing impatience: "Almost Ready for Petawawa Aero Trials"; "Assembling of Aeroplane is Tedious Work"; "Baddeck No. 1 Will be Tried at Petawawa Early Tomorrow"; "All Ready but Wind too High"; "Aviators Again Disappoint

Those Who Would See Them Fly"; "Doubt on Its Ability to Fly"; "Aerodrome Flew 100 Feet at Petawawa Camp Trial"; "Aerodrome Comes to Grief While Up Fifteen Feet"; "Disappointed Aviators Make Decision—Will Return To Baddeck."

Casey took the media glare in stride, even when he was made the brunt of their "attacks." In diarizing those events Casey remarked, "The Toronto News had a little jest on me to the effect that while they always understood me to be temperate, there was reason to believe that I took a drop too much at Petawawa. Kass was very much annoyed when she heard of it and was on the point of writing an indignant letter to the Editor when the joke dawned on her."

Casey and Douglas were very careful to heed Bell's advice and took meticulous efforts to test the machine and motor of Baddeck No. 1 on the ground before attempting to get airborne. McCurdy made this abundantly clear when interviewed by a reporter from the *Pembroke Standard* on August 10.

Of one thing the public can rest assured and that is that there will not be even a preparatory test until we feel sure that we are good and ready. I do not think anyone need be particularly anxious to see this aerodrome leave the ground for the first time. We shall have many of these preliminary tests, one of which will probably be about as interesting as another, before we can feel warranted in having her leave the ground for a real trial. In the first trial we shall probably just bump around close to the ground, going not more than two or three hundred feet until we can satisfy ourselves that she is properly balanced and under perfect control. All this will take up a lot of time, and I would not even guess when we shall be ready to make a trial that will be worth looking at.

By mid-August Baddeck No. 1 had been up and down the runway a number of times with a few "hops" into the air and despite much tweaking never did demonstrate sustained flight. On the last of such attempts, after flying but seventy yards, the machine, seeming to be tail heavy, slid backwards, breaking the running gear and outer edges of the lower wing. To the uninitiated, not knowing just how much testing was required to rectify minor defects in a new machine, it looked more as if the pilots knew little about flying machines. It was a monumental disappointment, particularly for McCurdy who in Baddeck had flown Silver Dart successfully and repeatedly for miles at a time.

Casey's prediction that the misfortune with Silver Dart would quickly be forgotten with a successful flight of Baddeck No. 1 never materialized. The Petawawa jury had returned its verdict, and as Casey wrote, "the nays have it." If nothing else had been accomplished by all this effort, Silver Dart did fly what is now considered the first military flight trials in Canada at Petawawa. On a slightly lesser historic note, the shed built to house Silver Dart was the first airplane hangar built in Canada, and the final flight of the Dart, piloted by McCurdy with Casey aboard, represented the first passenger flight in Canada. Nonetheless, this was small consolation for the two aviators.

On August 15 a final account of the Petawawa trials appeared in the *Citizen*.

Following the accident to Baddeck 1 aerodrome on Friday Messrs. McCurdy and Baldwin have decided to take the disabled machine back to their workshops at Baddeck, N.S. where repairs will be made. They feel that the work will be done with greater dispatch there. So soon as the necessary repairs are completed, Mr. McCurdy states that Baddeck 1 will be brought again to camp and the trials resumed. "We should be back here in about three weeks and despite our seeming failures, we will make good here yet" was the aviator's reply.

That the two young aviators are keenly disappointed in the two disastrous endings to their attempts to fly here is quite evident from their downcast demeanor. They are not the same McCurdy and Baldwin of Friday afternoon before the second accident. Their bright and cheery manner is missing. Much sympathy is felt for them among the officers and soldiers of the camp.

Abruptly, on August 19, Casey, Kathleen, and Douglas packed up and returned to Beinn Bhreagh where a post-mortem was held with Bell. The performance of Baddeck No. 1 while in Petawawa was the subject of intense discussion and scrutiny before the machine arrived back in Baddeck on September 3.

It takes time to implement new technology and for people to come around to it. It is always easier to be a naysayer than an advocate. That is not to say that aviation in Canada did not engender support—it was simply a matter of not garnering support at the highest level. A few months after Casey and Douglas had returned home from Petawawa, MP Thomas Chisholm rose in the House of Commons in Ottawa imploring the government to take action in this new field of aviation. His address on February 16 was reported in Hansard.

> There is another matter which I think should be taken up by the government, and that is the encouragement of aviation. I think this government should have done something for Messrs. McCurdy and Baldwin when they attended the military camp at Petawawa last summer. We are told that the government gave them the use of some sheds on the grounds, but what the government ought to have done was to pay their way there, maintain them properly when they were there, and pay their expenses back again at least. They are considering in other countries the question of the navigation of the air and Canada should not be behind—why are we neglecting this very important factor in the defence of our country?

Casey and Douglas retained one ally in the militia. Major G. S. Maunsell, Director of Engineer Services, Militia Department, had been present at Petawawa for a number of the attempted flights, including the last one by Baddeck No. 1. He had full confidence in McCurdy and Baldwin and Baddeck No. 1, stating that "there was no doubt that the machine could fly." Within a few months he would prove himself to be correct when he flew as a passenger aboard Baddeck No. 1 in Baddeck.

CHAPTER 7

Aerodrome Park

Once back home in Baddeck, Casey gave considerable thought to reasons why Baddeck No. 1 had underperformed at Petawawa. He was perplexed, even to the point of reviewing photographs of both Silver Dart and June Bug in the air to reassure himself that they really did fly satisfactorily. It could be that Baddeck No. 1 was over-modified. As Casey would write in the *Beinn Bhreagh Recorder*, "The curved bow-control was a departure in Baddeck No. 1, and one which I think we must admit was a mistake under the existing circumstances. While it may not have caused the accident to Baddeck No. 1 it undoubtedly made the machine more sensitive. A tailless aerodrome with a curved bow control is about as sensitive a model as we can possibly build. In our efforts to improve the safety of the machine I think we are wise to going back to a tail and plane controls."

The fledgling Canadian Aerodrome Company was lacking in one important asset—a proper airfield. The invitation to Petawawa had been received just shortly after the company had begun, before they'd had time to investigate this need. In hindsight, had there been a testing ground in Baddeck in all likelihood the trials that took place in Petawawa would probably have taken place "at home" and perhaps with a different outcome.

In any event there was some exploratory work undertaken by Baldwin and McCurdy that summer. They had considered and dismissed a possible site in the outskirts of the village of Baddeck. Alec meanwhile had proposed looking into possible sites in the Baddeck River Valley, just a few miles west of Baddeck. With typical foresight he had already put out feelers and received helpful advice from local residents.

During the latter part of August Casey and Douglas reconnoitered both sides of the Baddeck River, from Red Bridge downriver to Bentick Farm, Intervale, where they found about three hundred acres of ideal ground, flat as a table and entirely cleared of trees or obstructions of any kind. The owner, Sandy MacRae, was very accommodating, asking for a mere ten dollars for which they could use the field any way they wanted for the rest of the season. Work began immediately on the construction of a shed for "Aerodrome Park."

On September 1, McCurdy wrote in the *Beinn Bhreagh Recorder*, "It is a comparatively easy matter to transport a fully assembled machine from our factory to these grounds by water all the way. The machine being placed on the *Get-Away* at Beinn Bhreagh can be towed by the *Gauldrie* up through Nyanza Bay to the Big Baddeck Bridge (lower) where, after making a short portage of about 20 feet to negotiate the bridge, the *Get-Away* can proceed with the machine directly to the shed at the river's bank. In about two weeks we hope to be encamped there with Baddeck No. 2."

It was September 3 before Bell managed a site visit to the new airfield. By then it was all but up and running; however, as his September 4 entry in Home Notes attests, he was impressed just the same.

Visited the Canadian Aerodrome Company's quarters at the Bentick Farm Big Baddeck yesterday, and am satisfied that Messrs. McCurdy and Baldwin have at last found a suitable place to try out their machines. It is a grand place for short jumps inasmuch as there are no trees to prevent a good landing. I should judge there is about a little better than half a mile for a straight-away flight, which should be ample room for two or three short jumps. Later, when the machine has been properly tuned up and longer flights are attempted, some perhaps across country, on their return to starting point the machine can easily find a safe landing, on any side within half a mile from its shed. Crossing rivers, brooks and streams can also be accomplished, and I should think that McCurdy or Baldwin might perhaps fly the whole length of the river later on from a mile above Bentick's Farm to the Red Bridge as a landing could easily be made on either side of the river.

So began an amazing chapter in the earliest days of aviation in Canada. These in some ways were the best of times for the Bells, Alec and Mabel, in the company of "their boys," Casey and Douglas. It was also a time for adventure that was shared with and participated in by other family and friends. Kathleen Baldwin had already proven herself to be an "outdoors person," and it wasn't long before she was camping out with the boys at the airfield on Bentick Farm. Kathleen spent so much time there in fact that Alec, getting scant news of developments from either Casey or McCurdy, pressed her into service as a diarist for the Recorder.

Reports were one thing but Bell was anxious to observe. To this end, the *Ugly Duckling* catamaran was converted into a houseboat and towed upriver where it was anchored just off the park where Bell could observe flying operations. Bell wasn't infirm, but much to Mabel's chagrin, he was not one to exercise. The houseboat, anchored in the river that ran along the new airfield, provided him with an excellent and well-equipped vantage point.

By mid-September Baddeck No. 2 had been towed upriver to Bentick Farm where testing began on September 17. Kathleen brought her Toronto friend Miss Darling to Bentick Farm where they camped together and took in all the action. Kathleen wrote an account on October 21.

We were awakened this morning by hearing Willie MacDonald's voice saying "boys it's a fine morning for a flight." We fell asleep and were next aroused by the buzz of an engine. We donned our dressing gowns and rubber boots, rushed out to the field in time to see John slowly rising into the air till he attained a height of what we thought to be 15 feet. Passing us he flew round over the Bentick Farm completing a circle. On the second round the machine rose higher until we imagined it to be perhaps 30 feet in the air, apparently responding perfectly to the will of the operator, who brought her down slowly and accurately to the spot by the riverbank from where she started.

Work had proceeded slowly at first, but by October 21 Casey and Douglas had made some thirty flights of varying distance and altitude in Baddeck No. 2, which by now had become a familiar sight in the skies over Bentick Farm. Visitors were witnesses to much of the test-flying at Bentick Farm. McCurdy noted on October 13 that his experimental flights that day were witnessed by Alexander Graham Bell, F. W. Baldwin, Willie MacDonald, Willie MacRae, John McDermid, Miss Darling of Toronto, Mrs. F. W. Baldwin, Dan MacRae and sister and lady, and McPherson Jr. of Baddeck.

Like Kass, Casey was impressed with McCurdy's flight with Baddeck No. 2 on October 21, remarking that "John made a splendid flight twice around the field this morning." The distance covered was about two miles in just under three minutes giving an average speed of 40 mph. "It was by far the prettiest flight yet being perfectly steady and finishing up with a perfect landing. The engine gave no signs of heating up and altogether it was most encouraging."

Both Baldwin and McCurdy were even more excited just two days later when on October 23 Douglas made seven circles of the intervale in just shy of eleven minutes. He said afterwards, "I thought I ought to come down but she seemed to fly so well, the engine showing no signs of overheating, that I went round once more. Soon I had entirely lost count of the number of turns... this so far is the most satisfactory flight we ever had."

All this excitement was tempered considerably when Mabel received news that her mother had died as the result of a motor vehicle–tram accident in Washington on October 20. Mabel and her then eighty-two-year-old mother where very close, and she quickly made plans to return to Washington.

Kathleen gave some insight into her own family history when she wrote a letter of condolence to Mabel on October 29. "I feel that I cannot properly express to you, dear Mrs. Bell, how great is my sympathy for you in your great loss—or perhaps you would rather I didn't say anything. My own dear mother's death was due to a terrible accident, and this always makes me realize more just what another's grief must be."

With late fall came the inevitable rains, which compromised the airfield. The Baddeck River overflowed its banks after heavy rainfall or during spring freshets. The intervale, made soggy with the retreating floodwaters, created more obstacles for the aviators beyond the inherent challenges of flight.

Despite the late October flooding at the airfield, Baddeck No. 2 managed to give one more performance before the flying season wound up at

Bentick Farm. It would prove to be the most successful effort to date and was described in detail in the *Beinn Bhreagh Recorder* by Charles Cox, Bell's secretary, who as part of his narrative humorously describes the difficulty in rolling the plane to a suitably dry takeoff point. "On November 1 at about quarter to five P.M. the machine was ordered from the shed and hauled to the starting point.... As the writer was one of the horses used in towing it to the starting point, he can truly state that had he not known beforehand that the machine he was hauling had already left the ground under its own motive power and gone into the air, no one present could have convinced him of the possibility of ever accomplishing this achievement."

In commenting on the actual flight Cox noted:

On the sixth lap McCurdy again crossed the river in negotiating both turns and flew directly over the aerodrome shed, the machine having perfect equilibrium. McCurdy kept this up for fourteen times round the meadow, manoeuvring at different elevations, and decided to make a landing....

I have witnessed nearly all of McCurdy's long flights in the Silver Dart, but never have I seen him give so satisfactory a demonstration as to the possibility of being able to produce a machine capable of being out on the market as an up-to-date flying machine. There is no doubt in my mind that Baldwin and McCurdy now have a machine (1) that is remarkably steady in the air (much more noticeable than in the Silver Dart); (2) that they are now in the possession of a good, reliable motor; and (3) that they are both now experienced enough to give satisfactory demonstrations to the public of their ability to cope with other manufacturers along these lines.

I consider Baddeck No. 2 to be the neatest looking flying machine I have ever seen in the air, to say nothing of the excellent workmanship found on her when inspected on the ground.

Pity that these flights could not have happened just a few months earlier at Petawawa or that the Canadian government hadn't sent military brass to Baddeck to be on hand for these performances.

Toward the end of November with winter approaching, Bell met with Casey and Douglas at The Lodge at Beinn Bhreagh to discuss a winter program for the Laboratory. Casey and Douglas were, after all, Bell's assistants in the Lab in addition to self-employed principals of the Canadian Aerodrome Company. Before Alec departed for Washington it was agreed that the ice, when it firmed up in Baddeck Bay, would allow flights for four aerodromes: Baddeck Nos. 1 and 2 as well as Bell's kite dromes, Cygnet 11 and Oionus.

The year ended on an auspicious note when, on December 3 Beinn Bhreagh was visited by the Governor General of Canada, Earl Grey, accompanied by his aide, Lord Lascelles. Various entries in the *Beinn Bhreagh Recorder* by some of those who participated give a clear picture of a great occasion, hosted in the absence of the Bells by Casey, Kathleen, and Douglas. Mabel and Alec had returned to Washington to deal with matters arising from the tragic accident that had claimed the life of Mabel's mother.

Knowing how anxious his employer was for news, Charles Cox sent a lengthy report in which he described the event from start to finish; some excerpts follow. "Mrs. Baldwin received the party at the Point on their arrival and they immediately started a tour of inspection on Beinn Bhreagh. They drove from the Point up the high Level Road, coming down to the Canadian Aerodrome Factory first. His Excellency shook hands with each individual in the Canadian Aerodrome Factory and was deeply interested in Baddeck No. 1, asking many questions in relation to its construction. Douglas and Casey ably explained in detail the mechanism of their machine to the delight of His Excellency."

From there the entourage went to the Laboratory, then the aerodrome shed where Casey "explained everything in an able manner" to his guests. Lunch at the Point was prepared and presided over by Kathleen who seemed a consummate hostess.

The "simple lunch" over, the party took the *Gauldrie* over to Baddeck Wharf where they set off for Big Baddeck in the pouring rain on two teams of horses with carriages. Despite the inclement weather the Governor General was in high spirits and was captivated by Baddeck No. 2 upon arrival at Bentick Farm. While waiting for a break in the rain, both Casey and Douglas entertained their guests with stories of their summer work with the aircraft. Douglas was bound and determined to get the machine into the air; Cox reported, "Douglas told me on the side he was going to fly anyway." Soon thereafter they took Baddeck No. 2 out of the shed. It was suggested that the Governor General could watch any flight from inside the shed and keep dry in the process. He, however, would have none of that. He asked for and was given a pair of rubber boots and "sauntered down the field with the rest of the spectators to be sure that he would miss nothing."

In far less than optimal conditions Douglas got the machine into the air and impressed the agent of the Imperial Government with a flight of three quarters of a mile, finally landing near the Bentick farmhouse. Wisely he chose not to try a second flight. The flying conditions as reported by Cox were abominable. "A hail storm came up just as McCurdy got into the air, and he said on landing that he could absolutely see nothing. His face was white and his eyes looked filled with tears, which of course was only rain water trickling down his face. Douglas did well and I am glad he made a flight for His Excellency, although I don't think there is another aviator in the world that would have gone up that day under such trying circumstances. He deserves credit for his pluck and determination."

Upon his return to Ottawa, Lord Grey wrote to the Bells to express his thanks for his recent visit to Beinn Bhreagh. Clearly he was very much taken with the Bells' "kingdom" and with the flying demonstration.

I was much attracted by the two young aviators and the pretty wife. They made my stay most pleasant and interesting. The weather was wet and conditions adverse to the realization of McCurdy's ambition to best the world's record. The more cautious Baldwin never committed himself to the expression of any such hope.

Although the weather conditions made it impossible for Baddeck No. 2 to show what she could do, she gave us a sufficient exhibition of her powers to enable me to realize more vividly than I have ever done before, what a big part the flying machine is likely to take in the life of the future. The anticipation that the flying machine will make "dreadnaughts" as obsolete as bows and arrows, and will also abolish Custom Houses, thus bringing about the parliament of Man and the Federation of the World, in accordance with Tennyson's prophecy, does not seem so extravagant as I had formerly supposed.

Bell was both pleased and satisfied with the Governor General's visit in his absence. It held out considerable hope for the future fortunes of the young aviators, something Bell seized upon in a reply he sent to Lord Grey December 17.

I was at first much disappointed that I could not remain at Beinn Bhreagh to give you a personal welcome. Upon second thoughts, however, I came to the conclusion that it was perhaps a fortunate circumstance for "my boys" that they should have the opportunity of meeting you by themselves without any person to come between. You would of course take their measure at a glance; and I felt it might be "the chance of their lives" to form the acquaintance of the Governor General of Canada in this quiet way, and that it might mean everything to them in their future careers. Having met Messrs. Baldwin and McCurdy you will understand, I am sure, how it is that, having no sons of my own blood, I feel a great affection for these fine young men and wish to help them to the utmost of my ability.

I am encouraging them to work together, for each supplements the deficiencies of the other. McCurdy is the progressive element, in the combination, and Baldwin is the conservative. Baldwin is par excellence the thinker and McCurdy the doer. McCurdy, high-spirited and ambitious, requires constantly to be restrained, while Baldwin, though quite a genius in his way, is of so retiring and modest a disposition that he requires to be pushed to show what there is in him. Both boys are the best blood of Canada, well educated and of high personal worth and character, and they will undoubtedly make their mark in the world.

If anyone had ever sought a good character reference, this would be it. As it turned out though, Earl Grey was unable to do much more for "the boys" than encourage them in their endeavours.

Not knowing, of course, that this would be the case, Bell wrote to Douglas:

It was great that you were able to make a good flight of one mile in the presence of Earl Grey and Lord Lascelles. The good impression created will be of enormous consequence to you in your subsequent dealing with the Canadian and British Governments.... I want to hear all about the interview with His Excellency. It was a great thing for you and Casey to have him all to yourselves without anyone to come between...I am very anxious to know whether the Governor General was empowered by the British Government to make inquiries concerning your success.

The whole method of approach seems to me to indicate that there is something behind his visit to Baddeck.

Then, almost in the same breath, Bell changed the focus back to his old preoccupation with the concept of a tetrahedral aerodrome, lamenting, "I wish very much that you and Casey would help me to get an aerodrome of pure tetrahedral construction into the air." It would not happen—Bell's protegés had already proven that the future of aviation rested in fixed-wing aircraft.

Early in December Casey wired Bell in Washington seeking his advice on how he should respond to a request received from T. Eaton & Company, which sought to use Baddeck No. 2 as part of an advertising gimmick for "a January attraction." Casey was obviously considering income-generating opportunities for the fledgling Canadian Aerodrome Company. In his response Bell made clear that he was not so inclined and offered his financial support. "The proper place of exhibition of a flying machine is the air, not a Department store...unwise I think to consider any proposition of the kind at present. I will see you through to the end of March. For the present seek only to perfect your machine and demonstrate its capabilities this winter on ice as a counter-blast to Petawawa."

Christmas was nearly upon them, winter was fast setting in, and Baddeck No. 2 was still in the shed at Bentick Farm. If the river iced up, the machine would be trapped there for the winter. In a letter to Bell dated December 20, Casey's account of how they managed to get the machine back to Beinn Bhreagh provides great insight into just how physical was their work in transporting the planes. First, however, is a short and humorous anecdote by manager Charles Byrnes demonstrating that Casey, as always, had time for humour, regardless of the task confronting him.

The *Gauldrie* left here on Friday the 17th at noon with the *Get-Away* in tow for Big Baddeck and returned on Saturday evening bringing Baddeck No. 2.

I had some misgivings about consenting to have the *Gauldrie* away for this length of time until I secured a very legal-sounding document from Mr. Baldwin which fully explained the gravity of the situation. I give below a copy of the above document, viz:

"This day, Friday the 17th, 1909 Anno Domini, being the last chance to rescue Baddeck No. 2 from the clutches of the ice, I, Frederick

Walker Baldwin of Baddeck, hereby request of Charles Byrnes the use of the mail and passenger ship *Gauldrie*, and assume all responsibility for interfering with her regular schedule. Also the wrath of any man, or collection thereof, who by this action may have to resort to oars.

Witness my hand and seal,
– F. W. Baldwin

Extricating Baddeck No. 2 from Bentick Farm before freeze-up was a very close call just the same, as Casey revealed in his account to Bell.

We got the machine in on Saturday after a couple of days' work, which was not without excitement. The ice very nearly nipped us. We took the *Gauldrie* up on Friday, towing the *Get-Away*. There was too much ice to get the *Gauldrie* through the regular channel, but it was possible to pole the *Get-Away* up through a different channel as she does not draw so much water as the *Gauldrie*.

We left *Get-Away* at the bridge on Friday night and the *Gauldrie* over at Nyanza. Then we went up to the shed and rowed down in the morning as soon as it was light. It was quite a job to pull, pole, push, and tow the *Get-Away* up the river to the shed but we got her up about eleven o'clock.

The machine was put on. All the tools, etc., in fact everything we had out at Big Baddeck. We left about one o'clock and got to the mouth of the river about a quarter past two. The machine would not go under the bridge so we had to carry it around. This took us about an hour and a quarter. Murdoch went on to Nyanza to get the *Gauldrie*, and the rest of us went right along with the *Get-Away*, which we got out OK and cleared for Baddeck in tow of the good ship *Gauldrie* about four o'clock. We got to Baddeck about six and had to leave the *Get-Away* in the harbor with the machine on board as the ice was too heavy to get up to the shed.

In February Baddeck No. 2 was fitted out with a new Kirkman engine. McCurdy, by now well established as the lead flyer of the two, began test flights off the ice on February 26, 1910. By March McCurdy was making multiple circles of Baddeck Bay while keeping the machine airborne for more than twenty minutes at a time.

Both Mabel and Alec were staying at Beinn Bhreagh during this time. Bell made sure the media heard about the latest flights. McCurdy and Casey had kept Major Maunsell, the aeronautical expert of the Canadian War Department, apprised of their latest successes, and he arranged to attend Beinn Bhreagh to witness first-hand the performance of Baddeck No. 2. He arrived the night of March 7 and was on hand to take in the remaining flights of this machine for that season. Of particular significance were two flights on March 9, of two miles each, in which Major Maunsell was carried as a passenger—Alec must have looked the other way. Maunsell was so impressed with his experience that he extended his stay, by which time yet more dignitaries had arrived on the scene.

Having heard of the latest aerial escapades at Baddeck, on March 12 the lieutenant-governor of Nova Scotia, the Honourable D. C. Fraser, appeared. He had been drawn by media reports that "droming at Baddeck is in daily practice and drawing visitors from far and near to the scene of activities." He was not disappointed.

A press dispatch originating from Baddeck and entered in its entirety in the March 17 *Beinn Bhreagh Recorder* provides a good account of this event.

The Lieutenant-Governor of Nova Scotia, the Honourable D. C. Fraser, and his son Allister arrived here last night. Governor Fraser was on the flying grounds at seven o'clock this morning just in time to witness McCurdy's first flight of the day in the aerodrome Baddeck No. 2. McCurdy flew up and down, around and around the Bay, covering in the eight flights in all about eighteen or nineteen miles keeping at a height of from fifty to one hundred feet. Citizens of Baddeck and farmers from around the country, on foot and in teams, flocked to the scene. In one instance the writer saw Mr. McCurdy in his drome fly right over a man who was hauling a load of hay across the ice.

Governor Fraser was very much excited over the flights and Major Maunsell watched the performance with intense interest exclaiming every little while to Mr. Fraser Junior, who was standing beside him, how pretty the machine looked and with what ease Mr. McCurdy brought it down. The Governor was very much impressed with Messrs.

Baldwin and McCurdy and spoke of the importance of the work they are engaged in.

"Why," said he, "just think of the different uses these machines could be put to if the Canadian Government owned them. Not only would they be imperative in time of war, but they could be used for the purpose of exploration in the North where now explorers encounter so many hardships and privations. Yes indeed, they could be an invaluable possession for Canada to have right on hand in time of war."

It was perhaps the most extensive, consistent, and impressive public demonstrations of flight exhibited by McCurdy to date. Both the lieutenant-governor and Major Maunsell, the expert observer from the Canadian War Department, were very impressed.

Mabel Bell became quite caught up in the excitement of the occasion, as she wrote later in the AEA Bulletin.

Yesterday was a day as is a day—a beauty, a dandy of days—and that old motor chose to balk! It would go for six minutes and then gradually lose power so that the aerodrome would come down. It came down just as if Douglas had meant it to come—perfectly—and on even keel without jar or flutter, but incerably [*sic*] down. It was the same old motor that had previously given records of fifteen and thirty minutes and had offered more—and no one could discover why she wouldn't go yesterday. It was colder to be sure, but she had been in as cold weather and had not minded. However, the flights that were made were dandies and His Honor, the Governor, who didn't know better, was wild with delight and said he would stand up for them in Ottawa, and Major Maunsell will also I am sure.

We had a very pleasant, or I might say, a very interesting week, for both the Major and the Governor are unusual people. The Governor—I could hardly help dancing with delight at the idea—looked as if he had just stepped out of a historical picture. There he was—stout old Peter Stuyvesant come to life. Big, oh big and burly with his great tall cane and cap and immense fur gauntlets—stalking around, master of all and everyone—and all very much at his service. And Douglas, the very ideal of the trim-knit wiry young coureur de bois—standing before the bluff old Governor straight and slim as a dart giving an account of himself to His Honor.

McCurdy couldn't have known it at the time, but years later he would assume the title and role of the man he was addressing—Duncan Cameron Fraser, Nova Scotia's ninth lieutenant-governor—when in 1947 McCurdy became Nova Scotia's twentieth lieutenant-governor.

There was never a picture more to delight the heart of a painter. Douglas in high, thick stockings reaching up to his thighs like the leather leggings worn by those 16th century men—a tight fitting short fur lined coat with wide fur collar closely turned up around his face—a close-fitting tasseled cap was on his head and big fur gauntlets protected his hands. And there was Papa—looking even alight beside the giant Governor in his fur lined coat of fine broadcloth and fur cap and fur gauntlets and snow white beard. Yes, he represented the rich courtly merchant prince. And there was the sparse figure of Maunsell—veteran soldier. Grouped around were other picturesque figures. Gardiner [Hubbard] in Norfolk jacket gracefully skating back and forth, Casey in fur coat and tasseled cap, other men in short fur or leather coats with high laced elk skin boots, and lithe active boys swiftly chasing the hockey sphere, spending themselves while waiting for the young knights' conference with his Honor should be over and he would mount his very modern chariot and be off with them all tagging after him.

It was interesting living then.

The Governor came to dinner and enjoyed himself. He really is a remarkable man who has made his way up from the ranks. He favoured woman suffrage in an able and diplomatic speech at dinner and urged the retention of Gaelic, reciting Gaelic songs to prove its musical qualities, and he told anecdote after anecdote, and they say he is one of the most popular Governors who ever occupied Halifax Parliament House.

Immediately following these flights, Reverend Joseph Freeman Tupper, a Church of England missionary in Baddeck, wrote to the *Halifax Morning Chronicle* "to confirm media reports of the brilliant aviation successes of Messrs. McCurdy and Baldwin." In his letter to the editor he wrote,

I have every confidence in the success of the Canadian Aerodrome Company and am filled to the brim with enthusiasm for the undertaking….We have an industry in our midst worthy of greatest encouragement…and permit me to say that the promoters are worthy of the success they have attained. Too often it is the case that clever men are not good men and their lives being so prominently before the public have a degrading influence upon the young. Thus their very achievements are the cause, in many cases, of lowering civilization instead of elevating it. This is not the case with those who are exciting our wonder at Baddeck. Messrs. Baldwin and McCurdy are almost model citizens as well as very profitable ones, while the whole staff can be spoken of in the highest possible terms.

Perhaps the village of Baddeck, nestled along the shores of Bras d'Or Lakes in Cape Breton in the northern extremity of the far eastern province of Nova Scotia, was just too small a place for inventions and events of such historic proportions. Had it been left to the Governor General, the lieutenant-governor of Nova Scotia, and Major Maunsell—and not the bureaucrats—the Canadian Aerodrome Company, and aviation in Canada, might have "taken flight." That was not to be. Bureaucrats had the final say, and, as Parkin put it, "through pettiness, ignorance, and futility in high places" the determined efforts to establish Canadian aviation by Bell, Baldwin, and McCurdy were all for naught.

Baddeck River Valley is much unchanged today from what it was over a century ago when Bentick Farm, part of a large grant of one thousand acres given to an original settler by the name of Jones, became Aerodrome Park, test grounds for the first aircraft built in Canada. It is my opinion that Bentick Farm, a.k.a. Aerodrome Park—a quiet, pastoral area in a beautiful landscape of river, meadow, and highland hills—should be declared a national historic site.

March 31, 1910, was the first anniversary of the dissolution of the AEA. It had been an exacting, often frustrating, but exciting time nonetheless for Casey and McCurdy. Mabel and Alec were about to set out on a world tour. Bell decided to close the Beinn Bhreagh Laboratory. The two associates would have no work there. Instead Bell offered to turn the Laboratory building, tools, and equipment over to the Canadian Aerodrome Company if the two proprietors could continue its operation. He wished them luck.

They would need more than that.

CHAPTER 8

Changing Fortunes
Bells and Baldwins

T
HE YEAR 1910 WAS PIVOTAL IN THE FORTUNES OF CASEY BALDWIN
and Douglas McCurdy who, until now so closely connected as college chums,
AEA associates, and most recently, business partners, for these two were about
to go their separate ways. The Bells, and in particular their mentor Alexander
Graham Bell, had greatly influenced their lives. For McCurdy this was a relationship that had been nurtured almost since birth. For Baldwin, the past four years
had brought both him and more recently his wife, Kathleen, into the Bell family.
Mabel and Alec had by this time come to regard both Casey and Douglas as sons.

Life for everyone during the past four years had been lived at a hectic pace
allowing little time for either Casey or Douglas to think much about their
own situations. That was all about to change. Once again the Bells would play
an important role in the events that followed. The catalyst was the decision
by Mabel and Alec to embark on a world tour.

Alec was now sixty-three years of age and feeling every year of it. He
had been re-energized with the experience of the AEA and subsequent efforts
to launch "his boys" into a new Canadian aviation industry. The AEA had
been a spectacular success, but hopes to take advantage of that success in the

commercial world had been unfulfilled. Bell was worn down by it all, and he and Mabel both felt that getting away while he still could was a good idea.

This was not the first time they had "escaped" to the continent as a means of relaxation. This time, however, it was different. During the past few years they had not only aged but had come to dote heavily upon Casey and Kathleen, who by then were virtually family. They couldn't see themselves getting along without them while at Beinn Bhreagh, and this dependency now extended to their time away. They wanted Casey and Kathleen to come with them on their world tour—a year in duration, all expenses paid.

By this time too, Kathleen Baldwin had become a formidable force, both as wife to Casey and also as a daughter-in-law figure to the Bells. Her marriage to Casey in June of 1908 had been a turning point in the fortunes not only of herself and Casey, but also of the Bells. Mabel Bell appears to have met Kathleen for the first time at the wedding, although she did exchange letters with her in the months leading up to it.

The wedding, which took place June 15, 1908, in St. Catharines, Ontario, had been postponed in order to enable the Bells to attend. Alec and particularly Mabel very much wanted to be present for the event. She and Alec had been making future plans for Casey and his bride since the engagement had been announced. The Bells had decided to construct a house for Casey and Kathleen on Beinn Bhreagh.

Mabel described both the wedding and the bride in correspondence with her mother, written while she and Alec were staying as guests of Glenn Curtiss at the Curtiss family home in Hammondsport. "I thought my own turnout of blue liberty satin and yellow hat with big yellow ostrich feathers the prettiest of any after the bride, but there were plenty of fine gowns, but not too many to spoil the effect of a country wedding. The new Mrs. Baldwin is a fine looking woman, but not much younger than Mr. Baldwin himself who has known her since they were children."

The wedding over, it was back to work in Hammondsport for Casey until July 16 when he and Kathleen arrived at Beinn Bhreagh. They stayed in the Point house at the invitation of the Bells while their cottage, "the bungalow" was under construction.

Any initial apprehension Mabel may have had over Kathleen quickly evaporated, as evidenced in this letter she wrote to Daisy soon after Kathleen and Casey had settled in at The Point.

I suppose you found her a bit difficult. She certainly takes little trouble to make people like her—yet, she grows upon one. Papa and she get along finely. They sing together every evening while Casey curls up in the big armchair listening. They are the nicest newly married couple to have around. I have not seen them a bit demonstrative—the utmost was when Kathleen tried to slap him once. They might have been married a dozen years; she is so matter of fact about taking care of his clothes and neither are the least bit shy of having me see them when they are partly dressed. In fact Papa has buttoned Kathleen's dress when Casey wasn't there to do it, and no woman handy! She is just absolutely unaffected.

Kathleen was quick to fit in and endear herself to her hosts, as Mabel wrote to her mother on August 5. "My company does not worry me in the least. My household never ran more easily. I see just as little or as much of my guests as I desire and there never was anyone more easy than Mrs. Baldwin. She is perfectly independent." When speaking on another occasion about a young lady who otherwise appeared much like Kathleen, Mabel remarked, "She has none of the savoir faire of Mrs. Baldwin who is exactly the same and perfectly at home talking with people of position or fishermen, but is quiet and ladylike."

Both Casey and Kathleen enjoyed being on the water. Casey was an inveterate sailor; one of the factors that influenced his decision to join with Bell at Baddeck was the incomparable sailing opportunity offered by the Bras d'Or Lakes. Before the month was out the newlyweds were taking advantage of excellent sailing in Casey's sailboat *Scrapper* as well as experiencing what it was to dine with the Bells in their beautiful home where they soon became regular guests.

In October of 1909 the "Baldwin bungalow" was nearly finished. It was a fine single-storey dormered cottage built near the Laboratory—undoubtedly in order that Casey could be near to work—on a rise giving a spectacular view up Baddeck Bay toward the village of Baddeck and Kidston Island. Kathleen was busy getting ready to move and already had all the house linen embroidered with the letter B, which she thought "seemed sensible." Mabel agreed; she wrote, "Mrs. Baldwin is making her bungalow very pretty. I particularly like her curtains; they are just plain burlaps home stitched, but they fit in most harmoniously with the rich brown colour of the wood. I suppose in a way she is in a hurry to get in, but we all get along beautifully here, so she is not worrying because she hasn't got her maid yet."

Mabel also kept close watch over Alec and his association with Casey. She wrote, "He and Mr. Baldwin are enjoying each other's society tremendously. Mrs. Baldwin is awfully good about it. She is a great athlete and can do anything she wants to and is altogether a very uncommon girl and very capable."

Even at this early stage in their relationship it was clear that with Kathleen now on the scene, the Bell–Baldwin relationship was growing ever closer. Casey devoted most of his time and energy working alongside Alec who grew ever more dependent upon him as a sounding board for his thoughts, and one whose counsel as an engineer he often, but not always, followed. For her part, Kathleen, ever mindful of Casey's working relationship with Bell, gave her husband great latitude while she went about the business of settling in at Beinn Bhreagh.

The bungalow was ready for occupancy by December 12 when, the following day, disaster struck and the bungalow burned to the ground. The Bells were back in Washington at this time. Telegrams were immediately exchanged. Even before the embers had been fully extinguished, manager Charles Byrnes wired Alec. "Baldwin bungalow destroyed by fire this A.M. Cause unknown and undiscovered. Masonry intact and contents saved. Building insured." A telegram from Casey to Alec followed. "Bungalow burned this morning lighting furnace preparatory to moving in. No explanation. Nobody hurt, few things saved."

It was shattering for Casey and Kathleen who had been so excited about the prospect of moving into their own home—their first as a married couple. Mabel too was distressed. She had financed and overseen the construction of the bungalow, which she liked nearly as much as the Baldwins. She was quick to respond by telegram on December 13. "Awfully sorry for you. Hope you saved your wedding presents. Of course go to the Point."

Before that day was over, Alec had already put plans in motion to move the Baldwins into The Point. Alarmed by the fire, he wanted to ensure that The Point had adequate fire protection. He telegraphed Davidson, the superintendent of Beinn Bhreagh's nursery department, "to have house opened for Mr. and Mrs. Baldwin. Try out the fire hose and get Babbington fire extinguisher. Can't afford to have fire at the Point." He followed this up with a telegram to Byrnes. "Write full particulars about fire and do everything possible for Mrs. Baldwin. Have telegraphed Davidson to open the Point house."

On December 14 Casey sent a letter off to Mrs. Bell giving her a full account of the fire. It is interesting to contrast his writing style from that of Kathleen—Casey very casual and folksy, and Kathleen more polished in her prose. Here is Casey's account.

> Our bungalow, or rather yours, is no more. We were looking forward so keenly to the opportunity of enjoying it and now there isn't anything but the foundation and two chimneys, which look like two huge tombstones.
>
> I telephoned to Byrnes to have the fire lighted Monday morning.
>
> MacKenzie who was putting on an outside porch lit the furnace. Kass left here about 9 o'clock and I followed about ten minutes later after getting Miss McCurdy to answer a letter for me.
>
> Just as I got down by the stable I noticed the smoke from the bungalow chimney. It struck me as rather black but did not alarm me until I came up the next slope of the road. The smoke suddenly burst out of several places at once and I ran the rest of the way as fast as I could. However, it was no use. You couldn't get within ten yards of the house by the time I got there.
>
> The man who had lighted the furnace and was working in the house didn't notice anything until the place was a mass of flames. There was no danger to the Lab as the wind was from the North so there was nothing to do but watch it burn. Kass steadied down and took it splendidly, but it was an awful wrench. Luckily we had the lamp you gave us here, and most of the silver.
>
> We haven't the least clue to the cause of the fire. The furnace had been tried out before and with a man right beside it everything should have been alright. The extinguishers from the lab could do nothing as the interior was burning fiercely before the alarm was given.

Charles Byrnes, head of the buildings department, and Casey could only speculate as to the cause of the fire, which remained a mystery. The building was insured for $1,400, or two thirds of the value of the woodwork, with nothing allowed for masonry. The foundation and two chimneys were "practically uninjured," with Byrnes estimating that the building could be rebuilt at much less than the original cost.

Bell was not entirely satisfied with Byrnes's explanation for the fire and directed that a full investigation be undertaken, perhaps with the assistance of the insurance company as "there may have been some defect in the flues connecting with the furnace that should be remedied when the house is rebuilt."

Casey and Kathleen found themselves back in the familiar surroundings of the Point house. It would now have to be kept open for the winter, or at least part of it, with the maid and kitchen staff kept on to accommodate the unexpected winter guests.

Kathleen was very mindful of the overwhelming generosity of the Bells when she wrote to Mabel on December 14.

> I forgot to mention in my letter yesterday how grateful Casey and I are to you for suggesting to keep the house open. I do think that you are awfully good to us—I have always thought so—in having us stay with you so long. You have shown just what a brick you are. I don't believe many people would have wanted us day in and day out as you have.
>
> Casey and I have been thinking things over and think we should contribute towards the expense of keeping the house open. I know that you were very anxious to have it closed as soon as possible and it does seem a pity that you cannot carry out your plans. Please let me know your ideas and if you will consent to this proposition.
>
> I was so glad to know from Mr. Byrnes that the bungalow was insured. What fools we were not to have insured all our things. Besides the silver I told you was saved, your lamp too escaped as it was up here and a mahogany butlers tray, carved brown tray, one plate side dish and vegetable dish, four plate candle sticks, one pair blankets, four pillows and some cushions.

Kathleen assumed the lead role in consummating a plan with Mabel. There was an abundance of correspondence between the two following the fire. Mabel was notorious for not dating her letters (she could have learned from her husband on this score), which for the researcher sometimes makes it difficult to follow the sequence of events.

With the decision made to keep The Point open for the winter, Mabel was quick to put forth her plan to Kathleen, a plan that was tweaked from letter to letter. Her first thoughts were that The Point might be occupied; Casey had previously invited a friend to stay there. In that scenario the western half of the house was shut down, the living room became a bedroom, the dining room a living room, and the paid staff was reduced from six to two. Mabel suggested that the two kitchen "girls" could live together in the kitchen, and Douglas McCurdy could have the round room and share the nursery as a private office for himself and Casey. Kathleen and Casey could use Mabel's private bedroom.

Within just a few days of making this suggestion Mabel was back to Kathleen with a more concrete plan.

My Dear Kathleen; you are a nice little girl and your letters are so satisfactory.

About the house: as I wrote you I thought you could easily be perfectly comfortable by keeping only half of it open, and having only two girls. This would reduce the expenses very greatly. Now, if it would make you feel any better to contribute towards the expense of living there, suppose we adopt this plan.

I should have to have the furnace fires lighted once in awhile anyway, so I will supply all the fuel you need and pay the expenses of keeping the house warm, and of one of the girls. This would I think leave you with just the same expense you would have if you were in your bungalow—one girl, and the market account.

Let me know what you think. My expenses here are pretty heavy and I would like to keep them all down as much as I can. At the same time I want first of all to be sure that you and Casey and Douglas are comfortable. Casey and his friend Norman Nichols were alright with only Mr. Byrnes.

I do hope that the arrangement I propose meets with your approval. I do like having you and Casey with us. It would be very lonely for Mr. Bell and me without you so I am very glad you will be with us when we return.

There would be a few other considerations, which subsequently increased the occupancy of The Point by two. Mabel wrote to Kathleen to say that Gardiner Hubbard, her late father's nephew and namesake, might be on his way to Beinn Bhreagh and if he stayed at The Point he would pay for his board or Mabel would for him. She thought that $6.00 per week would cover his share of living expenses and wages. "Remember please," wrote Mabel, "that it was you who suggested some such arrangement and that I particularly desire that it should not cost you more than living in your own house would."

As winter took hold at Beinn Bhreagh, Casey and Douglas were busy working on a custom order—the first for the Canadian Aerodrome Company—for Gardiner Hubbard. Gardiner had been to Baddeck that September and had witnessed flights of Baddeck No. 2 at Aerodrome Park. Suitably impressed, he determined to obtain a machine of his own. He commissioned the Canadian Aerodrome Company to build him an aerodrome. The company's first order was markedly different from anything previously built by either the AEA or Canadian Aerodrome Company. It was to be a single-winged aircraft—a monoplane.

Gardiner worked out plans with Casey, materials were ordered, and work was begun in a lean-to built into the shed housing the Baddeck aircraft. Nicknamed Mike, the radical, modern-looking aircraft was substantially completed by March of 1910. Numerous test flights were attempted into April with Gardiner as pilot on the ice of Baddeck Bay. The machine got into the air, but the flights were short and limited by the extent of reasonably sound ice for takeoff and landing.

Just the same, history had once again been made in Baddeck. These represented the first monoplane flights in Canada. Bell was enthused and immediately notified the press and the Governor General. Mabel B. McCurdy, who in addition to being Mabel Bell's personal secretary was also part-time Baddeck correspondent to the press, sent the following dispatch to the *New York Herald*, Associated Press, and the *Halifax Herald*:

Baddeck, NS, April 5, 1910: The Hubbard drome made nine successful flights over the remaining ice in Baddeck Bay carrying as aviator the designer of the machine, Mr. Gardiner Greene Hubbard of Boston.

The drome is of the monoplane type and resembles in its general features the machine with which Bleriot crossed the British Channel. It was constructed by the Canadian Aerodrome Company of Baddeck, Nova Scotia, and represents the first work of Messrs. Baldwin and McCurdy in filling an outside order. Mr. Hubbard is a son of Mr. Charles Eustis Hubbard, a prominent lawyer of Boston, Mass., and a nephew and namesake of the late Hon. Gardiner Greene Hubbard of Washington, DC, and cousin of Mrs. Alexander Graham Bell.

The flights this morning were at an elevation of from ten to fifteen feet in the air and did not exceed half a mile in extent on account of the limited area of ice remaining in the bay and its rotten condition. Considerable difficulty was experienced in wheeling the drome home, as at one point the ice gave way beneath its weight and it was half submerged in the water.

It is obvious that no further flights will be attempted here for some time to come. The ice is rapidly disappearing and it will be at least a month before the flying grounds at Big Baddeck will be in condition for experiments. The Canadian Aerodrome Company has closed its factory for the present, but it hopes in the course of a month or so to resume operations.

With the annual breakup of the ice in Baddeck Bay, Casey and Douglas were directing their thoughts as to how the company operations could be carried on from Baddeck after the ice went out. They had already concluded that Aerodrome Park at Big Baddeck was not suitable without substantially more capital invested to improve the ground. Their conclusion was that the future of the fledgling CAC would depend on whether their machine could be adapted to fly over the water.

Casey broached the subject with Bell, suggesting the use of a sandspit in Beinn Bhreagh harbour for takeoff and modifying the undersides of their machines to enable them to alight upon the water. Down the road the craft could be further modified to both take off and land on the water. Casey was in effect describing the theory and design behind what later would become seaplanes.

Bell was supportive of the idea. He agreed with Casey's opinion that Cape Breton Island was a poor place for an aerodrome factory if the machines are adapted only to start from and alight on land. As he wrote in the *Beinn Bhreagh Recorder*, "On the other hand Beinn Bhreagh and Baddeck are ideal places for such an industry if the practice flights can be made over water. It is of the greatest consequence therefore that the aerodromes should be adapted to alight upon water; and it would be very desirable also if they could be made to start from the water."

By the end of March, Baddeck Nos. 1 and 2 were being modified with the addition of a form of "toboggan" between the skids that would absorb the shock of a water landing. Wheels were to be left on to enable launching from Long Sand Point at the head of Beinn Bhreagh harbour. Work began on building a road as a runway for launching off the sandspit, Casey's plan being that following launch in this manner "practice flights could then be made over the Bay and the machine could alight anywhere desired upon the water and then be propelled by her own power to the landing place at the tongue of land and there be hauled up on her wheels and put into the shed."

The Hubbard monoplane trials and efforts to build a landing strip at Beinn Bhreagh represented the last real workings of the Canadian Aerodrome Company. There were thoughts of opening up Aerodrome Park later in the spring, but other factors came into play and changed everything. The first was the decision to close down the Canadian Aerodrome factory. Bell entered the event in the *Beinn Bhreagh Recorder* on April 5, 1910. "The Canadian Aerodrome Company closed its factory yesterday, April 4th. Waiting for better times. The ice has almost disappeared and nothing can be done in the experimental way until the aerodrome park at Big Baddeck is in condition for trial flights. This will probably not be for a month or more. Nothing has yet been heard from Ottawa and so Baldwin and McCurdy do not know what they have to rely on."

The factory would never reopen; the days of the Canadian Aerodrome Company were numbered.

During the winter months of 1910 Mabel and Alec were contemplating taking a round-the-world tour. This was the subject of considerable correspondence between Mabel and Kathleen, during the course of which Mabel encouraged her and Casey to join them on their twelve-month trip.

On January 10, 1910, Mabel wrote the following to Kathleen, who was in the habit of spending a month at a time with family in Toronto:

You'll know in plenty of time when we start our trip. I believe we'll go. It's now or never for us, and Mr. Bell has wanted to go for so long. But when—that's the question. Mr. Bell says he is bound to the boys until March 31st and then he will close up his experiments and start. Well, I am not going without another visit home—and a nice way would seem to be for us all to meet at St. Paul's and go on together by the C.P.

[train] to Vancouver and sail from there to New Zealand. I want to get at my farthest point as soon as possible so the greater part of the way will be a homeward one.

All our people know we are talking of it. The only thing that Mr. and Mrs. Fairchild know is that we want you and Casey to come. It doesn't seem advisable that anything should be known about this until the deal with the government is decided. It might be that Casey would have to stay. We wouldn't think of standing in his way if it were best for him to remain, but I don't believe we'd go in that case. However, time will tell—the only thing is that you will know in time for your Toronto month.

The Bells' travel plans developed further in the weeks that followed. On February 4, 1910, Mabel wrote to Kathleen, saying, "Mr. Bell and I think of sailing from Vancouver May 21st for New Zealand—there's no steamer between April 15th and that date, and the April sailing is too early. Will you and Casey come too?"

This decision, once made, would come to represent a pivotal moment in future relations between Casey Baldwin and Douglas McCurdy.

CHAPTER 9

The End of the CAC and the Start of a World Tour

I T WAS DECIDED. CASEY AND KATHLEEN ACCEPTED THE BELLS' INVI-
tation to join them on the world tour beginning in May 1910. They could
hardly be blamed for their decision to go. It was truly a once-in-a-lifetime
opportunity, made all the more special in the company of the world-famous
inventor and his wife. The art of cruising, which is now commonplace, had
not yet come into its own in 1910. It would be another decade before world
voyages were made fashionable by the Cunard liner *Franconia*. The Bells and
Baldwins, accompanied by Miss Christine McLennan, Bell's secretary, were
forerunners to today's globetrotters.

The affairs of the Canadian Aerodrome Company would be left for
Douglas to handle. He would be entirely on his own. Decision-making would
be left in his hands while the Bells were exploring the far reaches of the globe
with Casey and Kathleen, who to this point had been his almost constant
companions.

In the months before departure Alec was busy tying up loose ends. On
February 10, 1910, Bell presided over the first-ever presentation of the Samuel
P. Langley Medal for Aerodromics, named in honour of Alec's great friend and

aviation mentor, Samuel Pierpont Langley, late secretary of the Smithsonian Institution in Washington. This was a magnanimous gesture, given that the recipients were the Wright brothers, regarded by many, but not Alec, as fierce competitors of Bell and the earlier work of the AEA.

In his address Bell paid homage to Langley by saying "when we trace backwards the course of history we come unfailingly to him as the great pioneer of aerial flight." Fittingly, Bell also chose to quote Langley who, when speaking about the end of his career in 1901, said, "I have brought to a close the portion of the work which seemed to be specifically mine—the demonstration of the practicability of mechanical flight, and for the next stage, which is commercial and practical development of the idea, it is probable that the world may look to others."

Bell, who had received his inspiration to explore the intricacies of manned flight from this man, concurred and observed, "He was right and others have appeared. The aerodrome has reached the commercial and practical stage, and chief among those who are developing this field are the brothers Wilber and Orville Wright. They are eminently deserving of the highest honour from us for their great achievements. I wish to express my admiration for their work and believe that they have justly merited the award of the Langley Medal by their magnificent demonstrations."

Soon after this event Alec and Mabel made their way to Beinn Bhreagh. After all, Mabel was determined to "see home again" before she left. It was a short stay; on April 2 she and Kathleen left Beinn Bhreagh for Montreal. Kathleen was to proceed from there to Toronto while Mabel would continue on to Washington. She and Alec needed to be present there on May 9 when their new grandson, Alexander Graham Bell Grosvenor, would be christened at the Grosvenor home; among the distinguished invitees for the christening were US President William Howard Taft and his wife.

Casey and Mr. Bell set off from Beinn Bhreagh in mid-April, and at Saint John, New Brunswick, Casey left Bell in order to meet up with Wallace Rupert Turnbull at Rothesay, NB. Turnbull, a consulting engineer with particular expertise in variable pitch propellers, had met both Casey and Douglas earlier. Since then he had been following the newspaper accounts of their Baddeck flights. On March 8, 1910, he addressed a letter to them both, wondering about their experience with propellers. "In your early machines I note that you used the double curvature surfaces that I advocated in my paper. Did you find them satisfactory? Do you still use them? Did you find that they gave any measure of automatic longitudinal stability? I would like very much to know just how they work in a practical machine."

Casey wanted to bring Turnbull up to date on their experiments with different forms of propellers and other plans he and Douglas had for their machines. In March Casey and Douglas had talked about the possibility of entering one of their machines to represent Canada in the one-hundred-kilometre race for the Gordon-Bennett Cup at the International Aviation Meet to be held in October at Belmont Park, New York. In pursuit of this plan, before he set off on the world tour Casey was to canvas wealthy "sportsmen" in Toronto to try to raise the $10,000 required to build a machine. McCurdy pledged to do likewise on a separate trip.

On May 4 McCurdy, now alone at Beinn Bhreagh, received a short telegram from Bell that read simply "think you better join us Montreal Windsor Hotel May 9th." The Bells and Baldwins were due to leave on their tour the next day.

Within a day of McCurdy's arrival at the Windsor Hotel in Montreal both the Bells and the Baldwins were checked in. Douglas and Casey spent a day together in Montreal "looking up men interested in flying machines" and during this time also contacted Major Maunsell in Ottawa. He confirmed that the Militia Department had decided to purchase one of their machines under terms previously stipulated for the sum of $5,000.

There was still much going on with the Canadian Aerodrome Company when the next day the Bells and Baldwins bid farewell to McCurdy and set off on their journey. They departed Montreal on a good footing with full coverage of their brief visit given by the local media. Referring to the Canadian Aerodrome Company, the *Montreal Star* reported:

Aviation for the Baddeck syndicate of aeronauts has now passed the experimental stage…so confident have they now become of the practical utility of their plans that they have entered the field of commercial construction of aeroplanes. Though they have conducted their own experiments entirely in bi-planes, they do not restrict themselves to that line of manufacture. In fact, the first machine which they have made for sale was a monoplane which has been purchased by a Boston aviator. Thus, remarked Mr. Baldwin, "the United States is coming to Canada for its flying machines."

The Canadian government has been resting on its oars in the matter of experiments in aviation. Last year they gave Messrs. Baldwin and McCurdy the use of the camp at Petawawa as a ground for experimental flights, but since then they have done nothing. The formation of an aviation corps in connection with the militia has been mooted, but no action has yet been taken. Mr. McCurdy may discuss this subject with the department on his present trip to the federal capital. Speaking in this connection to a representative of the *Star*, Mr. Baldwin called attention to the fact that the first aeroplane in the Empire was built in Canada and expressed regret that the Government was allowing the Dominion to drop out of the premier place in the Imperial development of aviation.

Now on his own, McCurdy travelled to Toronto where he arranged for interviews in the local newspapers attempting to raise the ten or fifteen thousand dollars needed to place an entry in the Gordon-Bennett race. He was received politely, but in McCurdy's own words "they thought that the price was a little too steep." Likewise his efforts to attract capital from well-heeled Toronto sportsmen failed to amount to anything.

McCurdy went back to Montreal from Toronto where he met Mr. Lewis, the city editor for the *Montreal Star*. Lewis had made a point of telling Douglas that it was the policy of his newspaper to encourage aeronautics in Canada and for Canada. There was an aviation meet being planned for Montreal; Douglas discussed a Canadian entry and received encouragement from Lewis, strong enough for McCurdy to wire Casey in Victoria to let him know that the Canadian entry proposition was "cinched" and to ask that both he and Mr. Bell write him fully with their ideas on the machine to be built for this entry.

With that McCurdy was back to work at Beinn Bhreagh on May 19. He had perhaps bitten off more than he could chew—the Montreal "aviation week," scheduled for June 25–July 4, 1910, was mere weeks away. McCurdy would later relate to Bell that he tried to negotiate with the Montreal meet people for $5,000 to take a CAC machine there and fly at the meet. He ultimately compromised and settled on $2,500, explaining to Bell that "the only reason for me coming down to the figure was because I had to have the money." The Canadian Aerodrome Company was after all owned, operated, and financed by McCurdy and Baldwin. This was to be the company's first appearance at an airshow; the Montreal meet was the first to be held in Canada. McCurdy looked upon it as a watershed moment for the CAC.

On June 14 Baddeck No. 1 was packed into crates and shipped by fast freight from Baddeck to Montreal. Douglas, accompanied by his brother Lucien and Ingraham and Willie MacDonald, followed the machine to Montreal.

The meet, with ten flying machines, was reputed to have had at least three times the number of entries of any previous meet in North America. The pivotal flight took place on June 30. With McCurdy at the controls, Baddeck No. 1 took to the air and attained an altitude of fifty feet. Then, when turning round a pylon, "something went wrong with the works." The plane unaccountably swayed from side to side, then dropped heavily to the ground, smashed beyond repair. For McCurdy and Baddeck No. 1 the meet was over. The laurels at the meet were taken by the team entered by the Wright brothers and their machine, which attained an altitude of 3,130 feet and stayed in the air for more than forty-five minutes.

It was a crushing blow for McCurdy as well as a defining moment for the Canadian Aerodrome Company. First at Petawawa and now Montreal the CAC machines had failed to produce. McCurdy, beset by bills and with no working capital, was depressed and questioned whether the design of their planes was satisfactory. It was a lonely time for Douglas. He sold the engine salvaged from Baddeck No. 1 in order to pay some of the bills, then shipped the damaged machine back to Baddeck.

McCurdy had other plans. Although he still had work at Beinn Bhreagh outside the CAC, Douglas decided to throw his lot in with former AEA associate Glenn Curtiss who had taken to exhibition flying. McCurdy accepted Curtiss's offer to join him for one year. Curtiss was on the leading edge of a new American phenomenon—the age of barnstorming.

THE WORLD TRAVELLERS—ALEC AND MABEL BELL, CASEY AND Kathleen Baldwin, and Christine McLennan—set off from Montreal on May 10, 1910, via the Canadian Pacific Railway train bound for Vancouver. It was the first leg of their journey, a cross-country whistle-stop trip during which Bell would mix and mingle with the press at each major centre en route.

As the train continued westward Bell remarked on the vastness of the country, with his thoughts still occupied with flight. "The country we have been passing through this morning seems perfectly flat—extends to the horizon like sea—without a shrub or tree in sight. Ideal country for aerodromes."

By mid-May the troupe had reached Banff in the Canadian Rockies where they spent a few days at the Banff Springs Hotel. Casey and Kathleen were given free rein to come and go as much as it suited them while still respecting their roles as travelling companions to the older couple. Being considerably younger they were naturally more adventuresome. While Alec spent time talking bighorn sheep with the commissioner of the national park, Casey and Kathleen took off on horseback, riding up the mountain.

Mabel and Alec were a little less venturesome. They chose to walk from the hotel down into the village of Banff. There they followed a road marked "High Sulphur Springs" where by chance they ran into Casey and Kathleen just returned from their mountain climb, "so we all went into the bathing pool for a swim in the hot sulphur water with temperature of 113 degrees as it issued from the top of the mountain."

The Banff experience and the national park there impressed the travellers, particularly Casey Baldwin. Canada was at this time still a relatively young country and national parks were few, most being in the western part of the country. The national park at Banff would leave a long and lasting impression on Casey and figure prominently years later when he found himself in a position to promote a national park for eastern Canada, what would become Cape Breton Highlands National Park.

Arriving finally at Vancouver on May 19, the party was met at the depot by Arthur McCurdy—Douglas's father and Bell's former personal secretary at Beinn Bhreagh—and his second wife, the former Miss Mace. They had relocated from Baddeck to Victoria, British Columbia, a few years after Arthur left Bell's employ. After spending a night at the Vancouver Hotel, the Bells, Baldwins, and McCurdys took a "regular steamer" over to Victoria on Vancouver Island. Later that evening the Bells and Baldwins boarded the liner ss *Makura,* just arrived from Vancouver with Miss McLennan aboard. Together they set off the following day across the Pacific bound for Australia.

The ss *Makura* was constructed just two years earlier for the Union Steam Ship Company of New Zealand. It was small by today's standards but purpose-built as an ocean liner. The Bell entourage travelled first class on the ship that would be their home for the three-week voyage to Australia.

Bell used the long ocean voyage to reflect and to commit to writing thoughts and ideas in much the same way he did while on his houseboat back at Beinn Bhreagh. A week out from Vancouver he wrote, "Beautiful day after several storms. An albatross has been following the ship all day doing things that students of aviation would declare impossible—flying against the wind without a flap of the wing and overtaking the ship with ease although it makes fifteen knots, and all this with wide, motionless outstretched wings."

When not socializing with other passengers together with Kathleen, Casey spent much of his time in Bell's company. Mabel and Kathleen, both prolific writers, devoted considerable time to long letters home to family as well as making regular accounts of the trip by means of dictation to Miss McLennan. In a letter to her sister Marion and aunt Jess, Kathleen described their time in Honolulu as delightful; they were toured about and dined with Governor Freer and his wife. A few days later they went ashore in Suva, on the island of Fiji, where Casey bought a model of a Fiji dugout with an outrigger float on one side. While the others shopped, Alec was keeping in touch with events back home. He learned that Glenn Curtiss had just made an historic flight from Albany to New York.

Finally the voyage ended when *Makura* arrived at Brisbane, Australia, on June 12. The Australian press had been anxiously awaiting the Bells' arrival; interviews began as soon as the group stepped ashore. Bell took the first opportunity to note that Casey had been the first to fly publicly in the United States while giving credit to an Australian, Lawrence Hargraves, "for the current rage for aviation," saying that "he has done more probably than any other single individual living to attract man's attention to the possibilities of aviation."

The group spent most of July in Sydney where both Alec and Casey attracted a good deal of press, which was hungry for news about flight. At every opportunity Bell directed their attention to Casey as "the greatest aerodrome expert." While in Sydney Alec and Casey met with Hargreaves, the Australian aviation enthusiast. Their days were full and evenings sprinkled with dinner invitations.

The party then made their way to Melbourne. There Casey busied himself by calling upon the Canadian High Commissioner, Mr. Ross, and looking over a file of Canadian newspapers for any reports relating to aviation. The Montreal newspapers gave accounts of a recent aviation meet in the United States where "the McCurdy Brothers exhibited their Baddeck aerodrome and where Boston millionaire aviator Mr. Hubbard showed his monoplane."

It was a hectic few days in Melbourne. Everyone it seemed wanted a piece of the Bell entourage. Before leaving the city the Bells and Baldwins were guests of Prime Minister Fisher and his wife at Parliament House. Following that dinner all of them were admitted to the floor of the Senate and House of Representatives. The next night Casey and Bell attended the first annual dinner of Victorian Electrical Engineers where Alec made a fine speech and was elected honourary member of the fraternity. Casey, being an engineer, "had to respond to kindred institutions and could only think of the most commonplace remarks," as he put it. Characteristically Casey, modest to a fault, chose the shadows rather than the spotlight when sharing the stage with his mentor.

Casey and Alec were given a fine send-off by Colonel Burston, the Lord Mayor of Melbourne, and a group local notables. After a short layover in Hobart, Tasmania, the group boarded the ss *Moana* for New Zealand. Soon after arriving, Casey and Kathleen left on their own to tour the South Island. They were particularly taken with Queenstown, which Casey described as "the most picturesque little town I have ever seen....Although we were very loath to leave we didn't want to keep the Bells waiting so hurried back and met them the next day at Gore."

Casey spent time in New Zealand interacting with the native Maoris and learning some of their language. One phrase he picked up while at Wairakei was *kia ora*, which means "good luck" or "best wishes." The name *Kia Ora* was later given to a Bell motorboat.

On October 5, 1910, after returning to Sydney, Australia, aboard the ss *Moeraki* the group boarded the Japanese steamer *Kumano Maru* and set sail for the Philippines. With the regimen and rigours of land travel behind them for the present, the intrepid travellers found time to wind down aboard the ship. Alec described a fancy dress dinner party where costumes were expected. "Mabel appeared as Night, with four diamonds arranged like stars in the southern cross and one of the Thursday Island oyster shells made up to represent the crescent moon. Kathleen looked very sweet and pretty but I forgot what she was intended to represent. Casey was the most extraordinary looking object—got up as a Maori Chief with hardly anything on excepting a kiwi feather mat and tattoo markings on the face. Kathleen and Casey were called 'beauty and the beast.'"

Two weeks later, on October 21, the *Kumano Maru* arrived at Manila in the Philippines. The few weeks of sea time had given everyone in the troupe an opportunity to rest and gather up their strength for the next leg of their epic journey.

CHAPTER 10

Globe-Trotting & Barnstorming

I T WAS WELL INTO OCTOBER OF 1910. THE BELLS AND BALDWINS were halfway around the world and halfway through the twelve months set aside for their circumnavigation of the globe.

Throughout the voyage Bell had kept in touch with Douglas McCurdy through correspondence and increasingly by reading press clippings detailing McCurdy's new vocation as an exhibition pilot with the "Curtiss team."

Curtiss had been on Douglas's mind during those hectic days in June 1910 when McCurdy hastily prepared Baddeck No. 1 for transport to the Montreal aviation meet. On May 29 he had received a dispatch from the *New York World* stating that Glenn Curtiss had just won their $10,000 prize for successfully flying from Albany to New York. The newspaper asked if McCurdy would share his opinion of this flight. He obliged with a telegram in which he congratulated the paper for sponsoring the event and praised Curtiss for his accomplishment, which he stated "has done more for aeronautics and practical flying than anything yet undertaken in this country."

Douglas saw his future as mirroring that of Curtiss, whose recent success was an inspiration and a challenge. He possessed all those attributes he described in his account written for the *World*. He also had the ability and experience, which appeared to be bringing fame and fortune to his former associate, Glenn Curtiss. Douglas McCurdy craved similar success and glory. He also needed a job. The Montreal aviation meet might have afforded him that opportunity but ended in failure. Little wonder he was despondent. He decided to throw his lot in with Curtiss. It was only for one year—and Casey, his business partner, would be away throughout that period.

By September Douglas was flying a Curtiss biplane in exhibitions in the United States. He became known in the media as "the bird-man" and very quickly established a reputation as an accomplished aviator.

At the end of October Douglas arrived in New York to participate in the Belmont Park Exhibition Meet. The American media sometimes gave McCurdy more credit than he deserved. In the hype leading up to this meet he was described as "the foster son of Alexander Graham Bell—and the first member of the AEA to fly an aeroplane at Hammondsport when, in the Red Wing, he made the first public flight on record in America." In actual fact, he was not the foster son of Bell, and it was Casey Baldwin who was the first member of the AEA to fly at Hammondsport and who made the first public flight on record in America.

McCurdy flew well at the Belmont Park Meet but lost first place when he fouled two pylons in attempting to cut corners a bit too fine. The eventual winner received $3,000 prize money. McCurdy had to settle for $1,000.

America was mesmerized by the antics of McCurdy and his fellow demonstration pilots. There seemed to be no end to the new challenges thrown out to these fearless "bird men."

The steamer *Kumano Maru* with the Bell party aboard arrived in Hong Kong on October 24. Following a day of rickshaw rides, sightseeing, and shopping, the next day Casey and Kathleen ventured off on their own. For some weeks the two of them had been plotting to go to Japan where Casey planned to meet his half-brother, J. MacQueen Baldwin, who was an English Church missionary at Toyohashi. Casey had discussed their wishes with Alec, who gave the young couple his blessing for this side trip. So, the Baldwins reboarded the *Kumano Maru* and set sail for Japan. They would rejoin the Bells a fortnight later at Shanghai.

The ship had hardly left the pier before Kathleen was writing to her sister to express both joy for the opportunity to visit Japan and some remorse in leaving their travel mates behind. "We've had two days in Hong Kong and now Casey and I are on our way to Japan and will meet the Bells later in Shanghai. In a way I feel rather guilty leaving them as it means about three weeks that they will be alone. However, it's the chance of a lifetime and we hated to miss it."

Not only had Mr. Bell agreed to their going, he also paid the Baldwins' way. In the same letter, Kathleen wrote:

Mr. Bell is paying our expenses though we really didn't want him to— but he insisted. He gave us each bank notes for one hundred and ten pounds. Did you ever know such a man? He said he wanted to be sure of us having enough. Of course we won't spend a quarter of that, but we can use them for the running expenses of the party after we get back. Both Casey and I think it was very, very good of Mr. and Mrs. Bell to give us this perfectly glorious trip. It was quite unexpected as we had fully intended financing it ourselves, but Mr. Bell wouldn't hear of it—so our fairy Godfather and Godmother continue to wave their fairy wand.

Small wonder that Kathleen would effuse that "taking it altogether this is absolutely one of the most perfect trips I've ever had."

Fully two weeks later, on the evening of November 10, two ships arrived at the anchorage for Shanghai. The steamer *Manchuria* arrived first with the Bells, followed shortly thereafter by the ss *Princess Alice* carrying the Baldwins, who had enjoyed a great adventure in Japan. The group didn't stay long in Shanghai; Alec was anxious to leave as there had been a number of riots brought on by government efforts to contain the bubonic plague in that city.

News from Beinn Bhreagh was a welcome diversion for him. About this time Bell received a letter from Charles Byrnes with photographs of the new Baldwin bungalow and of improvements at the Central Wharf, including a new boathouse over the boat canal. Casey and Kathleen would return home to a brand new house, a virtual rebuild on the foundation of the first bungalow, which had been lost to fire the previous December.

After departing Shanghai the entourage spent more than a month in Manchuria and the Chinese cities of Peking and Hangchow before arriving back in Shanghai on Christmas Day, 1910. The travelling was taking its toll on everyone. Mabel required some medical supervision while Alec came down with a bad case of shingles.

Toward the end of January 1911, their travels found them in Ceylon where they spent two weeks, most of it at the Queen's Hotel in Kandy. It was an opportunity to rest up and allow Alec to recover from his shingles attack. Here Casey took time to catch up on his reading. At their hotel he came across a very good illustration in the December 28, 1910, edition of *The Car* magazine of the Italian Enrico Forlanini's latest hydroplane boat. Casey felt it was a great improvement over his earlier form, which he and Alec had seen illustrated in *L'Aerophile* magazine. The inventor and the engineer were planning to meet Forlanini in Italy toward the end of their voyage in hopes of seeing his latest hydroplane boat in action.

The thoughts of both Alec and Casey were turning now more toward "hydro" than "aero" surfaces. Before leaving on this voyage Casey had committed considerable time at Beinn Bhreagh experimenting with hydroplane technology. They only had modest success to this point with the Query, an early model "hydrodrome" or hydrofoil test craft, which had consistently failed to produce any kind of speed on hydroplanes. Casey and Bell chose this time together to debate the efficiencies of hydro versus aero surfaces. Casey, whose engineering prowess dominated the conversation, concluded the two distinct parts of the speed problem were resistance and propulsion and that efficient propulsion was key to their future success with hydrofoils. He would later prove this theory to be correct with the success of HD-4.

On February 1 Bell noted that he had just read in a newspaper of Douglas McCurdy's attempt to fly from Florida to Cuba. The *Times of Ceylon* reported on an attempt made January 30 where "ten miles from shore the aviator McCurdy fell into the sea but was saved." Nine lives and counting.

After curtailing their stay in India where Mabel was taken ill with dysentery, the group departed Bombay March 4 aboard the steamer *Malwa*, bound for Marseilles, France. For the first two weeks Casey unfortunately suffered considerably from dysentery. Mabel wrote to Daisy on March 17 expressing her concern about the state of health of the voyagers and her desire to return home.

I want to go right home and see you all, and I am not a bit interested in Europe after the East. It is so commonplace and threadbare. But I want Papa to get back his old interest in flying machines and this is his chance—the meet at Monaco April 1st. Then there is the hydroplane boat at Lake Maggiore.... I had thought the Meet was just about now so that the delay would be slight and am very much disgusted that we must wait, but Papa would never buy any motor without Casey and he ought to see himself what there is in the market.

The party arrived at Marseilles and the next few weeks were spent eventfully on the continent.

Back in America, Douglas McCurdy was having the time of his life barnstorming around the United States throughout the fall and winter of 1910. By December he was entertaining crowds at Norfolk, Virginia, but it was getting cold so he headed further south, to Florida, where the air was warmer and more suitable for flying. He decided to make a flight over open water—something that had never been tried to date in America. His course would take him from Key West, Florida, to Havana, Cuba, a distance of approximately one hundred miles. The *Havana Post* newspaper and the City of Havana had put up a prize purse of $8,000 for the first airplane to fly from United States to Cuba. The prize money, worth approximately $100,000 in today's currency, was too tempting for McCurdy to resist.

The flight—the one Bell read about in the *Times of Ceylon*—took place on January 30, 1911. Flying a Curtiss land model, McCurdy made it to within just a few miles of Cuba before a broken oil line forced him to ditch. He and the plane were retrieved by one of the four United States Navy torpedo boats that had been strategically placed along the planned route for just such a contingency. McCurdy was delivered to the dock at Havana where he received an enthusiastic welcome from the Cubans. Although his goal was not achieved, McCurdy nonetheless set a new record for the longest flight over water, a distance of ninety miles.

Before he attempted his crossing from Key West, McCurdy had arranged to have a second Curtiss plane in Havana. He thrilled Cubans with a demonstration then had this craft shipped to Palm Beach where from February 24 to March 6 he put on exhibitions and experimented with the wireless receiver in his plane. Wireless technology was quite new at this time and had been successfully demonstrated aboard ships while at sea. Attempting to do so in the air was a novel idea and taken up by McCurdy. With the assistance of a Marconi wireless engineer whom he had fly with him, McCurdy sent and received messages from points on land and from steamers off the Florida coast. This was believed to be the first experiment with the use of radio aboard an aircraft.

McCurdy's recent attempt to fly to Cuba had made him a hero in the United States and provided him with great advance publicity for an exhibition at Daytona Beach back in Florida. Civic leaders and hoteliers there, recognizing the potential of a flying exhibition as a tourist attraction, negotiated a contract with Glenn Curtiss for $3,500, stipulating that one of his pilots, J. A. D. McCurdy, would make a series of three flights off the beach. They were not disappointed. McCurdy's flights, which began on March 28, attracted immense crowds.

Not to be outdone, the neighbouring city of St. Augustine jumped on the aviation bandwagon. Arrangements were made with the Curtiss Exhibition Company to conduct airplane flights in conjunction with the Southern Championship Speedboat races hosted by the St. Augustine Power Boat Club. Large crowds were dazzled when on April 2 McCurdy made seven flights off South Beach.

It was becoming very hot in Florida. With spring now in the air McCurdy's thoughts were directed north once again. He had just completed a most successful exhibition circuit with the Curtiss aviators and aircraft. His year with Curtiss was nearing an end, and the world travellers, including his business partner Casey, were about to arrive back in America. McCurdy packed up and returned to Hammondsport.

The Bells and Baldwins were nearing the end of their circumnavigation of the world. For Casey and Alec at least, the remaining few weeks of the trip would largely be devoted to research and honing their collective thoughts on aerodromes and hydrodromes before getting back to work at the Beinn Bhreagh Laboratory.

They left Marseilles by train to Menton, France, conveniently located just a few miles away from Monte Carlo in the principality of Monaco. This was the venue for the annual motorboat exhibition and races, something that Casey in particular looked forward to attending. The travellers were joined in Menton by Gardiner Hubbard, Gertrude "Gipsy" Pillot—Mabel's neice—and her husband, Peter Stuyvesant Pillot.

Alec and Casey had been endeavouring to track down Signor Enrico Forlanini since arriving in France. The Italian engineer and inventor had by this time attained considerable success in the development of hydrofoil technology. They finally received a telegram from him saying he would be happy to meet them in Milan, Italy. Alec and Casey took the train—a tiring twelve-hour trip. Forlanini met them for lunch the following day. Alec would later describe him as a particularly gracious sixty-two-year-old gentleman who spoke little English, but they all managed to get by on French.

The next day they travelled together by train to Laveno on Lake Maggiore to see Forlanini's hydroplane boat, *Forlanini No. 7.* Bell was impressed to see how it operated on the water. "It was a beautiful and inspiring sight," he wrote, "to see this boat rising out of the water and travel at the rate of a fast express train. It makes about 45.6 mph or 73 km. I had a good long flight in the boat and then Casey and Mr. Lage [Forlanini's friend who helped as an interpreter] were taken aboard for a spin." It was the first time Bell had ever had such an experience. He was elated, and wired Mabel in Menton: "Both enthusiastic over our wonderful 'water-flight' yesterday at 45 mph."

The Motor Boat Exhibition at Monaco, reputed to be the world's largest and most prestigious, was held both "in water" as well as in facilities ashore. Alec and Casey very nearly missed out on the shoreside exhibition but for the intervention of Gipsy, who was accompanying them. Mabel wrote of the incident.

Alec forgets to record how they got into the Motor Boat Exhibition. It was the card admission [i.e., for invited guests only] and when they presented themselves at the door they were refused admission. They were about to turn humbly away when Gipsy suggested Alec should present his own personal card and display his red button. Alec refused to show his card himself but allowed Gipsy to do so herself if she desired. Nothing daunted, the child did so and there was an immediate transformation scene—and with many bows and smiles the doors were opened to Alec and the red button of the Legion d'Honneur of France and all his party. The incident was rather characteristic of both Alec and Gipsy, especially the former as, while he is quite willing to take advantage of the privileges rightfully his, he is never willing to personally assert them.

By April 9 the original group had made its way to Paris. Casey and Alec were focused once again on aeroplanes now that the Monaco boat show and the meeting with Forlanini and his hydrodrome were behind them. Casey had carefully made copious notes that soon would make their way with him back to the Laboratory at Beinn Bhreagh.

France in Bell's view was the world's leader in aviation technology. The airfield at Issy, just outside Paris, had been the scene of much experimentation and history-making flights by French aviators. Alec and Casey visited the flying grounds there a few times. The next few days were spent tracking down engine manufacturers. Casey visited the Gnome manufacturing plant, which he learned was very busy with the production of pricey motors.

The time spent by both Alec and Casey in France and Italy was key to their thinking about both aerodromes and hydrodromes. By the time he left Paris, Bell had reached certain conclusions on both subjects and chose to pen his thoughts into what would become a blueprint for further research and experimentation at Beinn Bhreagh.

I am satisfied that the French are developing the practical art of Aerodromics energetically and along scientific lines that I feel it will hardly pay me to spend much time in developing the subject myself.

It would undoubtedly pay therefore to ascertain by direct experiment whether tetrahedral structures driven by engine power would display in the air the same automatic stability they exhibit when flown as kites.

The aerial parts of the structures have already been developed and need only a suitable motor to drive them into the air. I would therefore like Casey to examine the different motors available so as to recommend a suitable motor for experiments with tetrahedral structures at Beinn Bhreagh—the structures to be raised from the water and to alight upon the water either with the help of hydro surfaces or of deep reefing displacement fins. This is all I propose to do at present in experiments relating to aviation. My idea at present is to make a contract with Douglas McCurdy or Curtiss (with the general advice of Casey) to put one of my tetrahedral structures into the air.

In relation to Casey it seems to me that he has developed ideas relating to hydroplane boats that are eminently practical and worthy of being developed. Should he devote himself specially to the development of a high speed hydro-surface boat he would have a subject that would be all his own; and he would have the chance of a lifetime to do a great thing for the world as well as for himself. My idea therefore would be to let him "gand his ain gate" on this subject and simply help him financially to make his experiments. I would therefore like Casey to examine carefully the different forms of motors available here and recommend the purchase of a suitable motor for his hydro-surface experiments.

Bell was anxious to place an order for an engine but wanted Casey's oversight and final decision on the motor. That decision still had not been made when it was time for the party to move on. It was determined that Casey and Kathleen would remain "some time longer on this side of the Atlantic so as to make a thorough examination of British as well as French motors before coming to my [i.e., Bell's] decision." The Baldwins, Bells, and Christine left Paris for London on April 23. For the next few days Casey and Alec toured about, visiting different places including the flying grounds at Brooklands Motor Race Track.

On April 29 Alec, Mabel, Christine, and Casey left for Liverpool, leaving Kathleen behind in London. Casey was to see the Bells off on the White Star liner *Celtic*, bound for New York. He would then return to London and complete collecting information about motors before going back to Paris and arranging for the purchase of Gnome motors for aerial work at Beinn Bhreagh. As the *Celtic* pulled away from the landing stage at Liverpool, the Bells waved back at Casey. One can almost feel a little anguish in Bell's journal entry. "He looked very lonely on the wharf as we waved our adieus—but we hope soon to meet again in Nova Scotia."

The Bells arrived back in New York on May 8. They were met at the pier by a number of friends including Douglas McCurdy, Glenn Curtiss and his wife, and the Bells' six-year-old grandson, Melville Bell. They had been away for twelve months. Mabel in particular was exhausted and vowed never to leave again.

As planned, Casey returned with Kathleen to Paris. While there he actually worked for six weeks at the Gnome manufacturing plant "to gain practical experience" before eventually acquiring the much-desired motor. The manufacturers had a policy that required one of their trained mechanics to travel with and install the motor. Casey chose to get on-the-job training in order that, once home, he might install the motor himself and thus avoid this additional expense.

Casey and Kathleen then made their way back to Liverpool where in late June they boarded the ss *Virginian* bound for Montreal. On June 28 Alec received a wireless message via Cape Race wherein Casey spoke of disembarking at Rimouski and Kathleen carrying on to Montreal and from there to Toronto. With Casey making his own way back to Beinn Bhreagh, Kathleen spent the month of July in Toronto before leaving there for Baddeck on August 7. A few days later she was reunited with Casey and Mabel, and on August 11 they were all together for a dance across Baddeck Bay.

It had been an eventful, long, and arduous trip. There were moments when they were all tested—physically and socially—but at journey's end, the bond between the Bells and Baldwins was stronger than ever. The worldly young couple settled into their new bungalow and resumed life on Beinn Bhreagh.

CHAPTER 11

Regrouping at Beinn Bhreagh

O N MAY 25, 1911, AN ARTICLE APPEARED IN THE *NEW YORK Herald* that was read with considerable interest by Alexander Graham Bell, who was still in Washington following the recent world tour. It was headlined "Mr. M'Curdy [*sic*] Plans Aeroplane Factory" and proclaimed, "Aeronautic circles were surprised yesterday by the news that J. A. D. McCurdy who has been one of the star flyers of the Curtiss Exhibition Company, is to sever his relations with that organization next week and start in business for himself as a manufacturer, teacher and exhibitor.

"In his new venture Mr. McCurdy it is understood will be associated with several capitalists who will afford him ample financial support. Articles of incorporation are to be filed at an early date and the work of constructing factory buildings, for which a site has already been selected, will begin at once."

Casey was still in Paris at this time and had no knowledge of this development. It was almost akin to a bigamous commercial undertaking, given that Casey and Douglas were ostensibly still partners in the Canadian Aerodrome Company. The McCurdy Aero Company was incorporated at Pittsburgh, Pennsylvania, on June 20, 1911.

McCurdy put on an exhibition at the Yale Aero Club with fellow aviator Lincoln Beachey. This flight proved to be yet another first, demonstrating the practicality of aerial bombardment. Douglas took the aeroplane up to around fifteen hundred feet, covering a five-mile course in four minutes. They then "dropped bombs" (fruit) upon a "battleship" (ground target) from a height of about seven hundred feet.

Toward the end of July Douglas was in Ontario to arrange and promote an air race between Hamilton and Toronto. His partner in this venture was a fellow aviator by the name of Charles F. Willard. The plan was for each to set off a few minutes apart from an airfield just outside Hamilton and make for Toronto. McCurdy would fly over open water directly across Lake Ontario while Willard would follow the shoreline to a waterfront landing in Toronto. Kathleen was in Toronto at this time and stayed overnight in Hamilton to see "John" before the start of the race. Both men succeeded in making the thirty-five-mile flight—McCurdy in thirty-six minutes and Willard in forty-three. They had recorded the fastest time flown between the two cities, but as usual, Canadians were unimpressed.

In mid-August of 1911 McCurdy very nearly came to grief as a now independent aviator. While performing in Chicago his plane came into contact with live wires, caught fire, dropped forty feet to the ground, and crashed. Remarkably he was unhurt, but clearly he was pushing his luck as he indicated in a letter to Casey dated August 29, the first communication between the two since they parted company at the start of the world tour over a year earlier. The letterhead was inscribed "McCurdy Aeroplane Company, Inc, 1780 Broadway, New York."

I have been wanting to write you for a long time but kept putting it off with the usual result of such a policy. It seems such a long time since I said goodbye to you and Kathleen at Montreal last year, and I want very much to see you again and further to have you working with me at the old game. I know you are quite happy where you are, for one could not help being contented when being with Mr. and Mrs. Bell, but the game of working in the commercial world in competition with others is exciting and I may say terribly strenuous and gives you lots to worry about all the time.

I told Kathleen about our company when I saw her in Hamilton and Toronto and asked her to tell you about our machine. Our idea is to establish one machine on the market as soon as we can and simply manufacture and sell. I don't want to do much more public flying as I can use my time to much more advantage here, but all the same we have to make our machines earn enough money as we go along to carry on the building and I can tell you it is mighty expensive, much more so than I had any idea of.

We had a good meet at Chicago and although I only had one machine available I flew all the time in speed events and won $2,400. Am going to Louisville tomorrow where we have a meet of three machines of my own and then fly in Cincinnati. After that I am going to take it easy and let the other fellows do the flying. Hope I will see you soon. Love to the Bells and Kathleen.

It appears from this letter that McCurdy hoped his friend and now former business partner would join him in his new company and the commercial world of manufacturing aeroplanes. Casey had a decision to make, one that would undoubtedly impact the rest of his career—and his life. He had returned to Baddeck and his home, a new bungalow at Beinn Bhreagh, flush with ideas old and new for the design and construction of hydrodromes. He also had the encouragement and financial backing of his mentor and benefactor Alexander Graham Bell to continue his work.

It soon became apparent what Casey's decision would be. He chose to stay, and he spent the rest of his life at Beinn Bhreagh. He threw himself into his work designing and testing "hydrosurfaces," the essential component that provided lift out of the water for his hydrodromes, which in nomenclature became known as hydrofoils. Casey was happy and fully absorbed in his work. Kathleen found time to travel back and forth to visit family in Toronto. Casey missed her. He wrote a letter on December 4 that described his work.

We have been very busy all day trying to get the machine ready for another trial tomorrow. The hydrosurfaces are not quite low enough to raise the control point completely out of the water. Of course we had a wonderfully smooth day today and tonight it is blowing up a bit. However we will soon get out and I am tremendously anxious to see what she'll do. Mrs. Bell christened her the "H.D." before leaving. "Hope-Deferred"; "Happy Device"; or possibly "Hunky Dory" etc. ad lib.

In the days that followed Casey was rewarded with successful trial runs with HD, which in one test attained a very respectable speed of 40 mph. With the Bells in Washington, during the winter of 1912 Casey continued in Beinn Bhreagh with the refinement of his hydrodrome prototype. He worked on his own with the help of the Laboratory staff and was increasingly enthusiastic about his progress and future prospects for his craft. He wrote to Bell:

Next year will, I think, be marked by tremendous strides in heavier-than-water work. The whole world is at last convinced of the possibilities of hydroplanes and it appeals to so many that development should be rapid. If we can only apply more power as successfully as we have used so far…. Back to the old advice…"Talk afterwards."

However I cannot content myself always with the present, and you are one of the few who do not always discount the future to present work, and, nothing but prejudice, which is getting weaker every day, makes us afraid to talk about 100 miles per hour on water.

It would take a few more years, but eventually history would prove Casey's prediction to be accurate. When eventually his hydrodrome was perfected Casey would have Bell to thank, in part at least, for his sound advice and constant, timely encouragement, such as at this moment. "Now is your chance to go ahead on the hydrodrome…think you should give attention to the best form of superstructure for a practical aerodrome. The HD is all very well for experimental purposes but if, as I believe, you are going to startle us with a fifty or sixty mile boat, public attention will be riveted on Beinn Bhreagh, and you should have completed, at least on paper, plans for a hydrodrome to be entered in races, etc."

Mabel kept in almost constant touch with Casey by correspondence throughout the winter of 1912. In March she was writing nearly every day encouraging both Casey and Douglas McCurdy who was also at Beinn Bhreagh to press on with completion of Bell's tetrahedral drome, Cygnets 2 and 3. On March 15 she wrote to Casey, referring to the Cygnet, "I don't want you and John to fail. You *must* get the thing up. I want you two to do it—in the face of every obstacle, the more the better." She signed off this letter "much love to you three children of my heart," referring to Casey, Kathleen, and Douglas.

Casey had just written to Mabel on March 12 describing ongoing efforts by both himself and McCurdy to get Cygnet 3 into the air. With "John" at the controls the drome got "within a hair of flying." Tracks in the snow revealed that at one place "all three wheels must have been up as they left no mark for about a foot on the snow."

As soon as she received this update Mabel wrote to Casey again. Bell had evidently "left it all with Douglas" insofar as testing of Cygnet was concerned. The challenges presented by winter weather conditions did not deter Mabel from exhorting Casey onwards. She asked that he "remember I am not going to be satisfied until the Cygnet has had such a trial as will demonstrate absolutely the impracticability of the cells" and advises Casey not to be deterred by money, which she will attend to "while I have still my own property." She reassured Casey that Mr. Bell remained confident that they were doing their best with Cygnet and then pointedly told Casey, "Mr. Bell must rely more and more on your help as he grows older."

This was a pivotal time for McCurdy. His heart was not in the tetrahedral drone. He had already experienced great success with the now proven biplane and saw other plans for his future in aviation. McCurdy made one last test run with Cygnet 3 on March 17; the machine crashed, effectively ending any further testing. On March 20 McCurdy left for New York, leaving Casey on his own—for good. It was small solace to Bell when McCurdy wrote from New York saying that "technically a tetrahedral structure had gotten into the air, albeit for only one foot, under its own power and carried a man."

Upon learning of this, Mabel wrote to Casey giving him her blessing to now continue with his work on hydrofoils. "Regarding the Cygnet 3—of course it was alright for Douglas to leave at once. There's evidently nothing more to be done and nothing to be gained by his staying. I wish Mr. Bell had talked over matters more decidedly with Douglas and you, and I wish we had gone up with you. But I didn't want to—that's the beginning and end and it's easy to be wise after the event. Anyway, we'll try again over the water, so go ahead with your hydrosurfaces."

Mabel implored Casey to keep a daily diary of all that he did and to send it off to Mr. Bell each night, thus making it easier to keep hold of what was going on. "I think it would have been so much better if Douglas had reported," she wrote. Her parting words to Casey, now alone at Beinn Bhreagh, were "Push forward, not back; up, not down; and keep fighting."

Mabel was never one to disguise her feelings when she wrote. She said it the way it was, from her perspective, and often with a great deal of emotion. If Casey had any thoughts of leaving the Bells and Beinn Bhreagh, they would have been considerably diminished, vanquished upon receiving Mabel's letter of June 9, 1912. In it, she reflected back on their time with the AEA and left little doubt that Casey and Kathleen were very much part of the Bells' future.

I looked over the ledger and saw all the figures we spent on the old A.E.A. and other things later—and now the day is done and my memory goes back over the years and days in the beginning. How I wanted that the money should be to put Mr. Bell's machine in the air, and his own bigger decision that it was to "get in the air anyhow," and that each was to have his chance. And every one of you boys except Mr. Bell himself has been in the air…but yet I do not regret one penny of all the money we've spent together. We've had our money's worth, every bit of it, having our experiences together, having the companionship and co-operation of you boys. It has been a very full and happy time to both Mr. Bell and me, and it is simply dreadful to think how dull and lonely our lives could have been but for all that you boys brought into it; how impossible it would have been for us to have gone around the world without you and Kathleen; how much it meant to us both to know that you are there holding the fort.

I am sorry for your sake Casey dear that you haven't yet been able to report the H.D. flying on the lake like a bird, but never mind, we know you are doing your best—and as I have already said, it's everything to us now to have you there with the Laboratories open to greet us, and to work along with Mr. Bell when he comes.

Our own children are very dear to us and life indeed would be terrible without them and the grandchildren. But you and Douglas and the rest of you boys and Kathleen too have approached us in a different way, and brought to us things the others could not, and all together have rounded out our lives in a most beautiful way. God bless you.

In the spring of 1912 Kathleen was pregnant; sadly, the baby was lost in a miscarriage. In an undated letter to Kathleen, Mabel wrote to express her sympathy and encouragement.

You have lost one little baby—that cannot be helped now—but your chance of giving birth to another living one depends very greatly on what you do now. As I understand it, it takes longer for a woman to fully recover from a miscarriage than a normal birth.

Make haste slowly. I am so afraid that by doing about as much as you can do every day you will delay your full restoration so long that there will be time for some harm to get ahead of the natural processes. Don't take any chances and be too careful…to me the greatest thing in life is wifehood and motherhood, and I want you to know them both. Casey should be a father—he will make a beautiful one.

Kathleen and Casey appear to have taken Mabel's advice to heart. By December of 1912 Kathleen was expecting again.

During the summer and fall that year Casey and Kathleen dined frequently at The Point with the Bells. Their bungalow was also fast becoming a regular venue for entertaining visitors to the estate. On July 30, 1912, George Henry Murray, premier of Nova Scotia, and Mrs. Murray, accompanied by two ladies from New York, called at the Beinn Bhreagh office and took afternoon tea at the Baldwin bungalow. Casey was being groomed by Alec to take over management of the Beinn Bhreagh estate. On November 22, following dinner together with their wives, Casey and Alec "had a conference on Beinn Bhreagh affairs." By the end of that discussion Casey had been made manager of the estate.

This was no small role and greatly added to Casey's responsibility and existing workload as manager of the Laboratory. Beinn Bhreagh had for years been operated as a business, primarily through oversight provided by Mabel. Alec had no time for business whereas Mabel had a keen mind, sharp eye for figures, and good business acumen. In this new arrangement she would continue to keep a watchful eye over things, but the day-to-day management would now be Casey's to handle.

Over the years Beinn Bhreagh had become a major employer around Baddeck with the various spheres of operation on the estate broken down into various "departments," each with its own manager. By the time Casey assumed his new role as general manager there was a farm department, building and wharves department, nursery department, and stable department.

The Bells wanted to revamp the original management plan, which up till then had allowed each department head to operate independently, with

separate bank accounts. They wanted Casey to take charge of the entire operation with a single "farm manager's account." They also wanted to make sure
that he received remuneration commensurate with his responsibility. The discussions between the new manager and Alec over salary provide interesting
insight into the character of Casey Baldwin. Casey was visiting with the Bells
in Washington in March of 1913 when he and Alec discussed "Beinn Bhreagh
matters," including the salary Casey was to receive as manager. At one point
Alec proposed that he receive $2,500 per annum with Casey providing his own
clerical help. Casey responded with an entry in Home Notes: "I would much
prefer to accept a salary of $2,000 and pay for my own clerical assistance."

Alec followed this entry with his own.

It is quite refreshing to find a man who is so conscious as to object to
receive a salary that he thinks out of proportion to the work. I think,
however, that he can make the work of value. I would propose to make
the salary $200 a month or $2,400 a year and let him provide such
clerical assistance as he needs…and I further propose that as neither
Mr. Baldwin nor I seem to be able to come to a definite understanding
on the subject that we call in a third party to decide, that is that we
submit the matter to arbitration and that we both select Mrs. Bell as the
final arbitrator in the matter and both agree to abide by her decision.

Casey's response: "I accept this."

In the end, after "recent conferences with Mrs. Bell" it was agreed that
Casey would receive an annual salary of $2,250 and "as Manager will pay rent
for his house calculated to yield five per cent on the outlay involved." Casey
was empowered to employ clerical assistance to be paid by the estate.

The Bells' commitment to Casey went beyond just management of the
Beinn Bhreagh estate. Writing in Home Notes on March 7, 1913, Mr. Bell
made his intentions clear.

While the Manager's duties relate more particularly to Beinn Bhreagh
estate, it is also understood that he shall have charge of all our property
in Cape Breton Island. We have property at Crescent Grove on the
Baddeck side of the Bay. We own an island in the River Denys Basin
and we also have wild land in the neighbourhood of Baddeck Lakes.

It may be possible also that Mrs. Bell still has a mortgage upon some property in Baddeck as security for a loan. It is the desire of Mrs. Bell and myself that Mr. Baldwin should represent us in respect to all property of any description whether land, stocks, bonds, loans, mortgages etc. that we have or may have on Cape Breton Island.

Alec signed off on this directive "as satisfactory to me and Mrs. Bell." Casey's entry followed immediately thereafter: "they are also satisfactory to me." With negotiations now concluded, Casey, who only a few years earlier had hardly heard of Beinn Bhreagh, now found himself in charge of the estate.

Life changed yet again for the Baldwins when on June 6, 1913, Kathleen gave birth in Sydney, Nova Scotia, to a baby boy. As Kathleen described it, "babe" was very thin and tiny and the doctor and nurse had to work hard over him to get his breathing started. "Dr. Kendall had to swing him back and forth by the legs. Altogether he was quite severely pommelled from what I can gather." Then the hospital burned down. Mother and child escaped with their lives and were taken in by the Kendalls for a week. During this time the baby showed signs of upset, but unalarmed Kathleen returned home with the child, then three weeks old.

The youngster "lost ground rapidly as soon as we got back," no doubt creating considerable anxiety for both his mother and Casey as a new father. After days of attempting different types of nourishment—Mabel at one point went over to Baddeck and got Archie MacDonald's wife, who had also recently given birth, to come over and "give our baby a feeding"—a wet nurse was brought down from Sydney via the *Kia Ora*. Within a short time, "babe" took on weight and recovered. The problem—failure to thrive—was summed up by Kathleen. "Dr. Kendall thinks there's very little doubt that all the trouble arose from the shock I received from the fire, though at the time there was nothing to lead one to suppose I had been affected by it." It was a rocky start for the young family and anxious moments for Mr. and Mrs. Bell.

The christening of little Robert Parmenter "Bobby" Baldwin later that year was a carefully planned "family affair" with a distinctly Kathleen touch. The Bells had chosen to remain at Beinn Bhreagh into the late fall. November 25, 1913, was the American Thanksgiving Day as well as Mabel Bell's birthday. Kathleen decided to celebrate that day with the Bells, beginning with the christening. Everything took place at the bungalow, including the christening by an Episcopalian minister from Sydney. The dinner that followed was attended by the Bells, Baldwins, and Keenans. (George Keenan was an American journalist, explorer, and one of the founders of the National Geographic Society. He and his wife were summer residents of Baddeck and close friends of the Bells.) Alec later wrote extensively of the event in Home Notes describing it as "a great day at Beinn Bhreagh."

In January 1914 Kathleen wrote to Mabel, who had agreed to be godmother to Bobby, enclosing some photographs of the baby and his mother that Mabel acknowledged with typical candour. "The photographs are splendid. I don't like yours so much but the baby's are lovely. I am very proud of my handsome little godson. Much love to you and Casey and my godson. Lovingly, MHB."

Little Robert had been the centre of much attention in his first few months. He not only had a godmother in Mabel, but Kathleen had also prevailed upon Bert and Elsie Grosvenor, her brother Reg in Toronto, as well as another relative, Gordon Fleck in Vancouver, to act as godparents to the youngster. Few children could ever claim to have had such parental oversight.

CHAPTER 12

For the Love of the Bras d'Or

T HE QUESTION, TOO SOON TO EVEN BE POSED, WAS WHETHER little Robert would inherit his father's and grandfather's passion for sailing. They say it's all in the genes. Casey's father, "Robert the Sailor"—one of several Robert Baldwins for whom Bobby was named—had gone to sea at the age of fifteen. Casey had followed in his footsteps when at the age of sixteen he secured passage as a deckhand aboard the ship *Honolulu* out of Saint John, New Brunswick, carrying a load of timber bound for Liverpool, England.

This was at the twilight of the era of "wooden ships and iron men," and Casey proved he had the mettle on this voyage, which he described in an undated letter to his Uncle Fred just after completing the crossing of the Atlantic. The following excerpts portray a young man who is both articulate and mature for his age: "The passage was a fair one of twenty-eight days and thoroughly enjoyable at all stages for me. Taken all around there is nothing like a sailing ship and although a few steam boats passed us easily when we had no wind, or a head wind, we had the pleasure of sailing serenely past several tramps in a fine run down the Channel." The crew on the ship was made up of many nationalities—Danes, Swedes, Spaniards. Casey befriended them all "by way of a little tobacco and a few judicious cigars."

For anyone who has never been to sea there is always great consternation about "mal de mer"—the dreaded seasickness. If Casey had been at all apprehensive about this condition he needn't have been, but he did address the subject in his letter.

Well, so help me Jimmy Johnson I was sick but once, and can get the Skipper and Mate to swear I never missed a meal; in fact I played an excellent knife and fork all the time. On this occasion we had only been out a few days and were in a heavy swell with no wind. Well at dinner time some salt beef hash with a lot of strong onions in it, which I tackled, evinced a strong desire to assert itself, and I had not the heart to refuse, hard as I strove to suppress it. So before both Mate and Skipper I was forced to beat an ignominious and hasty retreat. However I was very soon over this and as I say, never missed a meal.

Casey summed up the experience saying, "I will never regret being foolish enough to hunt up a windjammer to cross the western ocean." The trip would stand him in good stead later in life.

Casey would cross the Atlantic again, more than a few times and in sailing vessels much smaller than the *Honolulu*. He had learned to sail in small sailboats in the Muskoka Region of Ontario where his family had a summer cottage. He soon became a very accomplished sailor, so good in fact that in 1905, the year before he graduated from University of Toronto, he represented the Royal Canadian Yacht Club, Toronto, in the Canada's Cup held that year off Rochester, New York. Within a matter of months Casey was demonstrating his sailing prowess and racing skills in the waters of Bras d'Or Lakes in distant Cape Breton Island.

The Bras d'Or is not just any body of water. Quite the contrary, the "Arm of Gold" is in fact an inland sea, opening to the Atlantic to the north via the Great Bras d'Or Channel and to the south through St. Peters Canal, a national historic site. The Bras d'Or Lakes are tidal, but the tide is modest, averaging one foot. The salt waters are generally fog-free and very deep in many areas. The 650-mile shoreline is sprinkled with islands, many uninhabited, and a plethora of quiet, protected anchorages. It is a world renowned sailing paradise.

Undoubtedly Casey's primary motive in accepting Bell's offer to work with him at Beinn Bhreagh was the once-in-a-lifetime opportunity to employ his recently acquired engineering skills in working with an inventive genius. A close second was very likely the venue. Beinn Bhreagh was surrounded by water, the Bras d'Or Lakes on one side and Baddeck Bay on the other, with the village of Baddeck renowned as the yachting capital of Cape Breton Island. For Casey, as with Bell before him, it was a case of paradise found.

The Bras d'Or Yacht Club in Baddeck was just two years old when Casey arrived on the scene in 1906. It had been established in 1904 on the initiative of summer resident Charles Carruth, who became the first commodore; Arthur McCurdy, Douglas's father, was the first secretary. The club began without any property or clubhouse, and for the first number of years meetings were held variously at Gertrude Hall, the courthouse, and in members' Main Street offices.

Casey wasted no time in introducing himself, and he, Douglas McCurdy, and Thomas Selfridge all appear as new members in 1906. It wasn't long before they and members of the Bell family were playing active roles in the affairs of the club. At the annual meeting of July 8, 1907, Charles T. Carruth was unanimously re-elected as commodore. Douglas McCurdy was elected as a member of the governing board, and Casey Baldwin was elected "official measurer," already an early recognition of his racing experience.

Alexander Graham Bell also attended this meeting and when invited to address those gathered he gave his views on the elements of racing, in which he advocated "safety, comfort, and speed" and offered to put upwards of $250 for a trophy in furtherance of this thought. A few days later, on July 17, Bell wrote in Home Notes, "A great ceremony today on Kidston's Island off Baddeck at the raising of flags of the Bras d'Or Yacht Club. Douglas McCurdy as Master of Ceremonies 'did himself proud.' Everything went off well."

The yacht club and sailing was very much part of the recreational pastime for McCurdy, Baldwin, and Selfridge during the few summers they were together in Baddeck as AEA associates. In Home Notes for August 2, Bell recounts, "Douglas McCurdy's birthday—he comes of age today. Dancing party here [at the Point] in his honour. Lucien McCurdy arrived last night. Lieutenant Selfridge's twin brothers Jack and Woodford arrived a day or two ago. Lieutenant Selfridge and his brothers are off for Port Hawkesbury to bring home the new sailboat made by Embree for Lieutenant Selfridge and Mr. Baldwin."

Whenever he had time, Casey, often accompanied by Kathleen, could be found on the water sailing in one of his custom-made sailboats. He had three, all bearing the same name: *Scrapper*, *Scrapper II*, and *Scrapper III*. The choice of name was quite appropriate. With Casey at the helm, his Scrappers vied for every racing laurel and soon became well known, famous in fact, throughout Nova Scotia's yachting fraternity.

After returning from the world tour and with the work of the AEA behind him, Casey became very active in affairs of the Bras d'Or Yacht Club. At the July 18, 1912, annual meeting held at the courthouse in Baddeck—the last to be held off-site—Casey was elected commodore, a post he would hold for six consecutive years and then three more years in the early 1930s. In a short acceptance speech he stated that he was highly honoured to take the chair from such able predecessors and trusted that he would have the support of all the members to keep up the dignity of the club. Vintage Casey.

There were two significant matters discussed at this meeting: fundraising for a new clubhouse and choosing a contender to compete in the summer's Coronation Cup Races. Casey had assumed the chair at a pivotal time in the affairs of the club. He and others from Beinn Bhreagh combined their resources and spearheaded the building drive. By November the "yacht club building account" showed a balance of $1,014.65 toward the building of a new clubhouse. Donors of record included Casey Baldwin, Gilbert Grosvenor, H. G. Corson, Honourary Commodore Charles Carruth, Mrs. A. G. Bell, Mr. George Keenan, and Charles A. "Chal" Fownes. As well there were various donations in kind: a set of mission furniture donated by Mrs. F. W. Baldwin; a capstan from the ship *Crofton Hall* donated by Mrs. George Keenan; architect's plans for the clubhouse received from Mr. and Mrs. Bell; a ship model from Charles Byrnes; and proceeds from Dr. Bell's lecture and social.

At this meeting the secretary read a letter from the Royal Cape Breton Yacht Club in Sydney asking if the BYC would enter a yacht in the Coronation Cup Races to be sailed on Sydney waters August 31 to September 2. Casey offered his yacht *Scrapper II*, which was accepted "with great pleasure." It was a decision and an event that would help raise the prominence of the BYC in the promotion of yachting and good sportsmanship.

As Casey prepared for the Sydney race he expressed pleasure with the new marine railway at Beinn Bhreagh, which he had used to haul *Scrapper II* up in order to clean the vessel's hull for the race. As commodore he had also been busy with negotiations over securing land upon which to erect a club-house. On August 23, 1912, he made an entry in Home Notes of considerable importance to the club: "I, as Commodore, have just received a lease from the Government of Canada of a piece of property in Baddeck near the government wharf for the erection of a building for the Bras d'Or Yacht Club."

The Coronation Cup series attracted competitors from Cape Breton and the Nova Scotia mainland as well as a "spectator fleet," which included families from Beinn Bhreagh. Alec and Mabel stayed overnight in their motor yacht *Kia Ora*, which was anchored in Sydney Harbour near the coal wharf. Bell wrote of the event in Home Notes. "The yacht race for the Coronation Cup began Saturday, August 31st at noon. We followed the yacht fleet out to the open ocean and returned to Sydney for gasoline. Mabel and I went up to the Sydney Hotel to look for Bert and Elsie [Grosvenor].… When we returned to the *Kia Ora* the foremost yachts had returned and we found that Casey Baldwin was the winner."

The following month, with the Coronation Cup now "home" at the Bras d'Or Yacht Club, members got together for a clambake on Beinn Bhreagh harbour. The September 24 entry by Mr. Bell in Home Notes describes the occasion.

There were no clams, oysters being substituted. There was quite a large gathering on the shore of waterfall harbor, off Beinn Bhreagh harbor— bonfires, baked oysters, chicken, sandwiches, bread and butter, ginger ale etc. The *Scrapper* and *Alexander* [Bert Grosvenor's yacht] were anchored nearby, decorated with lanterns, also numerous boats and motor boats on shore. Supper was followed by Gaelic songs. I contributed a brand new song which had been composed this evening at the dinner table at BB Hall by the distinguished author Alexander Graham Bell, assisted by Miss Fletcher, Mrs. Bell, and Melville Grosvenor. This was sung with great gusto, the chorus being taken up readily by the men of the BYC. The following is the song, dedicated to the Bras d'Or Yacht Club by Beinn Bhreagh friends:

Verse 1:
Once upon a summer day
The Scrapper II went forth
It sailed away to Sydney Bay
For prizes in the North.

Chorus:
Oh! The Yacht Club of Bras d'Or
Success for evermore!
The Scrapper II, and Baldwin too
The Yacht Club of Bras d'Or.

Verse 2:
The Halifax boat, and the Louisburg boat
And the Sydney boats were there.
The breeze was strong, the course was long
And spray was in the air. (chorus)

Verse 3:
The Halifax boat was in the lead
Poor chance for the Scrapper II.
But the Commodore, he swore a swore
With the bold MacDonald crew. (chorus)

Verse 4:
And they beat that Halifax boat
Though it was almost neck and neck
And returned from sea with the C.U.P.
To the glory of Old Baddeck. (chorus)

On July 13, 1913, Commodore Baldwin presided over the annual meeting of the BYC, held for the first time in its own clubhouse. It was a propitious moment for Casey and the members. By 1915 the debt incurred for the building would be entirely paid off. As recorded in the club's minutes, at the conclusion of business the ever-popular Casey continued a tradition by "treating the members to cigars and refreshments." Casey had obviously discovered the secret of how to retain a crowd.

The rest of the month of July 1913 was very busy at the BYC. Yachts from Halifax, Sydney, and Louisbourg began arriving for the Coronation Cup Races, which BYC was hosting and defending this year. It was a big event. Baddeck Harbour was filled with yachts, and the steamers *Blue Hill* and *Aspy* were loaded with excursion crowds from Sydney and North Sydney.

When it was all over, Casey in *Scrapper II* finished second, and the Coronation Cup was relinquished to the winning yacht, *Gem* out of Halifax. Casey was the consummate sportsman. For him, it was not the winning but the sport—be it football or competitive racing—that was all-important. He was humble in victory and charitable in defeat. Whether on the gridiron or the water he always gave much more than he took from the sport.

The following year, 1914, the Coronation Cup series was hosted and defended by Halifax in September as the winds of war blew across the Atlantic. Casey and his crew of "MacDonald boys"—W., Al, and Archie— sailed *Scrapper II* to Halifax from Baddeck for the races in which she tangled with two Halifax yachts: last year's winner *Gem* and *Windward*. The latter vessel was well named, for it sailed to windward very well and won the series over *Scrapper II* because of it. The three races were hotly contested with *Scrapper II* winning the first, losing the second by a mere fifteen seconds, and then the third to *Windward* "in weather conditions which more favoured the Halifax boat," as reported in the *Halifax Daily News* on September 9, 1914.

The Halifax newspapers made much of the Coronation Cup and wrote more about the loser than the victor. "The *Scrapper II* made a splendid showing in the series…she made a gallant, plucky effort to lift the famous trophy, and the sporting spirit of her genial skipper is greatly appreciated by local yachtsmen. The humorous Bras d'Or ditty entitled 'They say the old *Scrapper* she ain't got no style' has been the popular air of the yacht club [the Royal Nova Scotia Yacht Squadron] since the speedy little boat's arrival here."

When Casey returned from Halifax on September 7 he found he had a visitor who had arrived in his absence. Mr. William Washburn Nutting, editor of the magazine *Motor Boat*, had arrived a few days earlier having sailed single-handedly from New York in his cutter yacht *Neresis*. He was en route to Battle Harbour, Labrador, and, as so many were wont to do, called in at Beinn Bhreagh to pay his respects to Dr. Bell.

A single-handed sailor attracted a good deal of attention and respect from yachtsmen. Nutting, no doubt through some effort by the commodore, was both well received and sent off by the Bras d'Or Yacht Club. The American guest was treated to a reception and informal dance at the clubhouse and a special farewell the following morning with a canon salute from the government wharf. This was not the last that Casey would see of Mr. Nutting.

Alexander Graham Bell was not an infrequent visitor to the BYC. On more than one occasion he was asked to address the club, which he did on October 23, 1914. Following dinner that night at The Point, Bell, Casey, and three gentlemen visiting from Ottawa traversed the bay to the yacht club in the *Kia Ora*. Casey that evening was the recipient of a beautiful silver cup presented to him by the club in appreciation of his immense contribution to it both in the advancement of sailing as well as his inexhaustible energy as commodore.

Dr. Bell very appropriately chose this occasion to speak to the members "upon the work in which Mr. Baldwin had been engaged since he came to Baddeck." It must have been quite an eye-opener for those gathered about that evening as Bell began his overview, with the tetrahedral tower followed by an account of the work of the AEA; Baldwin making the first public flight in America in a heavier-than-air machine; and noting that a great many of the improvements of the AEA were due to Baldwin alone. The recitation of achievements continued with reference to the Canadian Aerodrome Company and Bell reminding everyone that Baddeck No. 2 was still preserved in one of the aerodrome sheds at Beinn Bhreagh. Before he finished, the gathering had learned how Casey was currently working on the latest improvements to flying machines "in what are now called hydro-aeroplanes that rise from the water and alight upon the water" and how these improvements originated with Mr. Baldwin's experiments. The point may well have been lost on this audience, but speaking of Casey, Bell made it known that "His experiments were communicated to his associates McCurdy and Curtiss at Hammondsport, New York through the Bulletins of the AEA and were repeated there. It was Glenn H. Curtiss's introduction to the art of hydro-aviation. He carried on the experiments and produced his celebrated flying boat which has become the model for the most advanced flying machines of today. These flying boats can be traced back directly to Baldwin's experimenting at Beinn Bhreagh."

If this wasn't enough, Bell concluded his address with reference to Casey's HD "in which he now has the fastest motor boat in the world of its power, making 50.6 miles per hour with a 100 HP motor."

The members of the BYC this night had been treated to a talk covering matters of historic proportions by the world-famous inventor who, throughout his address, gave credit to the inventive and engineering genius of an individual whom by now they had adopted as one of their own—Commodore Casey Baldwin.

TOP: *Laboratory Buildings, Baddeck Bay, Beinn Bhreagh.* BOTTOM: *Baddeck No. 2 aboard* Get-Away, *under tow by* Gauldrie *to Aerodome Park.*

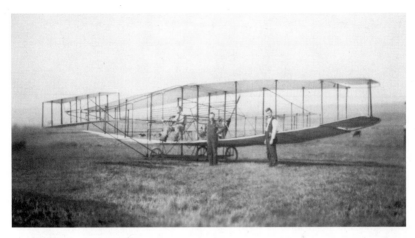

TOP: *Casey at controls of Baddeck No. 2 at Aerodome Park on Bentick Farm (note cattle grazing in background).* BOTTOM: *Aerodrome Park, Bentick Farm, Big Baddeck as it appears today.*

TOP LEFT: *Portrait of Kathleen Baldwin.* TOP RIGHT: *Mabel and Kathleen fashionably dressed during World Tour.* BOTTOM: *Baldwin Bungalow, Beinn Breagh, destroyed in December 1909 fire.*

TOP: *Constructing lifeboats in Laboratory on Beinn Bhreagh during the First World War.* BOTTOM: *Aftermath of Halifax Explosion, December 6, 1917.*

TOP: *Casey and Kathleen on steps of bungalow with Betty and Bobby.*

CHAPTER 13

A Call to Arms

A<small>T MIDNIGHT ON AUGUST 4, 1914, THE BRITISH EMPIRE, INCLUD</small>ing Canada and the independent colony of Newfoundland, went to war with Germany.

At the outbreak of the war the United States maintained a policy of neutrality. Alexander Graham Bell was an American citizen who had spent more and more of his time in recent years at his Canadian home in Baddeck, Cape Breton. With Canada now at war, Bell was faced with a dilemma as to whether he should continue experiments at Beinn Bhreagh "which might find an application in warfare." He couldn't just close down the Laboratory without risking much of what had already been achieved in research and experimentation and putting many valued and long-term employees out of work. His solution was to reconfigure the Laboratory into a virtual shipyard, overseen by Casey, in the construction of naval gigs and lifeboats for the Canadian Department of Naval Service and Imperial Munitions Board. By this means the workforce could be maintained, and it was hoped that the experience gained might by war's end give rise to the establishment of a self-supporting boatbuilding industry.

As for Bell, he chose to abandon his experimental work at Beinn Bhreagh— this lasted until the United States entered the war in April 1917. His decision, however, did not prevent Bell from devoting thought to hydrodromes and improvements to the HD and passing along those observations to Casey as he progressed with the new prototypes HD-2 and HD-3.

CASEY WAS A CANADIAN CITIZEN. HE TOO HAD A DILEMMA NOW THAT Canada was at war, and it would be much more difficult to overcome than that of Dr. Bell's. To enlist or not to enlist was a question Casey agonized over for months. Had the decision been his only to make, it is most likely that he would have joined up; however, he had a close affinity for family, a family that included Alec and Mabel Bell. They, more than anyone else, would influence Casey's ultimate decision on the matter. The pressure on him was enormous and was exacerbated by the advice and direction that the Bells, fearing for his life, continued to heap upon him. Letters Casey received from the Bells were frequent and pointed during a time that for Casey, wrestling with his conscience, must have been very rough.

To add to the difficulty of Casey's decision, Kathleen was pregnant and expecting their second child early in 1915. Memories were still fresh from the difficulties encountered with the birth of Bobby, concerns that were very much on Mabel's mind when she wrote to Casey in late August 1914.

Kathleen told me last night that you were talking about going to war. May I tell you why it seems to me that it would not be right for you to go at present?

I recognize that there are times when one's duty to one's country must override any other consideration. My own father was one of the first to volunteer in our Civil War and did not go because he was thrown out on account of disability, his being so short-sighted as to be nearly blind without his glasses.

But at present it seems to me that your wife has the first claim on your consideration for she is in a condition where she will require her husband's care and love more and more for the next few months. She has to face suffering for which you are partly the cause—and you should be by her.

Then even if she were personally strong enough to do without you, or rather if you felt that the mental and physical suffering she must face was after all a temporary condition which she could soon forget, there is the further consideration that all this worry of mind and body will have a permanent effect on her and your child. Her suffering may be a passing thing, but I think that you would find that nearly every scientific man would tell you that the mother's condition and emotions at this time affect her child throughout all its life. If a mother is well and happy the chances are that the child will be a strong and happy minded one who can do his or her duty to the world with all his ability, while when the mother is born with nervous anxiety and exposed to nervous shock and dread, the child's much more likely to be nervous and even below par all its life.

For these reasons it seems to me personally that you should not think of leaving Kathleen for the next few months. Later, if the war continues and the Empire seems to need help it will be the time to consider again whether you and men of your position should go. Much love and sympathy to you both—and please don't think me presumptuous or pushing into your affairs but I do love you both very dearly and I feel Kathleen is very pathetic.

This was a pretty heavy burden to thrust upon Casey and one that he took to heart in a personal note addressed to "Dearest Mrs. Bell" handwritten a few days later and hand delivered to Mabel at Beinn Bhreagh Hall.

I'm not sure but I think you are right, but it takes almost more than I've got in me to stay at home.

If Kathleen would be worried and depressed to a dangerous extent then it is clearly up to me to stay. On the other hand, were Kathleen her normal self she would be the very last to think of it and if she should revert to her normal self, with her normal clear-headed courageous outlook, what then?

I do feel strongly that for obvious and particular reasons every able bodied Canadian should offer his services and let the government decide whether he should go to the front or stay home and grow wheat. I can do nothing in the wheat line but have had three years militia training in the Engineers and a smattering of several kinds of military work. For this reason I feel I should go and would cheerfully and willingly, but it is not the reason it is hard to think of staying at home.

I have friends in every rank of that 20,000 and a good many who will miss me and wonder what could keep Casey out of it. I hope I am doing the right thing as it is the hardest thing I have ever done.

A mother's love is a great and wonderful thing which makes up for a lot. Goodnight—your own Casey. Don't show this to anybody.

The raw emotion and undisguised love a mother has for a son and a son for his mother is clear and unequivocal. Casey's conscience was in a tug-of-war between duty to country and commitment to family. Mabel may well have shared Casey's letter with Alec, despite Casey's request for confidentiality. Dr. Bell wrote to Casey on August 21 to say that "he was much troubled by Mrs. Bell's statement that you are seriously thinking of volunteering for the present war." Bell was concerned about Kathleen, whom he felt was "far from well"; in fact he was shocked by her appearance, leading him to conclude that Casey "should consider very carefully any steps that would take you away from Kathleen at the present time." He suggested that Casey could better show his patriotism and service to his country by using his expertise in offering his services to the Canadian government "to install submerged hydrosurfaces upon some high-powered boats. Anyone can go off to war as a volunteer, but no one but yourself can develop without delay, and at the very moment it is needed, this simple means of increasing the speed of high-powered boats." It was a compelling argument.

Casey reluctantly decided to remain home, at least for the present time. Alec's suggestion as to how he might best serve his country without enlisting gave him some solace. Casey took his mind off the enlistment conundrum by focusing his energies on continued experimentation with hydrodromes, overseeing the transformation of the Laboratory into a virtual shipyard, and attending to the management of the Beinn Bhreagh estate. He reported regularly by letter to Mabel who was his go-to person in Washington. Alec stayed aloof from management matters, preferring to let his wife run those affairs, but he kept a watchful eye on operations and on Casey to whom he wrote on January 15, 1915, candidly expressing his thoughts on the estate.

Glad to see your undated letter to Mrs. Bell about the affairs of the estate, just received I believe. For I generally fail to see letters directed to Mrs. Bell, whereas letters directed to me she always sees. I really am very glad to know that you are giving attention to the affairs of the estate and trying to plan out economies. From the point of view of the man who provides the money to run Beinn Bhreagh, it costs altogether too much. It is only Mrs. Bell's strong desire to keep the place in our own hands and our hope that you may be able to reduce our expenses that make me hold onto it. I am not a businessman and I can't plan out the economical management of a large estate. My natural desire would be to get rid of it as much as possible, rent all that we don't want for our own use, or sell it, but Mrs. Bell wouldn't hear of such a thing. Our hope therefore is in you, and I trust you may be able to show that we really do get back, in one form or another, what we put into it. And that you can point out where economies can properly be effected.

Casey's future and the continued existence of Beinn Bhreagh were linked; Dr. Bell was in effect placing the future of the estate in Casey's hands. Its continued existence might well have depended upon how well Casey was able to keep expenses in check and run a tight ship. Mabel was the glue that held it together. Casey would continue to take instruction from her as they both strove to maintain the estate.

It appears from the tenor of Bell's letter that Casey, in typical fashion, may have suggested that his salary be reduced or done away with as a cost-cutting measure. Bell was quick to nix that suggestion. "Allow me to suggest, however, that it is a very poor plan to propose economizing by cutting off the salary of the Manager! Such a thing cannot be thought of for a moment. It is the business of the Manager to *manage* so as to save his own salary by the economies he effects, and that is what I believe you can do if you put your mind to the matter."

In late January 1915 with Kathleen just weeks away from childbirth, Mabel, now back in Washington, continued to exhort Casey to remain fast and stay at home. "It makes me heartsick to think of all that you are suffering and I am afraid will suffer...no one can decide for you what is right to do. I myself trust you absolutely—I am absolutely certain that no man living is more resolute to do what seems to him right...whatever you finally do I love you and respect you and am always your loving Mabel...you are always my very, very dear boy."

Elizabeth "Betty" Baldwin came into the world at Toronto on March 14, 1915. Dr. Bell was pleased and relieved. He wrote to Kathleen on March 22 to congratulate her on the coming of "Kathleen Junior." Casey visited briefly with Kathleen and "baby Betty" in April in Toronto before a trip to New York where he was to stay with Stuyvesant and Gipsy Pillot.

While in Toronto Casey met up with Douglas McCurdy and learned from him of plans he and Glenn Curtiss had to start up a Curtiss branch in Toronto and fill an order for fifty machines for the British government. McCurdy and Curtiss also planned to start a school of aviation to train men for the Royal Flying Corps. As Casey later recorded, "I think they are also going to build wing tips [ailerons] which Curtiss was formerly building in Fort Erie…and at some point come under the Curtiss patent."

Casey and Douglas were moving in different directions. McCurdy was focused on the commercial side of aeroplane manufacturing and providing the means of training pilots for the Canadian and British governments. Casey was now totally committed to his ongoing work, including management of Beinn Bhreagh, and to family, his own as well as his extended family—Mabel and Alec Bell, godparents to his children, who by this time effectively stood *in loco parentis* to Casey and Kathleen.

The deep bond that had developed between the Bells and the Baldwins was frequently the subject of Mabel's correspondence and was sometimes mentioned by Alec in Home Notes. On August 30, 1915, the *Get-Away* and *Swan* house-boats were rafted up at Little Narrows Pond when he wrote, "This morning *Kia Ora* arrived at the Little Narrows Pond with Miss Schmidt and Mrs. Baldwin and Master Robert Baldwin. As they approached the *Get-Away*, little Robert, catching sight of me called out 'Gampie, Gampie' and held out his hands. The poor little fellow has no grandparents of his own and so I stand for Grandpapa. He does not however call Mrs. Bell Grandmama, but 'Godmammie,' because she was sponsor for him at his baptism. He seems to be as fond of Mrs. Bell as she is of him and calls out 'Godmammie, Godmammie' whenever he sees her."

In early December 1915, with the Baldwin family snug at home in their bungalow, Mabel wrote to Kathleen the following:

I wonder if you and Casey have the least idea how dear your beautiful home is to me. It came over me most powerfully how much it added to my happiness here [in Washington] and how I loved it, this evening….

It is such a lovely home with you and Casey and Bobby and the baby—not simply that your things appeal to my aesthetic sense, but that the spirit of it is so sweet. You are all so thoroughly nice together. I like coming and seeing you about your work, Bobby playing happily by himself, and Casey in and out with his pipe and his papers and books around. Everything is so fine and simple, unaffected and cordial. It is good to come into that atmosphere and to bear its memory away. I know no home where there is more of this charming home feeling with so much friendliness to all beyond its walls.

I want you and Casey to know how I feel and to say again how much I love you both and my precious god baby and his sister. Your very loving friend, MHB.

This type of regular positive reinforcement was obviously sincere, but also an effective means by which Mabel ensured that the Baldwins would remain part of her life and that of Dr. Bell, their anchor at Beinn Bhreagh.

This is not to say that Mabel could not be critical of Casey on occasion. With the Bells wintering in Washington, they depended on correspondence to keep them apprised of estate matters under Casey's oversight. Casey was not the most punctual or attentive writer, a trait made abundantly clear when Mabel wrote to Kathleen expressing her displeasure at not having heard from him. "Tell Casey he must send me some account of the farm [department].... Honestly, I think he is taking unfair advantage of our patience and absolute trust in him. He is keeping from me information which I am entitled to and for which I have asked him many times. I don't think he is treating me right."

As it happened, Casey had already sent a letter off to Dr. Bell with an account of the farm that crossed Mabel's letter in the mail. Meanwhile Kathleen sent off a testy reply defending her husband.

You certainly did give Casey a call down. If you have been "mortified" about not having reports as to the number of pounds of milk per cow and the sex, age, weight, and colour of the calves and chickens, I am equally mortified at your having to have found it necessary to write as you did. As a matter of fact Casey did send you a report though it probably wasn't as full a one as you would like.

Casey is certainly no businessman and you knew it when you asked him to take charge. I know he is much to blame and I feel that I might have helped him more in his work. If you had given explicit directions as to wanting a full report, say once a month upon everything connected with the place, it would have been done I have no doubt.

In May 1916 with the war still raging, Casey found himself at home alone caring for the two children while Kass was in Toronto. Casey had managed to stay away from the recruitment office up until now but obviously still remained bothered by his decision not to enlist. As would appear from a letter to Kathleen dated May 16, his sentiment was still close to the surface. "I suppose Jack and Alex will take transport at Quebec, not Halifax. I would like very much to see them but at the same time would feel rather sheepish waving a handkerchief on the wharf. Have no doubt Reg [Kathleen's brother] feels much as I do—it is not a pleasant role."

The Laboratory was still the scene of feverish boatbuilding activity. Beinn Bhreagh produced literally dozens of craft, so many in fact that it had its own "fleet captain," old Captain Murdock MacDonald. Apart from the gigs and lifeboats built for the navy, Casey also oversaw the construction of a small fleet of dinghies for members of the Bell family and additions to the recreational fleet, including the sailing houseboats and motorboats.

Perhaps the best work to that time, and the boat best remembered, was the *Elsie*, a yawl designed by American George Owen and gifted by Dr. Bell to his daughter Elsie and son-in-law Gilbert Grosvenor. The *Elsie* was a beautiful craft, fifty-six feet in length and having a beam of twelve feet. Built in the Laboratory by Walter Pinaud and launched in the fall of 1917, *Elsie* soon became well known around the Bras d'Or Lakes where it still sails today, although no longer owned by the family.

By March 1917 Casey had decided to enlist. It had been almost three years since Canada had entered the fray, during which time Casey, heeding the Bells' advice, had remained home close to his wife and children and contributing indirectly to the war effort through the Laboratory at Beinn Bhreagh. He no longer felt so constrained and took steps to enlist by writing to the Department of Naval Service in Ottawa on March 19, 1917. In this letter Casey pointed out that he was anxious to offer his services as a Canadian Naval Volunteer and made mention of his experience as a yachtsman as well as his experience as manager of the Bell Laboratory where he had been employed "chiefly on design, construction, and operation of hydroplane motor boats. I should prefer some sort of active sea service and am willing to go overseas if necessary."

Casey's application was supported by impressive references including Dr. A. G. Bell of Washington, DC, and Commodore Amelius Jarvis, J. Ross Robertson, and J. A. Lash, KC, all of Toronto. Casey immediately wrote to Commodore Jarvis, whom he had only met casually through earlier yachting experience, to say he hoped "that in using your name I have not abused a very slight acquaintance." He also addressed the obvious question as to why he sought to join up so late in the day by remarking, "I have been held down by peculiar obligations to Dr. Bell's work for so long that I am now desperately anxious to get in somewhere, where lost time may be made up."

Kathleen was stoic about it all and seemed resigned to have Casey go. In early April, just after Casey had sent off his application, she wrote, "Casey has been talking off and on all through the winter about going into the Motor Boat Patrol Service, preferably overseas. I didn't want to think about it even. He is really determined to go."

The months dragged on with nothing of substance being offered to Casey. By the latter part of July, with still no developments, Casey wrote to Jarvis to thank him for efforts made on his behalf and to seek his advice as to what he should do.

Captain Pasco, formerly in charge of the Patrol down here, suggested that we build boats for the Halifax Dockyard, so we took a contract to build fourteen gigs. While these boats were building I thought I could get away and leave things running here, at least on a small scale. This however proved impossible and I am now confronted by the problem whether to close down our shop or give up all hope of active service. Mr. Bell will not continue the boat-building plant unless I undertake to operate it, so that it is very difficult to make a decision. We have a facility here and first-class equipment with a really good opportunity for expansion, if a decent sized building program could be arranged. There is a great opportunity to develop an important boat-building industry here, either on small boats or large, and it is this opportunity which places me in such an awkward situation.

While Casey noted that he would greatly value his opinion, Commodore Jarvis left it up to Casey to determine his own best course of action. Casey had made up his mind when he wrote to Jarvis once again to say, "I judge from you not saying anything to the contrary that you think my own personal services, for what they may be worth, would be better employed boatbuilding than on Patrol Duty."

The decision made, Casey's fight with his own conscience was put to rest, or at least ameliorated somewhat. He had put himself forward in service to his country only to learn himself, and with the concurrence of those in authority, that he was most useful right where he was, in keeping with Bell's earlier advice.

Then, in a strange twist of fate, an opportunity arose for Casey to contribute directly to the war effort in a way he never could have imagined. Through it Casey would be able to give of himself in a manner that few others, even among those who served, could have done.

On December 5, 1917, Casey made an entry in Home Notes describing the current state of affairs at Beinn Bhreagh and said that he was "much encouraged by the progress that has been made." Winter was beginning to settle in with ice forming in the harbour. The Bells were still in residence but due to pack up and return to Washington in a few days' time.

As Alec made preparations to depart for the winter, he composed some thoughts and written instructions for Casey regarding his work with hydroplanes over the winter months.

I would recommend Mr. Baldwin to make any towing experiments he desires with the Cigar model [hydroplane] before the ice closes in and then go ahead and build a full-sized cigar body. Whatever changes he will desire to make on the full-sized machine will relate to the form and arrangement of the hydrosurfaces. The Cigar body itself seems to be satisfactory and there is therefore no reason why we should not go ahead and build it full-size to accommodate two, two hundred HP engines and operating staff.

I have to be in Washington on the 13th of December and I am seriously considering the advisability of returning here so that Mr. Baldwin and I can continue our discussions relating to hydrosurface boats. Previous experience assures me that if I remain in Washington, the whole subject will be dropped until well into the Spring. We have time during the winter to build boats of full size and arrange all the details of hydrosurfaces to be employed, so that by the opening of navigation in 1918, we can have full-sized vessels with powerful engines installed ready for trial.

From Bell's comments it is clear that Casey worked best, at least in Bell's mind, when Alec was on hand. He didn't require supervision at all but needed a little motivation and encouragement, which was derived from Bell's presence.

The following morning both Casey and Bell awoke, or were awakened, to a new reality that would change these plans for days to come and provide that unsuspected opportunity for Casey's unique contribution to the war.

The morning of Thursday, December 6, 1917, was cold and clear in Halifax, Nova Scotia, when the French munitions ship *Mont Blanc* collided with the Belgian Relief ship *Imo* in the Narrows of Halifax Harbour. The collision resulted in the world's largest man-made explosion to that time and obliterated much of the North End of the city with a loss of some two thousand lives. The blast was heard and felt in Baddeck, 175 miles away. The calamity paralyzed the city and gave rise to a massive relief effort from Western Canada, the United States—and Beinn Bhreagh.

Entries by both Casey and Dr. Bell in the Beinn Bhreagh Recorder as well as letters written by Mabel provide a graphic and riveting account of the disaster and its aftermath. Casey reported:

A great many people on Beinn Bhreagh heard the explosion and felt the vibration. Our window shook violently and Kathleen remarked that there did not seem to be any wind to make it rattle. She then presumed it was Margaret shaking something up in Bobby's room, and we didn't think anything more about it. The window vibrated so violently that you could see it shaking, and the vibration lasted for several seconds. I did not hear anything like an explosion, but several of the men in the Lab heard what they described as an explosion or rumbling, and remarked about it at the time to one another.

Almost immediately everyone on Beinn Bhreagh initiated steps to determine just what had happened. Details were uncertain but through the Baddeck

telephone switchboard they soon learned of the "Halifax Disaster" accompanied by great loss of life. There were immediate concerns in the Baldwin family,
for Kathleen's nephew, Jack Kingstone, was attending preparatory school at
the Naval College near the Halifax Dockyard.

As they attempted to gather as much intelligence as possible, a winter storm
set in creating havoc in travel and downing telephone and telegraph wires,
thereby cutting off communication. This didn't stop Mabel Bell, who by the
evening of December 6 had arranged to ship a quantity of relief material from
Beinn Bhreagh, "the first things that left Baddeck." Mabel further reported,
"We shipped a bale of six blankets, three of Mr. Bell's dressing gowns, and
a heavy winter oxford coat of his, a lot of woolen underwear, a couple of
flannelette children's nightgowns that Mrs. MacLeod knocked up in a hurry,
and some things of Margaret's and Christine's which I credited to them as
of yesterday.... We are now cleared out and have only about enough for our
own emergency needs."

Others living on Beinn Bhreagh also contributed clothing and blankets,
including Kathleen who, according to Mabel, sent off "three big boxes."
Mabel, writing to Gilbert Grosvenor, described Kathleen as "my great admiration these days. She has arisen to the emergency like a heroine. Kathleen
worked her sewing machine all day Sunday making baby things for those we
were told were most wanted. She really is a wonder, and doesn't know it which
is more wonderful still."

The Halifax explosion radically changed Casey's immediate plans, as noted
in a December 11 letter from Mabel to Bert Grosvenor.

It was hard for Casey to leave [for Halifax] and he wanted more time
if he did go. Election day comes December 17th and Casey wants to
be here to cast his vote. (Politics here are running terribly high, and I
wouldn't have believed the girls I know could talk and act as they are
doing. The liberals can't subordinate party to National issues.) Also he
wanted to be in Washington at the same time as Mr. Bell. However,
he was just starting for Halifax for a day before joining Mr. Bell on the
train when the disaster upset everything. Casey thought best to wait a
day before trying to get to the city and then came the first of the great
storms. Finally he got off Saturday.

If Casey was at all fazed by this change in plans, he didn't show it. From the moment of the explosion he went into action. His recordings provide considerable insight into the scene in Halifax and the relief effort mounted within the city and from Beinn Bhreagh.

I intended to leave for Halifax on Friday December 7th as we could get no information about Jack Kingstone, but the northeast gale then blowing made it impossible to reach the railroad. On Saturday the 8th we heard that a construction relief train was going through so I left on the afternoon Blue Hill, taking chances on getting on this train, or some other train that might be allowed into Halifax. Station Agent at Grand Narrows told me the road was paralyzed as no wires were in operation and west of the Strait everything was blocked by snow. He was sure no relief train could be organized in Sydney as there were no cars. All passenger trains which had left Sydney since the accident were blocked at Point Tupper or Mulgrave.

Casey managed to get aboard a freight train "packed with telegraph linesmen" early that evening. "Some grub I brought made things pleasanter," he wrote, "as the men were dead tired and sandwiches helped out the commissariat." They arrived at Point Tupper about midnight, followed by the construction train, which Casey made his way aboard with the help of Captain Noble, the Provost Marshall for Nova Scotia, and several men Casey knew from the steel company.

We were busy all night straightening things out so that the unit could work effectively when we got there. The train consisted of seven freight cars full of lumber, glass, window sashes, roofing paper, nails, clothing, stoves etc. One empty car to be converted into a bunkhouse and one car full of provisions and a military cook stove. For accommodation we had a small broken down passenger car of about eighth class, resurrected from some-where for the purpose and a discarded freight van. The eighty workmen who formed the party were packed into the passenger car, and the foremen and officers of the party shared the van with the regular train crew.

The train got to Truro by noon on Sunday, the ninth. Here, hoping the wires would be fixed, Casey telegraphed Bell to advise that the news was worse. Carpenters were badly needed, and he asked that Bell "have Byrnes organize every useful man for hard outdoor work" and advised that he would wire more instructions upon getting more definite information from Relief Headquarters in Halifax. Casey observed that Truro was full of people held up by authorities from getting to Halifax and had already received some five hundred wounded persons from the city.

> Our train picked up seven more cars of relief supplies and we pushed on slowly getting to Halifax about eleven P.M. Sunday night. Our train was one of the first to be taken to the new deep water terminals at the south end of the city. The North end terminal was still impassable, being littered with piles of shattered rolling stock. I went straight up to the Halifax Hotel which was headquarters of the reconstruction work. I told Colonel Lowe we could bring a number of useful men if they could be got through. He wired at once to Mr. Bell and gave me a pass for myself and men with order to be carried on any train.

R. F. Lowe, the Manager of Reconstruction Halifax, sent the following telegram to Bell at Beinn Bhreagh immediately upon meeting Casey: "Thank you very much for your offer conveyed to us by Mr. Baldwin. Would be very glad to have you bring us as many handy men, carpenters etc, with their tools, and report to me at Halifax Hotel. Try and arrange to arrive in daylight so we can get them houses as that is the hardest obstacle we have to overcome. Wire reply how many are coming and when."

Bell received this telegram just before the Laboratory closed on December 10. Bell read it to the men and called for volunteers to go to Halifax. Almost to a man, they stepped forward. Bell recounted most of their names, which included Walter Pinaud, Willie MacDonald, Roddie MacLean, William Stewart, Duncan Davies, Malcolm Doherty, Angus Ferguson, John MacFarlane, Roddie Manuel, Roche MacLean, Dan Campbell, Neil Campbell, John McIvor, and James MacLeod. Bell telegraphed both Lowe and Casey to advise of the Beinn Bhreagh contingent; rather than wait longer the group, led by Walter Pinaud, set off right away for Halifax.

While his men were on the way, Casey went about trying to find Jack Kingstone. Eventually with the help of Dr. MacDonald, brother to Ned MacDonald who was proprietor of the Halifax Hotel, Casey learned that

Kathleen's nephew was on board the cable steamer *Mackay-Bennett*, which a few years earlier had attained international fame when it retrieved and brought to Halifax most of the bodies found on the site of the sinking of the *Titanic*. It was no easy matter to locate the steamer now.

> I knew she must be somewhere north of the Plant Line Pier so I started my search from that point. The only way to do was to work along from pier to pier, and this was by no means easy in the dark, especially as the piers were piled up with all sorts of obstructions. The wave caused by the explosion had piled small boats of all sorts up on the piers, and there was a general mess of driftwood and wreckage from schooners which there had been no time to clear away. Finally, after boarding innumerable schooners and rousing up their crews, I found MacKay-Bennett [*sic*] about 2 A.M., and found Jack snoozing his head off in most luxurious quarters.

Casey went with Jack Kingstone to pick up his things at what remained of the Naval College. There was another northeaster blizzard raging,

> and it was pitiful to see the struggles of some people on the streets trying to carry home clothes and other supplies which they had obtained at the relief stations. Every kind of conveyance was being used, from hand sleighs to baby carriages.
>
> I did not see any real distress in Halifax except indirect evidences of it, like the women and children standing around poorly clad in the biting snowstorm at the relief stations where they were distributing clothes. I enjoyed taking two or three of the stragglers from the outside of the crowd and going shopping with them. We went to the most convenient shops and got what we could....I heard lots of pathetic stories about men who could not be dragged away from the ruins of their houses where their whole families had been destroyed.

That night Casey and Jack managed to board a sleeping car bound for Sydney. They arrived at Grand Narrows the following day at 2:00 P.M. where they met Pinaud and the Lab crowd on their way to Halifax.

Having secured Jack safely in the bungalow, Casey was off again to Halifax with another half-dozen men from Beinn Bhreagh. They arrived around noon on the thirteenth. It had been a cold, wintry week since the explosion. Casey searched out the rest of the Beinn Bhreagh party and found them at the curling rink, which had been converted into a large bunkhouse. Casey described the work undertaken by the "Beinn Bhreagh Contingent," which got underway in earnest that afternoon.

The work assigned to us was repairing the Blind School…covering windows with beaver-board and roofing paper and repairing the glass roof over the auditorium…that finished, Mr. Lindsay, Colonel Lowe's first Assistant took me to the Sacred Heart Convent which was reported in bad shape. The building did not look any too comfortable, but the Mother Superior politely but very firmly refused any assistance, so Mr. Lindsay gave me a large district which had been more or less neglected and was occupied principally by poorer people. We started on Brunswick Street and covered a large area from below the Citadel to down to the waterfront. I made notes of this district on my way through with Mr. Lindsay and got a truck that night to get material to be ahead of us.

Next morning I got up to this part before the men had left for work to try and find out who were the most deserving of assistance. I don't know when I have ever enjoyed anything more than interviewing the occupants of what seemed to be the most badly smashed houses….

In the meantime another storm had picked up, a southeast gale was blowing which ripped up all the temporary repairs which had been made on other parts of the Blind School. None of our work had given way however and I am sure it will stand until they can get glass.

Construction Relief material was by this time coming in by train-loads and the ten motor-trucks with "Massachusetts to Halifax" on them were doing splendidly, so that it was possible to get material that was out of the question before this. Among other things I got a few cases of glass which we put in where it was most needed at the Blind School…. By Friday night the work at the Blind School had been pretty well finished up and Saturday morning we started to do what little we could in one day along Brunswick and Market Streets.

In a letter to a friend, Mabel remarked, "Casey is very enthusiastic for him about our Boston Relief train and the relief ship. He said they were splendidly organized and the ten trucks the ship brought were worth hundreds of horse teams, and any amount of public oratory in cementing the friendship between the countries."

Casey concluded his account of the Halifax relief effort with praise for the work of the Beinn Bhreagh workforce. "As we were going back [to Baddeck] that night I had a lot to do arranging transportation, but worked time in to have one round of inspection of the houses we had repaired and it was a satisfaction to see that we had been able to make several of them quite comfortable."

The contingent left Halifax that night. They would most probably have remained longer but for the federal election of December 17, 1917. Baddeck, it seems, was a political hotbed, and everyone, including the Laboratory workmen, wanted to be at home in order to exercise their right to vote.

The evening before the election was spent by Casey, Kathleen, and Jack Kingstone at The Point where Jack gave a first-hand account of his adventures in Halifax at the time of the explosion. He was very fortunate to have escaped with his life.

It was a trying and traumatic time for everyone as the year came to an end. Casey's personal war was over. Dr. Bell would allow his manager a little slack before picking up the traces again in the New Year.

CHAPTER 14

Personal Loss and the Curtiss Affair

B Y 1917 WHEN THE UNITED STATES ENTERED THE WAR, CASEY had designed, built, and tested three different models of the hydrodrome. As was the case years before when building aircraft, each succeeding model was an improvement of its predecessor. HD, HD-2, and HD-3 had proved conclusively that heavier-than-water machines, borne on "planes" or "foils," were capable of high speed when sufficiently powered and might potentially be of interest to the US Navy.

With the United States now in the war, Dr. Bell's stance on not undertaking work at the Beinn Bhreagh Laboratory that might be seen as aiding the war effort evaporated. Both he and Mabel now considered it their duty to make some personal sacrifice as a war contribution. As a means to achieve that end, Mrs. Bell offered to pay the cost of constructing an experimental submarine chaser using the hydrofoil principle. Dr. Bell and Casey agreed to contribute their services without any form of remuneration. This was a very generous proposition involving a cost far in excess of anything that could be expected to be borne by a private individual. The only concession sought, and ultimately granted, was the co-operation of both the US Navy Department and the Canadian Department of Naval Services in arranging for the supply and entry into Canada duty-free of engines and propellers.

The war took on a personal character for both the Bells and the Baldwins in the midst of all of their work. Casey was thunderstruck when he received a confidential letter dated July 20, 1918, copied to Dr. Bell from Colonel Lang, General Staff Officer with the Canadian Militia and Defence at Halifax. In it Lang drew attention to a serious intelligence matter involving an employee at Beinn Bhreagh.

> I receive many letters and one has come today in which your name is mentioned. Very grave charges are made against Miss Schmidt—now known as Smith—who has for the past ten years been private Secretary to the Bells. These charges place great suspicion on her integrity and loyalty and mentions that when you are away she is often writing in your office until late in the morning. There appears to be sketches of submarine chasers to which she has access and the letter charges her with making communications on long distance phone with code messages which appear finally via Sydney at a wireless station eighteen miles from the Mexican border. Please let me have a confidential statement about this and let all personal feelings towards this lady take a back seat. There is no need for me to say more.

This came as a most unwelcome shock to Casey and to Dr. Bell in whose employ Miss Schmidt had been. As manager Casey was responsible for her, but quite apart from work (she oversaw the women employed in the Lab), Gretchen Smith had become a close personal friend of both Casey and Kathleen. They frequently did things together—attending socials and dances, meetings of the Young Ladies Club, and sailing. Gretchen had also become a favourite of the Bells.

At some point, before Casey received this letter, Gretchen had changed her surname to "Anton-Smith." Her decision to do so was not readily apparent nor did it appear to arouse any curiosity on Beinn Bhreagh. She continued to work and socialize, particularly with Kathleen. Her behaviour did not cause anyone to doubt either her integrity or loyalty. The Department of Militia and Defence of course did not reveal the name of the informant, who quite possibly was an employee of the estate. The Bells, particularly Mabel, were sympathetic, even though their reputation was being impugned through it all. Mabel had her own suspicions too as to who might be responsible for the "spy affair." It was a very uncomfortable time for Casey as estate manager, not to mention a great distraction from his work.

Although it is unclear whether she was formally relieved of her duties, November 13, 1918, appears to have been Gretchen Anton-Smith's last day at Beinn Bhreagh. It was an eventful day. That morning everyone had gathered at the Laboratory Wharf to see the HD-3 perform, and both Mabel and Kathleen were given rides around Baddeck Bay. In the evening the Laboratory staff gave a party at the new storehouse in honour of Gretchen. Dr. Bell spoke and pointed out that Gretchen's work was "especially wonderful because it had been undertaken and carried on under very discouraging circumstances."

A few weeks later, on December 9, Mabel wrote to Alec in Washington expressing sadness over the loss of Gretchen. "I feel dreadfully but see its necessity. Gretchen was the whole thing. Under her everyone worked steadily, easily and intelligently, coherently. Miss Appleby, Casey says, has sufficient ability but she lacks self-confidence. So without Gretchen the girls have disintegrated, and the house is so forlorn and unhomelike that I don't see how anyone who lived there with Gretchen could stand it."

The new year, 1919, began on a sad note for Casey when in January Mabel's niece Gertrude "Gipsy" (Grossman) Pillot died at her home in New York of Spanish influenza and pneumonia. Gipsy had always been a great favourite around Beinn Bhreagh and had developed a very special relationship with Casey. The two of them spent much time together at Beinn Bhreagh the summer before she died.

In the months immediately following Gipsy's death Mabel exchanged correspondence with both Casey and Kathleen about her. To Casey Mabel expressed her eternal gratitude for the time he had taken that summer to make Gipsy's last days so wonderful.

Out of your own suffering came the opportunity and power to make that last summer one of the most wonderful and heartfelt in her life— to bring light where all was desperate darkness. She told me over and over again how much you had given her of new courage, new and bigger ideals—how much that really knowing you meant, and her letters repeated this.

She told me all you were to her—how much you gave her this summer that was wonderful and beautiful and new so that it was like a new world. So I know that I have you to thank in large measure that this last summer of her life was in spite of everything a happy one. She did so enjoy those long happy days and nights with you and Kathleen on the boats and the motor trip with the free untrammelled life—the youth restored....If there were nothing else I had to love you for it would be for what you did for her this summer. For she was very dear.

I am so glad you and Kathleen learned to know and love her....And I am so glad she came here at last and had a happy time and that you helped make it so.

Casey was very emotional about Gipsy's death, as is apparent from a letter he wrote to Mabel at this time.

For the present at least it is impossible for me to talk about Gypsy [sic] and I find it very difficult to write. It is quite useless to try and grasp the idea that she is really gone, leaving this world in general and some of us in particular so much the poorer. I was not only dazzled by Gypsy's loveliness but was fond of her in every possible way. Apart from everything else she was the best friend I have ever had—she was the only one who really knew what I was trying to do and why, and I miss her terribly now. Please do not think this is any disloyalty to Kathleen and you and Mr. Bell. If I gave anything to Gypsy it was the tiniest fragment of what she did for me...there are many things I would like to tell you about her and some that I must, but I can't do it yet.

About this time, Dr. Bell received a telegram from Georgina McCurdy, Douglas McCurdy's aunt who had raised him and his siblings following their mother's death. In it she announced that Douglas was finally on the road to matrimony having recently become engaged to Margaret Ball of Woodstock, Ontario. The wedding took place on April 2, 1919, and later produced two children, a daughter, Diana, and a son, J. R. D. or "Bobby" McCurdy. It was fully eleven years since those heady times of the Aerial Experiment Association (AEA) and the excitement surrounding the Baldwin wedding in 1908. A great deal had happened in the interim; Douglas and Casey had gone their separate ways, and recent events involving patent rights emanating from the AEA days had compromised their relationship.

It was a complicated matter that dated back to the dissolution of the association and, as Mabel called it, Glenn Curtiss's "defection." Curtiss had effectively disengaged himself from the AEA even before it was wound up, and with the knowledge he had gained as an associate with the AEA, immediately entered the commercial world of aviation in the United States. He was, after all, a businessman. Curtiss was quick to take advantage of manufacturing opportunities for aeroplanes brought about by the First World War. This inevitably led to patent issues and in the case of competitors like the Wright brothers, litigation. It also brought Curtiss and, by association, McCurdy into conflict with the original surviving members of the AEA, particularly Casey.

Early in 1914 there was a move toward amalgamating the Wright Company and the Curtiss Company into a single entity that would take in the interests of both as well as all other flying machine interests in America. Dr. Bell was approached about the AEA patents as they might pertain to such an amalgamation; he referred the matter to Charles J. Bell as trustee of the AEA. Charles's lack of initiative on the matter may have cost the AEA an opportunity to realize upon their patents. Alec commented in Home Notes of April 23, 1914, "Mrs. Bell and I are much disappointed that Mr. C. J. Bell does not seem inclined to take the initiative in utilizing the AEA patents. He is perfectly willing to serve as Trustee, but does not wish, he says, to be put in the position of a 'promoter.' Mrs. Bell has been stirring up Mr. Douglas McCurdy to see whether he cannot do anything to advance the interests of the AEA by approaching various people upon the subject."

In fact Douglas had taken some action and had written to Mabel on April 21 to apprise her of same. "The aviation consolidation scheme is progressing and there are at least three separate efforts made to effect the consolidation, all in different ways," he wrote. "Anyway, it looks that the AEA patent is a desirable element in whatever form the consolidation takes, and that an offer will ultimately be made for its purchase.

"The thing has gone too far to drop out of sight now so you may expect some action soon. I will let you know."

At this point it appeared as if Douglas was still "in the AEA camp" despite the fact that he was associated with Curtiss. Nothing came of this, however, which led Mabel to approach her son-in-law Bert Grosvenor to do what he could to promote the AEA patents. It was obviously very much on her mind at Christmas of 1915, although she did manage to wait until the 26th to write a compelling letter to Bert.

> I have thought of asking your help in doing something with it [the AEA patents] as Casey frankly admits he is no good in such matters, and will do nothing about it, but have not done so before because of the feeling that you are already shouldering quite as much care and responsibility as you have the physical strength to bear.
>
> Since however you have spoken of it, another point has occurred to me. If, as you say, Curtiss is making millions from machines using features basically covered by our patents, Mr. Bell and I should have our share in these profits, and it is in your interest and David's [Fairchild, her other son-in-law] to see that we get it for ultimately it will belong to your wives and children. If they be large, it is certainly not right that they should go by the board for want of a little pushing.
>
> I spoke to Mr. Bell about what you said and he replied that he wished you would take hold, and I am sure he really does want to have something done, he feels much more strongly about it than Casey, but he never did care much about money, and he never would have made anything out of the telephone but for my father. No, I don't think this is fair…and I hate both to see father's claims ignored and unknown, and money earned through his brains and his generosity going to one who seems to have betrayed his confidence.
>
> It is possible that Curtiss and Douglas, who is working with Curtiss, may be willing now to come to terms if they are properly approached.

Unlike Mabel, Casey was pretty much indifferent toward the utility of the AEA patents. He chose the forum of the Beinn Bhreagh Recorder to voice his thoughts. On March 25, 1915, he wrote:

> I had a letter from John McCurdy who says he is starting up a Curtiss branch in Toronto. In part John says "Of course it may be advisable to arrange with the A.E.A. in some way satisfactory to them." What his idea is I'm sure I don't know as the A.E.A patents seem to be about as useful as Hague Conventions to the Kaiser. I do not bear Curtiss the

slightest ill-will and from his point of view I have no doubt that what he did was alright. The fact that as a member of the A.E.A. he chose to manufacture and contested his infringement suit without acknowledgement to the A.E.A. cut the ground from under the A.E.A. patents, so much so that I don't see that they can ever be of any commercial value. Glen [sic] simply tried to put the A.E.A. machine up against the Wrights without the backing of the A.E.A. patents which were the necessary credentials for the machine. The result of this very short-sighted policy was naturally disastrous all round, and I don't see any sense at this late date of considering the building of Curtiss machines under A.E.A. patents, whether in Canada or in the United States or in Timbuctoo [sic].

In his concluding remarks on the subject Casey demonstrated yet again an unflinching modesty and understatement of his contribution toward the success of the AEA. "It is not a personal feeling, as my own contributions to the accomplishment of the A.E.A. was a drop in the bucket, and I have been repaid over and over in ways which mean far more than kudos or gold, but when I think how much time, money, hard work and greatest of all, inspiration you and Mrs. Bell put into the A.E.A., I would like to see someone have the grace to admit that it did do some original work and not a little towards the practical development of the modern machine."

The AEA patents became the subject of "negotiations" a few years later, culminating in the "purchase" of same by Curtiss through the AEA trustee, Charles J. Bell. Those discussions came to a head on December 29, 1916, when McCurdy arrived at the Bell home in Washington via Toronto and New York. According to Bell's recordings in Home Notes, that day McCurdy had a conference with Charles J. Bell and submitted a proposition to him from the Curtiss Aeroplane Company to purchase the patents of the AEA. The consideration was to include cash "for the amount expended in the defense of the patents," as well as stock in the Curtiss Company, one half to be preferred and the other half in common stock.

Discussions continued over the course of the next few days. While Dr. Bell attended a meeting of the Volta Bureau on December 30, Douglas and Charles met again to continue their talks. The following day Dr. Bell sat down with Charles to review the details of McCurdy's proposition, which by then had been clarified to provide for a purchase price of $4,000 plus stock. The

AEA trustee countered this with a demand for "payment in cash of all monies expended by the AEA, plus stock considerations." Dr. Bell estimated that the total cash outlay for the AEA was about $50,000, which included the $35,000 put in by Mabel, the $10,000 by Dr. Bell, and about $4,000 put in by the associates to defend their patents. The matter was for the moment in gridlock.

There was confusion about just what the Curtiss offer as advanced by McCurdy entailed. Clarification was sought during January when correspondence was exchanged on the matter. Interestingly, on January 8, 1917, Douglas wrote to Mabel Bell on the subject, saying, "I did not have much luck with Mr. Charles Bell" with his offer of $4,000 cash and $25,000 in common and $25,000 in preferred stock. Speaking of Charles, McCurdy wrote,

> He turned the proposition down cold and would consider nothing but $75,000 cash. I think he is making a mistake and may regret it later on. I doubt whether Mr. Charles Bell will get so good an offer from anybody else, and of course as time goes on the Curtiss stock will become more valuable. I thoroughly believe in the prospects of that Company especially as we have got Mr. Keys [financier Clement M. Keys] on the board and Executive Committee. I am convinced that Curtiss wants to do the right and fair thing and appreciates as I do Mr. Bell's part in his and my success.

Whether McCurdy knew it or not, Mabel harboured hard feelings toward Glenn Curtiss that would have influenced her thinking on all that was happening at this time. Those thoughts were only revealed subsequently in correspondence with family members. On March 13, 1919, Mabel wrote to her daughter Daisy about marketing opportunities for the hydrofoil, lamenting the fact that they had not profited from the old AEA experience with aircraft, which she attributed to Curtiss. "We would have been rolling in wealth now if we had had a businessman in our AEA. Curtiss was the nearest approach to one we had, but he was not honest and over-reached himself. Of course he is rich enough now, but he could have got plenty of money himself a more honourable way and let us have some too if he had been more broad-minded at the start. We are trying to find someone now and that's why I wrote you."

Daisy's husband, David Fairchild, appears to have taken a more supportive stance regarding Curtiss, prompting Mabel to set him straight in a lengthy letter in April 1919. "I feel so sure from the tone of some recent letters to Daddysan [Dr. Bell] and me that you really can know very little about Mr. Curtiss's relations to the old AEA, that I feel I want to tell you something about them and the reasons why we cannot give him either respect or friendship." She then went on to describe the AEA, which she depicted as "a great, a marvelous success. Yet very few know this. Fewer still the magnitude of that success.

"Curtiss, who knew every secret of the AEA, tried to find other methods [of biplane construction] and failed utterly. Those biplanes you saw flying overhead and thought of as Curtiss biplanes are not really Curtiss biplanes at all—they are Baldwin biplanes constructed on AEA principles, just as are every other biplanes now flying. The world does not know this, but Curtiss does, and it is due to him that the world does not."

Mabel continued, coming to the defence of Casey who, like her husband, shunned affairs of business.

The spirit that influenced Casey to turn aside from promising openings and devote himself to experimental work in the field, which every practical businessman would at once denounce as chimerical and impractical to a degree, was not one which would naturally fit him to cope with men like Curtiss. Besides there were reasons which will appear. To understand the situation at the close of the AEA life, it is necessary to bear in mind that Curtiss was much the elder, after Mr. Bell, in years and experience, especially the last. From boyhood, circumstances had forced him to battle with the world. As a consequence he was versed in its ways and was now with a flourishing business of his own, which could easily be combined with the making of aeroplanes to the profit of both. All he needed was more capital and already he knew where he could get it.

The other Associates were mere enthusiastic boys, totally inexperienced in business, absolutely trustful of him. They were full of eagerness, fresh from college, but with no definite plans or prospects. None of them, or Mr. Bell either, could have conceived that Curtiss was already scheming to betray them all in such a way as to make it practically almost impossible for them to reap their fair share of their mutual labours.

He owed his introduction to the AEA to his own energy and enterprise in having the fastest and lightest going motor then known in

America. But, the equipping of his shop, the training of his men, and the doing of the experimental work he owed to Mr. Bell's money, his brains, and those of the other Associates—all unobtainable otherwise. Curtiss himself had contributed little of value, apart from the fitting of his motor, to the development of the aeroplanes.

The following comment left little doubt as to Mabel's feelings:

> Glenn Curtiss stands before the public, a conspicuous figure, whose notice pleases, a millionaire, a successful man who has developed a wonderful new industry. Casey Baldwin does not. Mr. Bell's name is rarely mentioned in connection with aviation. But it is for us to judge privately who are the better men, who one wants for one's friend. Is it the one who broke his word, and when his foot was securely on the top of the wall of success, not only refused to lend a hand to those who had given their shoulders to help him up, but kicked them down—or the one who even now finds a word of excuse for Curtiss: "He wanted to be straight, but he needed the money and got into a cut-throat crew."

It was a profoundly revealing letter, which Mabel concluded by making reference to the present and the challenge of marketing the hydrofoil, and issuing a plea for help—for Casey's sake.

> So, the question I am asking today is, must the experience of the AEA be repeated, or is there any way by which some honour and pecuniary reward may be assured to those who have rightfully earned them. Casey is much more alive to the desirability of getting something in return for our expenditures than he was, chiefly for Mr. Bell's and my sakes. But how? He needs help. It is no use saying he should come down and compete—he cannot do that. What I am looking for is someone who is willing to be the leader of a forlorn hope, for this is about the size of our job. Where shall I find him?

As for the offer to purchase the AEA patents, Mabel of course shared the letter she received from McCurdy with Alec. He didn't think that it "tallied" with his recollection of what Charles Bell had imparted to him so asked the trustee if he would furnish him with a written statement of what passed between McCurdy and himself that he could send to Mr. Baldwin and Mr. Selfridge.

Charles Bell immediately wrote to Dr. Bell saying that McCurdy had "made no actual proposition" but suggested a deal might be reached if Dr. Bell would accept about $4,500 cash and $40,000 in par value of the stock of the Curtiss Company. "My counter-proposition was: the same amount in cash and some proper form of obligation from the Curtiss Company for $75,000, which I understand from you was the amount of money which you and Mabel had put into the AEA. Judging from the balance sheets I saw of the Curtiss Company I was not favourably impressed and could not see any permanent value in their shares, and believed it was wiser to take a deferred obligation of the Company itself rather than shares of stock in it."

On January 17, 1917, McCurdy wrote to the trustee on letterhead of Aeroplane Products Limited of Toronto to clarify any confusion in the proposition he had left with Charles Bell during his recent trip to Washington. In this letter McCurdy reiterates that the Curtiss Company was offering "approximately $4,000 cash and also to transfer to you as Trustee $25,000 par value of Curtiss preferred and 250 shares of the Curtiss common."

As for the suggestion made by Charles Bell that the Curtiss Company provide cash of $75,000 or a form of deferred payment for that amount guaranteed by a note from the Company, McCurdy's response was clear. "I beg to advise that the Curtiss Company do not feel themselves in a position to pay, or obligate themselves to pay any more cash than the before-mentioned $4,000."

McCurdy then made the following statement, demonstrating that he was clearly on the side of Curtiss, with whom he shared a common mindset toward the negotiations:

"It seems to me that if these patents are to be of any value that they should aid in making the Curtiss Company more valuable, and a just return would be derived from the increased value of the stock, and I, together with Mr. Curtiss, speaking as members of the now defunct Association, feel that the above offer is fair and just."

Commenting to Dr. Bell on this letter, Charles Bell repeated his previous observation about the financial standing of the Curtiss Company. "As I have informed you before the Curtiss Company is by no means in strong financial condition, but it is quite possible that if the War keeps up a complete change in their affairs might take place and their stock become valuable, so that there is a speculative possibility." He left it with Dr. Bell to discuss the matter further with him before he replied to McCurdy.

These meetings and negotiations all took place while Alec and Mabel Bell were at home in Washington. Casey was home at Beinn Bhreagh and does not appear to have played any active role in the proceedings. He and Dr. Bell shared a common disinterest in business affairs. Alec may have deferred to Mabel in the end. She voiced her thoughts on the subject in an undated letter to Alec.

> I had several conversations with Douglas about his proposition to Charlie, and he said the same thing each time, that the proposition was based on the idea that your expenditures for the A.E.A. amounted to $5,000, and that Mr. Curtiss wanted to reimburse you for your outlay on the A.E.A. as an acknowledgement of his indebtedness to you. It was in short not a question of what the patents were worth to the company, but of appreciation of what you had done for Mr. Curtiss through the A.E.A. He told me they were doing a large business but the cash capital was too small to warrant their offering more cash. The question in my mind is whether Charlie is wise in rejecting the proposition altogether. Is it not better to have half a loaf than no loaf at all?

In late February Charles Bell received a letter from Mr. Keys on behalf of Curtiss enclosing a cheque for $5,899.49 covering the cost of the AEA patents and defending them; other stock consideration was yet undetermined. Dr. Bell was in a quandary. In terms of the cash offering, he felt that "the greater part of this amount will come to me personally for money advanced by me." At the same time he didn't want to take the cash for himself, as he never expected to receive any benefit "when other members of the Association receive only stock of very questionable value." He refused to accept the money, suggesting rather that it be apportioned to the several interests of all—Mabel to receive 35 percent of stock and cash; with Dr. Bell, the estate of Thomas Selfridge, Baldwin, McCurdy, and Curtiss to receive 13 percent each. Fair to a fault, he also suggested that they set aside some money as a honorarium in recognition of the services of Charles J. Bell as AEA trustee.

The matter appears to have been concluded in this manner, and the counter-offer appears to have been taken off the table. Ultimately all that was received was little more than reimbursement for the original AEA patent cost, as well as some stock in the Curtiss Company. In an entry by Bell in Letter Books of August 4, 1917, he notes, "My shares of Curtiss Aeroplane and Motor Corporation have been sold and the amount received $3,748.57 has been deposited to the credit of my GRO account with the Washington Loan & Trust Company."

The whole matter involving the "purchase" of the AEA patents by Curtiss through McCurdy as his associate and go-between was unsettling to the Bells and Baldwins. Neither Alec nor Casey, being of the same temperament, said anything much about the matter. Mabel however was a different matter. She was quite prepared to voice her concerns, as evidently she did in correspondence with McCurdy after the purchase went through. There appears to have been some question as to whether McCurdy received more than he was entitled for his proportionate share of the AEA patents. Mabel confronted him on this early in 1918. On January 9 he replied, not to Mrs. Bell but to Dr. Bell.

I have received a letter from Mrs. Bell which places me in an extremely embarrassing position. She points out that in the distribution of the money and stock received by me from Mr. Charles Bell as Trustee for the AEA, I received a proportion not in accordance with the original agreement, nor in accordance with the amount paid by me to Mr. Charles Bell as the assessment pertaining to the Patent Litigation.

Mrs. Bell also points out that you were deeply disappointed that I did not make voluntary restitution. This is of course news to me that any inequitable distribution was made, as I received from Mr. Bell what he said was my proportion, and it never occurred to me to analyze the situation to determine whether or not the Trustee was correct in his figures.

Whatever the situation is at the present time, I should be only too glad to do what is right, and if you will kindly let me know how much I received in excess of the correct amount, I will gladly straighten the matter out.

The issue appears to have been resolved with the intervention of Dr. Bell and an exchange of correspondence between him and McCurdy, who wrote on February 7,

Many thanks for your letter of January 24th. I am very sorry indeed that there was any chance for a misunderstanding with regard to the distribution of the receipts of the patents of the AEA. It is a matter which I would have given a great deal to prevent occurring and one which I regret extremely. I remember at the time the assessment was made on the members of the AEA that I was not in a position financially to make any greater contribution than appears on the Trustee's books. I therefore am enclosing my cheque for $200 made payable to you as I know no better way of doing it as the trusteeship is now dissolved. I am very grateful to Mrs. Bell for bringing the matter to my attention and I hope that any doubt or disappointment in your mind will be cleared up.

It was a case of too little, too late. The damage had been done. Although not fatal, this incident did undermine the bond that McCurdy had shared with the Bells dating back to his childhood. The "disappointment" that the Bells, particularly Mabel, felt toward McCurdy was not "cleared up" and became even deeper in the months that followed.

The Curtiss Company did well during the next few years and following the entry of the United States into the war. That success, however, brought the company under the scrutiny of the United States Internal Revenue Service, which was questioning whether the company had made excessive profits over the valuation of certain "intangible assets," including Curtiss patents that in 1913 had been valued at $200,000 but which by 1917 were calculated to be worth some $7 million.

In April 1920, with his case about to be heard before the Income Tax Commissioners, Curtiss scrambled to gather evidence to show that the value of the "intangibles" was the same or little different in 1917 than in 1913 and thereby refute any claim by the IRS for any income tax liability. On April 9, 1920, Douglas McCurdy provided the Curtiss lawyers with a sworn affidavit in which he agreed that the two essentials of successful flying machines—the structure of the machine and the controls—were invented and developed "by Curtiss and his associates prior to 1913." No mention was made of the AEA.

The Curtiss attorneys then approached Casey, who at that time was with Dr. Bell in Washington, with a request that he help provide them with affidavit evidence supporting the Curtiss position on valuation of what was essentially the old AEA patents. It was not a good move on their part. Casey and Dr. Bell reviewed the materials provided to them by the Curtiss attorneys, which included the McCurdy affidavit. To quote Bell, "on looking over these papers with Mr. Baldwin I was really quite shocked by the misstatements contained in them."

In his April 20, 1920, entry in Home Notes, Dr. Bell was clearly very upset but did not want "to be dragged into the Curtiss affair." When Curtiss called him on the subject he "expressed no opinion and said nothing, but Baldwin gave him a very frank statement of his impressions." First Bell and then Baldwin made entries in Home Notes that expressed their feelings on the issue.

Bell wrote, "The patents were sold to the Curtiss Company for a consideration that did not at all express any estimate of value of the AEA patents, but did express the goodwill of the Associates towards Mr. Curtiss personally and the feeling that the patents should belong to the Curtiss Company as Curtiss himself was one of the patentees and a member of the AEA."

Casey replied:

> I feel exactly as you do about it but don't care to contribute to this series of Life and Noble Deeds that seem to be the tenor of the affidavits. Besides being inaccurate, all the statements are so contrary to the spirit of the AEA work that it is very distasteful. The question is whether we want them to modify their account of the AEA work to conform with our ideas or tell them that we don't care to have anything to do with it. Curtiss's point of view that because the material is not to be published, it doesn't matter how inaccurate it is seems to me to be quite beside the mark, and all their talk about playing up the Curtiss trademark seems to me a poor excuse and very stupid policy.

Later that day, April 20, Casey had an opportunity to express himself even more emphatically when he met with the barrage of Curtiss attorneys at the New Willard Hotel in Washington. Casey's remarks, later written up in Home Notes, made it abundantly clear where he stood on the matter, and it was not with Curtiss and McCurdy.

> I told them very briefly that the whole statement was a deliberate misrepresentation of the facts and that I would be very glad to go over it,

clause by clause, and point out the most specifically untruthful statements and the most offensive of the many incorrect inferences.

I went on to reiterate…that it was stupid now to pretend that the
chief asset of the Curtiss Company from a patent point of view was
anything but the patents of the AEA and the experience in construction
gained through this early work.

I did not correct the part about Curtiss being the first one to appreciate the advantages of flying from the water, but told them that this
claim was of the same order as a lot of their other claims and that if they
would take the trouble to look up the AEA work which they professed to
know they would find that Dr. Bell had always been in favour of flying
from the water and we had done the first work on the subject in Nova
Scotia. (Curtiss admitted where the idea came from and that it was not,
to say the least, a one-man conception.)

Toward the end of the interview Casey was asked if he would provide an
affidavit stating "that as valuable as the early germs [i.e., AEA patents] were,
it required the practical genius of Curtiss to bring them to fruition." Casey
summarized his reply thus: "I thanked them and said I'd be very glad to pre-
pare an affidavit outlining the development of the AEA patents, their value, the
reasons why all machines now used them—but that I would tell them frankly
where the AEA patents came from and would treat the subject in the same
spirit that the AEA had been incorporated, without dragging in personalities.
I could not subscribe either to the view that this work was valueless without
the culminating practical genius of Curtiss."

Clearly, the Curtiss attorneys would get no help from Casey. He ended his
recording of the event by saying, "They concluded that they could get along
without my testimony.…After a very pleasant and frank talk with Curtiss I
came home having enjoyed myself immensely."

A couple weeks later, on May 4, Casey and others were meeting with
Dr. Bell in Washington about matters relating to the HD-4 when Douglas
McCurdy made an unannounced visit to the Bell home. Dr. Bell described
the occasion.

Mr. McCurdy took me on one side and explained that on meeting
Mr. Baldwin in Toronto he had learned that we had been very much

disappointed by the affidavit that he had made in relation to the AEA matters for the benefit of Curtiss and he had come down specially to assure us of his loyalty to the old AEA, and his appreciation of all that we had done during the AEA days; that his only desire in making this affidavit had been to help Curtiss and not at all to reflect upon the work of the AEA. He seemed much distressed about the matter and said that the affidavit had been prepared by the Curtiss lawyers and that he had signed it without much consideration, and was sorry he had done so. He said he had seen Mrs. Bell and had expressed to her his kindly feelings towards us all and his regret at the way in which the Curtiss lawyers had worked his affidavit. He felt that he had been caught, and was so distressed about the matter that he had come right down to Washington specially to let us know that he felt very badly about the matter and that he was loyal to us and to the AEA.

Whatever Dr. Bell's feelings were he chose not to record them. Rather he completed his entry by noting that it was after midnight before Mr. McCurdy took his departure whereupon Bell and the others continued with their meeting. It appears that Douglas was not invited to stay the night. It had been an awkward situation and, following so closely upon the heels of the distasteful patent matter, became a defining moment in the Bell–McCurdy relationship.

It seems Douglas McCurdy was now out of favour with the Bells and Baldwins, as suggested in a letter from Mabel to Kathleen at this time.

I write to ask that as a personal favour you call on Douglas's wife and be nice to her. She at least has no part in anything that has passed. And as for Douglas himself—I cannot forget that he was my very dear little boy that I have loved and cared for just as I do your own little Bobbie. A mother can never take her love from her child no matter what happens—and I loved Douglas only less than I did mine and one of my sister's who also came very close to me as a little child. I must go on caring for Douglas and I ask that you and Casey do not make it any harder for me than you can help. I know how Casey feels and I am asking much of you both. But I never forget that it is to Douglas that I owe Casey, and all the dear comradeship he and his have given Mr.

Bell and me.... [A]ll this doesn't mean that I haven't been hurt, and very deeply, particularly by Douglas whom I especially loved.

These had been trying times for everyone, especially Casey. In a very short period he had lost a close friend and confidante in Gipsy Pillot, parted company with a valued employee and personal friend in the person of Gretchen Anton-Smith, and was now enduring a jaded relationship with his old friend and associate Douglas McCurdy over the Curtiss affair.

CHAPTER 15

World Water Speed Record and Other Maritime Milestones

T HROUGHOUT THIS STRESSFUL TIME, CASEY DID HIS BEST TO remain focused on his work with hydrofoils. HD-4 was radically different in appearance from the three earlier models. Casey who, with input from Bell, had designed and then built and tested all three prototypes had by now determined that a cigar-shaped body carried on three sets of reefing hydrofoils with aerial propeller propulsion was the ideal configuration. Design and construction of the craft was carried out throughout 1917 and into 1918; it was finally launched on October 10. Considerable time was lost waiting for delivery of the promised Liberty engines, during which period smaller 250 h.p., twelve-cylinder Renault engines were employed for test purposes.

The craft had a cylindrical hull some sixty feet long, about six feet in diameter and rounded at both ends giving it an appearance or shape similar to a dirigible. The wooden hull with six bulkheads, three of which were watertight, was built strong and was covered with an outside skin of canvas embedded in marine glue. A rudimentary cockpit about four feet wide and eight feet long, with "controls" and a thirty-inch diameter steering wheel, sat just forward of the two engine mounts. The weight of the craft with three men aboard was in excess of five tons, necessitating a great deal of power.

The Bell Laboratory continued to amaze even the most ignorant and casual observer with its high level of expertise and craftsmanship in the manufacture of kites, aeroplanes, and now hydrofoils. HD-4 would prove to be one of its crowning achievements. Casey, who enjoyed a good cigar, named HD-4 "The Cigar."

Test trials late in 1918 were impressive with speeds exceeding 50 mph, even with the under-powered Renault engines. It was an amazing time on the waters in and around Baddeck, with the hydrofoil craft, Casey at the wheel, roaring around the harbour. Local residents had become somewhat accustomed to this sort of thing with the testing of earlier models, but The Cigar was something quite different, and mesmerizing. At one point Mabel, wishing to experience the craft herself, prevailed upon Casey to "take her for a spin" from Beinn Bhreagh to Baddeck and back. Not to be outdone, Kathleen had Casey take her and Bobby for a ride. Alec preferred to watch from shore.

The HD-4 had been tested and performed admirably but required more powerful engines. The delay in delivery of the 350 h.p. Liberty motors was a frustrating time for Casey—and Mabel. She wrote to Casey regularly from Washington to keep up his morale and encourage him to use this time wisely lest others who might be engaged in similar hydrofoil work take undue advantage of what he had accomplished to date. Casey knew that delay was costly; he was concerned about expenses associated with the development of the HD-4. Mabel, ever money conscious, attempted to allay his concerns.

> Do not worry too much over the how and where the money has gone—prove that it has been wisely spent. It is important of course that you should know where and how it has all gone that you may avoid making the same mistakes, if mistakes were made. But an attitude of depression is not the one to take. It will not get you anywhere. And there is no reason why you should take it. On the contrary you should feel that you cannot be too thankful that you have been as successful as you have been. The HD-4 at 53 mph is one great big fact that can't be got around.

Mabel then drew Casey's attention to her experience with her father, a "promoter" for Dr. Bell who was content to invent but both unable and unwilling to market the subject of his inventions, most notably the telephone. She encouraged Casey to seek out his "Mr. Hubbard."

What you have to do, and with as little delay as possible, is to see that no one takes the glory of that accomplishment from US—and if possible, get others to take hold of it now and practically demonstrate its great utility. I realize fully that this is asking a very great deal of you. I realize now, if never before, Mr. Bell's indebtedness to my father. But for him it seems to me quite possible that Mr. Bell might never have won fame or money—simply because he did not know how to push himself. If only we had such a man as my father to help us now! You and Mr. Bell could go calmly on working away experimenting and developing—the work you are both fitted for, and in which you find your happiness. It only needs that you meet the right man.

Mabel was unrelenting in her efforts to encourage Casey with his development of the HD-4.

I want to see you and Mr. Bell justified in the eyes of the world before I die—and to be justified involves the HD-4's being used, and used as your and Mr. Bell's product. In short, I want some money success— not, I honestly think I can say, because I want the money, but because of what it represents. I believe in you. Mr. Bell believes in you. Kathleen believes in you. Gipsy believed in you, and if circumstances were against our having the correctness of our belief proved before the world we'd never say anything. But you see you have in your hands the proof of that correctness. All you have to do is to produce it.

I could be satisfied to have had you and Mr. Bell demonstrate the correctness of your and his theories about the HD and leave it at that. But I do want my own and Mr. Bell's judgment of you and your ability vindicated by the world. This is why I so want it to be known and to have boats built commercially after it. You see, in this way my—our— own personal credit is bound up in your success. I want to show the Charles Bells, the Kerrs, and all who have doubted *my boy* that they were wrong—utterly, absolutely wrong. All that money which worries you is not too much to pay for that. Please believe this, for it is perfectly true.

Finally, two 350 h.p. Liberty engines, the same were used on the HS flying boats of the US Navy, arrived at Baddeck on July 14, 1919. (The Curtiss HS flying boat was an amphibious aircraft powered by twelve-cylinder Liberty engines, large numbers of which were built for the US Navy from 1917 to 1919.) A few modifications were made to the HD-4 to accommodate the heavier and more powerful engines before testing could commence. With the new Liberty engines installed, history was again made at Baddeck when, on September 9, 1919, HD-4 covered a one-mile course at a speed of 70.86 mph, the fastest any watercraft had gone up to that time. It might not have happened at all. As HD-4 was on its way to the place laid out for the trial, the craft struck a submerged wooden crate causing some modest damage. It was quickly repaired and The Cigar was not denied its big day.

Casey's record-setting trial of HD-4 didn't receive near the publicity as did the flight of Silver Dart. A brief account appeared in the *Sydney Post* on September 11, 1919, with the headline "Bell Makes New Record," the first of many such instances in which Bell would be given credit for the HD-4. Within the body of this article it was acknowledged that "the boat was designed and built by F. W. Baldwin of Baddeck with the assistance of Alexander Graham Bell," but this misleading banner understated the significance of the event and focused public attention upon Bell rather than Casey as the person most responsible for this remarkable accomplishment.

Buoyed with the success of HD-4, Dr. Bell and Casey enlisted the assistance of Casey's brother-in-law, John F. (Jack) Lash—a Toronto lawyer married to Casey's younger sister, Grace—to provide legal counsel on patents and other matters. With his assistance, a company, Bell-Baldwin Hydrodromes Limited, was set up on June 26, 1920, with Lash as president and the head office at Baddeck.

The month after HD-4's record-setting trial, October 1919, William Washburn Nutting, yachtsman and editor of *Motor Boat* magazine, was back in Baddeck, this time by land. Six years earlier he had arrived for the first time when he single-handedly sailed his twenty-eight-foot yacht *Neresis* to Labrador. His time in Baddeck had been short, ostensibly to secure provisions for his voyage, but he met up with Casey and had enjoyed a memorable social visit at Beinn Bhreagh and fine camaraderie at the Bras d'Or Yacht Club. Nutting had been very interested in Casey's work with hydrofoils and was disappointed that his then current prototype, HD-3, was not fully operational. Now that HD-4 was built and test-proven, Nutting had returned to compose an article about it for his magazine and to renew his acquaintance with Casey. It was a rendezvous that would have lasting impact, both on their relationship and on the yachting world.

Nutting wanted to share Casey's accomplishment and the latest in hydrofoil technology with the boating world. His article, "The HD-4—a 70 Miler With Remarkable Possibilities Developed at Dr. Graham Bell's Laboratories on the Bras d'Or Lakes," was published in *Motor Boat* on October 25, 1919. The account is largely technical in that it describes the configuration and detailed construction of the craft. Nutting did, however, write of his own observations about both the feat of engineering represented by this craft as well as what it was like to ride in HD-4 at speed.

One of the most interesting of the many strange things that have come from Dr. Graham Bell's laboratories is a weird-looking glider that recently has been tearing about the peaceful Bras d'Or Lakes at the rate of 70 miles an hour.

The HD-4 is not a hydroplane in the usual sense of the term. It is the successful development of the idea, by no means new, of lifting the hull clear of the water by a system of submerged planes not a part of the hull itself. In other words, it uses the denser medium to obtain the lift and takes advantage of the low resistance to propulsion offered by the air. An ordinary hydroplane, of course, utilizes the lifting principle and dodges much of the resistance of the water, but is comparatively inefficient in that it uses only the lower and by far the less important surface of the plane.

Now step into the cockpit and we will take a ride, and if you want to hear anything for the rest of the day stuff some cotton into your ears before the motors are started, for they are not muffled. Over goes the starboard motor with the crackle of a machine gun and those on the dock scurry from the cyclone caused by the whirring propeller. The mooring lines are cast off and we slip out into the lake at about ten knots.

Baldwin gives the air to the port motor and the exhaust becomes a continuous roar. At fifteen knots you feel the machine rising bodily out of the water, and once up and clear of the drag, she drives ahead with an acceleration that makes you grip your seat to keep from being left behind. The wind on your face is like the pressure of a giant hand, and an occasional dash of fine spray stings like birdshot.

Baddeck, a mile away, comes at you with the speed of a railway train and you brace yourself for the turn as Baldwin drives her through the narrow passage inside the island. You feel that she is going to skid as he starts to make the turn at full speed, but she does not. Just as the struts of the rudder set are sufficient to steer her, so are those of the main planes sufficient to keep her from slipping. Even more startling is the fact that she doesn't seem to heel a degree as she makes the turn. It is unbelievable—it defies the laws of physics, but it is true.

Then Baldwin gives you the wheel and timidly you start to try it out. You feel that something must surely let go if you give her any helm. But nothing does and you find that she steers with the ease of an automobile. As you get accustomed to the speed your confidence grows and soon you find yourself out of the cockpit lying over the edge of the deck on your stomach to see for yourself what is going on below. The "preventer" at the bow is entirely clear of the water except for the tip of an occasional wave, and all the main sets are out except for the two lower ones on either side. Each square foot of submerged steel is carrying over 2,000 pounds.

Baldwin designed the HD-4 to demonstrate the possibilities of the type for carrying loads at extreme speed, efficiently, and with comparative safety. When you come in from your first ride you are convinced. If you have ever flown, you know that flying is a dull business, compared to skimming over the surface of the water at 60 knots, and for this reason there undoubtedly will be a future for the type for sport as well as for the more serious things at which Dr. Bell and Mr. Baldwin have been aiming.

Nutting's article was subsequently reproduced in its entirety with photographs in the Smithsonian annual report for 1919.

Casey and Nutting were cut from the same cloth—they shared a common passion for the water and boating. One day late in the fall of 1919 found the two of them in one of the innumerable safe anchorages around the Bras d'Or Lakes conversing at length about cruising opportunities and what in their minds might be the ultimate cruising yacht. An additional presence that evening was one Johnny Walker, who lent much to the flavour of the discussion, and by the time he was exhausted Casey and Nutting had come up with what they felt would be the best form of cruising yacht. Their thoughts were subsequently communicated to William Atkin, a leading yacht designer who promptly designed a craft incorporating the features put forth by the proponents. The keel was laid in the boat shop at Beinn Bhreagh early in March 1920.

The ice soon left the lake, spring arrived, and the forty-five-foot ketch designed by Casey, Nutting, and a bottle of Johnny Walker was launched July 3, 1920, just four months in the making. With a good many Baddeck people present, the launch went without a hitch. Kathleen undertook the christening and, exactly to time, smashed the bottle and stated for all to hear, "I name thee *Typhoon*." The vessel was a beautiful work of craftsmanship, which inspired its co-designer to state: "Casey Baldwin and his crew of Nova Scotian boat builders constructed a vessel that will last more than a lifetime." Nutting would be proven correct.

Casey and Nutting had hoped that with this vessel they might demonstrate to the yachting world that a sailboat of this size and standard could transit the Atlantic in the same relative safety and comfort as afforded by larger seagoing craft. This wasn't just talk—they intended to prove their point. To this end they planned to set sail from Baddeck for Cowes, Isle of Wight, UK, on July 17, 1920. They hoped to arrive there in time for the British International Cup races for motorboats vying for the Harmsworth Trophy on August 10. Getting the boat fitted out and provisioned in the few short days between launch and departure was a feat in itself. Through it all Casey and Nutting became the darlings of local as well as international media.

At home the adventure generated considerable interest and excitement both on the street and in the press. The July 20 edition of the *Sydney Post* made much of it, in haste and with some inaccuracies, describing the vessel as having been built under Bell's rather than Casey's supervision, as had been the case with coverage of HD-4. *Typhoon*, it was stated, would fly the Bras d'Or Yacht Club burgee of blue with an arm of gold. Nutting, who was made an honorary life member at a reception given at the yacht club, remarked about the send-off that he was grateful to Casey "who delivered a few intelligent remarks about the purpose of the boat and the cruise and really made the whole venture sound quite rational. Up to that time I had been somewhat in doubt as to just how to explain the thing."

The voyage was made in just over twenty-two days with *Typhoon* arriving at Cowes just a day before the start of the races. It was an amazing demonstration of seamanship in a crossing made in record time, often in adverse weather and entirely under sail. The small auxiliary motor had failed just after leaving the Bras d'Or. In his typical understated style, Casey wrote to Kathleen upon arrival at Cowes, "Luck was certainly with us all the time. When the motor went dead and we couldn't do anything with it I would have sold our chances for making a decent passage for a little less than the smallest coin I can think of, but to go back would not have done so we pushed on.... On arrival here we have been swamped with kindness and all sorts of interest in our little venture."

The English media had a field day reporting on the small Nova Scotian-built vessel that had just mastered the Atlantic and stood proudly amongst the *crème de la crème* of world-class yachts gathered at Cowes for the Harmsworth Trophy Races. Nutting later wrote of their reception in his book *Track of the Typhoon*.

Our coming to Cowes had been like that of a modest burglar; not so our awakening several hours later, after getting some rest—the first undisturbed sleep we had since leaving Baddeck. It seems that Cowes had heard of our departure from Baddeck and had been expecting us—but not so soon. We were jolted into consciousness about eight o'clock by the arrival of the Customs authorities, whom we received in our pajamas. The irrepressible Casey, seizing upon the opportunity as an event demanding a certain amount of hospitality, broke out a case of Canadian rye and in consequence the formalities incident to entering our ship were brief indeed. The little informal health certificate which our friend, Dr. McAulay had scribbled the midnight of our departure from Baddeck was accepted and we were given the formal certificate of "pratique." This finished, we were the legitimate prey for a horde of newspaper correspondents, photographers and movie men. With an admirable disregard for convention Baldwin insisted on being photographed in his luridly striped night gear much to the disgust of the Skipper, who endeavors to maintain an air of dignity and respectability at all times.

At some point it was found best to move *Typhoon* to a more convenient mooring, a feat that was accomplished with many helping hands whose "assistance was a bit sketchy from over-participation in Casey's hospitality," wrote Nutting. "For the three weeks that our ship remained at Cowes there was scarcely a moment that some interested visitor was not aboard. The Royal Yacht Squadron sent us an invitation to make use of the Castle, and the Royal London Yacht Club made us Honorary members during our visit."

The royal yacht *Victoria and Albert*, with the royal family aboard, had departed shortly after *Typhoon* had arrived; however, one of the first to visit aboard *Typhoon* was General John Seeley, the Lord Lieutenant of Hampshire, "who came onboard and welcomed us in the name of the King and expressed a regret that His Majesty had left without an opportunity to inspect our ship, in which he felt the sailor King would have been interested."

It seems that Casey soon became somewhat blasé about royalty. According to the skipper, "Several days after our arrival a modest sort of man rowed in by a dinghy with a couple of ladies, evidently wishing to come aboard. Casey, who was standing in the companionway, smiled reassuringly, but after several unsuccessful attempts to muster courage to invite himself aboard, the retiring gentlemen rowed away. We found out later it was the Duke of Leeds."

For the present, their mission accomplished, Casey was homeward bound as a passenger aboard a transatlantic liner. He had work to do back at Beinn Bhreagh. Nutting rousted up new crew and sailed *Typhoon* back to New York. He managed to make it there safely although he dearly missed Casey whom he admired both as an inventor as well as a yachtsman. "Casey may have had limited ability in the galley," he wrote, "but any such short-comings were excusable in light of his expert seamanship and cool judgment and iron nerve that were the despair of those who faced him on the gridiron—and his never-failing humour, all of which make him the best man on the water that I have ever known."

Their spectacular crossing of the Atlantic and the considerable media attention it generated had the desired effect. In a boating world which to that point was much focused on racing both at the yacht club level as well as off-shore racing like the America's Cup, the *Typhoon* in "Casey's little venture" had managed to direct attention to the sport of sailing through cruising. If anything, for Casey, always an avid racer, the Cowes experience increased his desire to promote cruising. He had already set those wheels in motion even before *Typhoon*'s Cowes saga.

While plotting the design and construction of *Typhoon*, Casey and Nutting had been part of a small group gathered one evening late in 1919 aboard the Grosvenor yawl *Elsie*. The others included Gilbert Grosvenor, Jim Dorsett, and William A. Wise Wood. The subject of discussion was the concept of a cruising club for all manner of craft, both motor and sail.

From this modest beginning, the Cruising Club of America was born in the winter of 1921–1922 with William Nutting as commodore and the mandate "to stimulate an interest in seamanship, and the navigation and handling of small vessels." Casey and Nutting's experience of the Royal Cruising Club at Cowes provided the prototype for the new undertaking in America. Among the objectives of the Cruising Club was the desire to "be an active force influencing others to make adventurous use of the sea." Casey and *Typhoon* had shown the way. The Cruising Club of America continues to this day with the same objective and makes the Bras d'Or Lakes in Cape Breton a regular part of its cruising agenda.

While in the UK, Casey had taken a side trip to London where he met with some members of the British Admiralty to discuss hydrofoil technology. Dr. Bell was travelling in Scotland in October of 1920 and wrote to the Secretary of the Admiralty on October 25 to follow up on Baldwin's visit and the discussion he'd had with the Admiralty involving a modified form of hydrofoil, specifically for use as a towing target, a "raft" topped with fabric-covered vanes (targets) and capable of being towed at high speed for air or surface target practice. According to J. H. Parkin, "The idea of a target for naval gunnery practice, carried on hydrofoils, apparently occurred to Casey sometime during the experiments with the HD series of hydrodrome. After his return from the voyage of the *Typhoon* to England, he began to develop his ideas…. Casey discussed, in a general way with members of the Admiralty Board, the advantages of a hydrofoil system in the design of a light easily towed high-speed target as compared with the conventional displacement type requiring enormous power to attain a speed of 30 knots."

Casey and Bell had subsequently discussed the concept and put together concept drawings for targets built on the hydrofoil principle, incorporating a superstructure built of tetrahedral cells. In this letter Bell enclosed blueprints for both a fifty- and a one-hundred-foot model for consideration. With the Great War just recently ended, though, interest in warfare technology was at a low ebb. Casey couldn't have known it at the time, but he would still be engaged in promoting the concept of hydrofoil targets twenty-five years later, after the end of the Second World War.

Meanwhile back in Washington Bert Grosvenor at Mabel's urging had been corresponding with officials of the United States Navy about the HD-4, which appeared to be in limbo while they awaited "an expression of opinion as to the Departmental policy on boats of this type." "Hurry up and wait" appears to have been the credo of all defence departments in Britain, United States, and Canada in dealing with first aeroplane and now hydroplane technology. Construction and testing of hydrofoil targets continued at Beinn Bhreagh late in 1920 and over the ensuing few years while discussions and sea trials were ongoing with naval officials.

By 1920 Casey, quite apart from the voyage of *Typhoon*, had acquired a reputation as one of the most outstanding sailors in Nova Scotia. Much of that had been gained at the yacht club level while racing competitively as representative of the Bras d'Or Yacht Club in *Scrapper* and *Scrapper II*. Soon after returning from the UK, Casey was busy making plans for *Scrapper III* with construction beginning the following February after a brief closure of the Laboratory.

During the summer of 1920 while Casey had been preoccupied with *Typhoon*, yachting enthusiasts up and down the Atlantic seacoast had been caught up in excitement arising from press coverage of the America's Cup. What became the most animated topic of conversation arising out of the event was the fact that the final race had been cancelled due to too much wind. Twenty-three knots of wind was considered excessive for these "extreme racing machines," but to old salts, like those who fished the Grand Banks in schooners out of Lunenburg, Nova Scotia, and Gloucester, Massachusetts, this was nothing but a stiff breeze. Talk began and interest spiked in the potential for an international race of "true" sailing vessels, working schooners or "salt bankers."

This concept caught the imagination of a group of businessmen and sporting enthusiasts in Halifax, Nova Scotia. Led by Senator William H. Dennis, newspaper owner and publisher, they established the International Fishermen's

Cup Race and donated the *Halifax Herald*'s International Fisherman's Trophy, which would be awarded annually to the fastest vessel in the North Atlantic fishing fleet. The race would only be open to vessels that had spent at least one season engaged in commercial deep-sea fishing on the Grand Banks. It was a marked departure from the America's Cup—more like the old days of "wooden ships and iron men" and determining who was the hardiest of the hardy, Lunenburgers or Gloucestermen.

As with any race, there were rules and from time to time the need for interpretation and enforcement. These competitors would for the most part be hardbitten fishermen/sailors with little time or interest in the niceties of rules and regulations. The Dennis consortium needed an arbiter for just this eventuality, and Casey Baldwin was their choice to fill that role.

At the first championship in October 1920, issues arose during the elimination races to determine a challenger for the American entry. In the elimination race held off Halifax on October 11, there were eight contenders—six schooners from Lunenburg and two from LaHave—each issued a number. Number 8 was assigned to a schooner that was conceded to have a very good chance of winning. The skipper, taking umbrage with being assigned the last number in the pack, promptly refused to compete and prepared to sail home. Casey was brought in and through his quiet tact and diplomacy, managed to persuade the captain that his number in no way reflected their estimation of his schooner's chances. It was not the only time Casey's personality would prevail and quell squabbles among the fishermen. Although not an active participant in the races, Casey's easy rapport with the fishermen, aided by his Irish wit, frequently helped ease tensions and smooth troubled waters. He proved to be invaluable in the success of the fishermen's races in this and succeeding years.

During March of 1921 Casey spent considerable time in Toronto with Jack Lash, the lawyer of Bell-Baldwin Hydrodromes Limited, working on patents for the hydrofoils. The Bells were wintering at Beinn Bhreagh, and during some of this time Kathleen and the children stayed at The Point with the Bells and Miss Catherine Mackenzie, Dr. Bell's private secretary.

Over the course of several days, correspondence and telegrams were exchanged between Beinn Bhreagh and Toronto. Casey advised that he and Lash were hard at work on a tender for the Admiralty and that Lash had initiated steps to secure patents in England and Japan. Patent applications as prepared by Lash made their way to Beinn Bhreagh where they were signed by Mabel and witnessed by Kathleen and Miss Mackenzie before being sent off to the American Consul in Sydney, Nova Scotia.

That winter Kathleen learned that she was pregnant and expecting a third child. She decided that this child would be born in Halifax. The Bells agreed to look after Bobby and Betty in Washington. With Kathleen's due date drawing near, on August 13 Casey set off for the city—by sailboat. His newest yacht, *Scrapper III*, had been launched, sailed, and found to be a fine craft, a worthy successor to his first two boats of that name. Casey was in Halifax when on September 1 Kathleen gave birth to a baby boy, news that the proud father immediately communicated by telegram to Dr. Bell. Alec acknowledged it by telegraphing Casey at the Halifax hotel where he was staying: "Congratulations on arrival of 'Scrapper No. 4.' Bobby sends love to mother and little baby brother, but Betty at school has not yet heard the news. Love and best wishes to Kathleen."

Casey remained close at hand in Halifax until September 10 when he set off on *Scrapper III* for the return trip to Baddeck. He had put together a crew composed of his good friend Dr. Archibald MacMechan, provincial archivist, and Victor Mader. Casey wrote about the voyage after returning to Baddeck on September 15. "So many things have happened since leaving for Halifax on August 13th that I hardly know where to begin to give an account of myself. The important point is that Kathleen and the boy who seems to be generally known as Scrapper IV are getting along splendidly. Kathleen is so well that it is already quite a job to keep her in bed."

That was all he wrote of Halifax and the birth—the rest of his write-up is all about sailing and the voyage home. Casey summed it up by saying, "The whole trip was one of the best cruises I have ever been on."

Dr. MacMechan had nothing but praise for the skipper. "Anyone who has ever had the luck to be shipmates with 'Casey' Baldwin knows what the terms 'navigation' and 'captain' mean. The most agreeable of companions, a master of his art, cool, resourceful, vigilant, unselfish, untiring, he inspires confidence from the moment he takes command. In danger and difficulty he is serene and unperturbed; he does the right thing at the right time, never sparing himself and always taking the heavy end of the stick."

"Scrapper IV" eventually received his proper name: Patrick Alexander Graham Bell Baldwin. Kathleen had discussed what to call her newborn son with Daisy, who may have played some part in the name ultimately decided upon. She wrote to Kathleen on September 24 while she was still in the hospital in Halifax. "I wish you wanted to call him for Daddysan. 'Graham' is the only namesake Father has that he cares anything about and he loves you and Casey next to Elsie and me—and it's a very close next. It's purely my own idea that he'd like it, but I should—in his place. Lots of love, Daisy."

Casey and Kathleen were now proud parents to three children. Happy times were enjoyed by both the Baldwin and the Bell families in the miracle of birth. Too soon Beinn Bhreagh would experience the emptiness of death.

CHAPTER 16

Stand by Casey

C ASEY WAS BACK INTO A MORE REGULAR WORK ROUTINE AT THE
Laboratory by late September of 1921. Despite his prolonged absences
from the shop that summer, both he and Dr. Bell had kept up regular dialogue with naval authorities in Britain and Canada and United States regarding
hydrofoils. During the summer of 1920 officers from the Admiralty as well as
the US Navy had visited Baddeck to witness test trials of HD-4. Discussions were
ongoing on both sides of the Atlantic and south of the border about potential
use of the HD-4 as a high-speed torpedo carrier and also the concept of using a
tetrahedral structure mounted on a hydrofoil platform as a towing target. Both
concepts involved a great deal of design work and eventually, testing.

Casey was more hands-on in design, construction, and testing while company president John Lash was busy preparing tenders and endeavouring to
obtain patents for the various variations of the HD-4. Dr. Bell continued to
provide oversight and use his influence wherever possible in letter-writing.
It was clear, however, that his health was failing. It also became increasingly
evident that there was no will "in high places" in either the Admiralty or the
US Navy to buy into the concept of the HD-4 as a torpedo carrier.

Toward the end of September Casey wrote to Captain Hose of the
Department of Naval Services in Ottawa to advise that he was soon to remove

the engines from "our experimental boat HD-4" but before dismantling her entirely was anxious to know if towing tests could be made to determine horsepower requirements for towing targets. There was no motorboat at Beinn Bhreagh of sufficient power to effect a tow, thus Casey's request that the department provide a destroyer for that purpose. On September 27 the destroyer *Patriot*, one of the first units of the Royal Canadian Navy, steamed into Baddeck under the command of Lieutenant Charles T. Beard. It was yet another head-turning experience for Baddeckers when, during the next day, *Patriot* made eleven runs, in both directions, over a one-mile course with the HD-4, stripped of her massive Liberty engines, in tow.

The HD-4 performed well. Detailed records of the tows were made and results shared with naval authorities in Britain, Canada, and the United States. No sooner had *Patriot*'s wake receded from Baddeck Harbour when Dr. Bell penned a note in his characteristic polite and engaging manner to Captain Hose in Ottawa.

> The *Patriot* arrived here the morning of the 27th and left the following day, the 28th, after a series of successful experiments in towing the HD-4. Mr. Baldwin and I will be glad to send you a copy of our notes of these trials when completed, and hope very much that this work has not interfered greatly with your program. We were very glad to have the opportunity of meeting the fine officers of the Canadian Naval Service who gave us every assistance, and wish to express again our appreciation of your co-operation. If we are prepared to take advantage of your kind offer of further assistance next Summer we will communicate with you later upon the subject.

Bell followed this up by offering the HD-4 to the Canadian Navy for use as a target, but the offer was not accepted. As J. H. Parkin wrote in *Bell and Baldwin*, "So it came about that the once-fastest craft afloat was beached and lay on the Beinn Bhreagh shore for decades, a silent relic, recognized by few, of a great technical achievement."

Negotiations involving tow targets continued into 1922. The Bells spent the winter of 1921–22 in the West Indies and Florida. Bell minded the heat of the Caribbean and was anxious to return home to the cooler airs of Cape Breton. Before leaving from Florida he, Casey, and David Fairchild worked collaboratively in attempting to raise interest there in the hydrofoil. By June, some success had been achieved with the US Navy in the further development of high-speed towing targets. Toward the end of that month Casey and Jack Lash were in Washington where they signed a contract with the Navy Department, later expanded upon by Casey in Home Notes.

> Our contract with Navy department is to deliver within 180 days at the Navy Yard, Norfolk, Virginia, 2 high speed towing targets generally in accordance with design submitted by A. G. Bell; targets to be delivered unassembled at the Norfolk Yard; dimensions will be approximately 48 feet in length by 10 feet in height; capable of being towed in moderately rough weather in the open sea on a towline not less than 400 yards long at a speed of not less than 25 knots. If targets satisfy the conditions it is agreed that the two targets will be paid for at $5,000 each. Import duty if any to be paid by the Navy.

The timeline for delivery was tight. Casey quickly initiated construction and experimentation with test models—smaller, ten-foot ones that were capable of being towed behind *Dundee*, one of the Beinn Bhreagh motorboats. Work and testing went well into mid-July while other members of the Bell family began to arrive for summer at Baddeck.

Rather ominously, it was also during this time that Bell's physician, Dr. Roy from Sydney, was spending more time at Beinn Bhreagh attending to Dr. Bell. In Washington that spring a diagnosis had revealed nothing alarming in Bell's condition. His personal secretary at that time, Catherine Mackenzie, speculated that perhaps Bell would not permit a full examination. "Bell always insisted on prompt and expert medical attention for any member of his family, but he was a bad patient himself. He didn't want doctors taking liberties with him; he resented their medicines, and their diets, and their orders to take exercise."

That summer Dr. Bell was failing—losing energy but not, however, his keen interest and desire to see Casey succeed in exploiting his great success with HD-4. No one, including Mabel, was overly concerned or alarmed, just mindful that Alec was feeling all of his seventy-five years. For all intents and purposes, life continued as it always had at Beinn Bhreagh.

Bell's death came quickly and took everyone at Beinn Bhreagh by surprise. Miss Mackenzie, who was close at hand toward the end, wrote:

Undoubtedly Bell knew that he had a very short time to live, yet he was sure that his fierce spirit could sustain him until he should have completed all his plans—for the Laboratories, for the Recorder. And no one in his household could believe that the end was measurably near. He rested rather more frequently than usual, he drove to his office only occasionally, sometimes he went to bed for whole afternoons, but he had often done that when he was bored. Dr. Roy recognized his weakened state as pernicious anemia, and specialists were summoned from the United States. But they did not have time to arrive.

Alexander Graham Bell drew his last breath about 2:00 A.M., August 2, 1922, at home, his Cape Breton home on Beinn Bhreagh. Late in the day on August 1 he gave his final dictation to his faithful secretary Catherine Mackenzie.

I want to say that Mr. and Mrs. Bell—we have had both—had a very happy life together, and we couldn't have had better daughters than Elsie and Daisy or better sons-in-law than Bert or David Fairchild, and we couldn't have had finer grandchildren than the grandchildren we've had....

I wanted to talk things over with Mr. Baldwin. (Daisy asked if he was referring to the HD.) Yes—I don't understand it all, I can't do it now, but just as a general principle is that we want to stand by Casey as he has stood by us, so that is all the suggestions that I can make. Want to look upon Casey and Kathleen as sort of children and grandchildren so far as we can with people who are not related to us. (To which Daisy said, "Yes, Daddysan, we understand and all of us feel the same.")

Present at Dr. Bell's death were Mabel, David and Daisy Fairchild, Catherine Mackenzie—and Casey. He was devastated. His mentor, the man who for the past seventeen years had stood *in loco parentis* to him, was gone.

Bert and Elsie Grosvenor were travelling in South America at this time. That very day, seemingly with an iron will, Mabel wrote a letter to Elsie describing what had happened and how everyone had been taken offguard by her father's passing.

There was absolutely no organic trouble present—it was just that he had no reserve strength—and went at the last, not suddenly, but far more quickly than anyone expected.

In the afternoon he had revived and was very bright and sent for Catherine and said he wanted to dictate a statement to her and she did and I enclose a copy. You see what he said of you and Bert and his grandchildren and of Casey and Kathleen. I know he has been much worried about the Navy contract fearing that it was not as absolute as Casey and Mr. Lash insist that it is because it is not in the regular contract fashion and he was so very anxious that the work should go through. Later he felt so much better that he discussed the target with Casey with all his usual clearness and interest—talking about the corner pieces etc. and urging Casey to get them together and have the target out for trial on the water. And Casey said he would get it out today and he must come and see it and he replied, "I hope so."

I am going to carry on his work as far as I can just as if he were here, and consider that the successful completion of the HD and its introduction into practical use as the last and most fitting tribute to his memory, and this one great last wish. For seventeen years Casey has stood by us and WE, father and I, are going to stand by him now. Father and I know Bert and David's love and absolute devotion to us, but both Bert and David's bent lies in other directions than Father's, and Casey filled a place that neither with all the love in the world possibly could. And Casey has given us both a love I believe as great even as Bert's and David's. So he is to me my third son-in-law and I am blessed indeed that I have these three beside me in the hours that lie ahead of me.

What is most apparent from this letter is Mabel's need to fully express to her daughter Elsie how strong and unbreakable was the bond between the Bells and Baldwins, and in particular their unshakeable commitment to Casey. Daisy, like her mother, was quick to put pen to paper. She also wrote to Elsie on August 2.

The end came about two this morning. Mother, David, Casey, and I were with him. We scarcely knew when he stopped breathing. I will tell you all about it Elsie darling when I see you but I really cannot write of it. It was really very sudden the last few days. Yesterday afternoon Daddysan dictated a few last words to Catherine which will be sent to you. It was evidently very much in his heart and it is now mother's greatest preoccupation that we should all "stand by Casey as he has stood by us." Casey is father's and mother' boy in a way that no one else could ever be. His work is father's work. His home is here on Beinn Bhreagh, and their mutual love and devotion is stronger than ever. Please write Casey—his heart is broken.

Alexander Graham Bell was born a Scot, chose to become an American citizen, but long before he died had determined that his final resting place would be atop his "beautiful mountain" at Beinn Bhreagh, Cape Breton, Nova Scotia. Not long after discovering Baddeck, Bell had made this wish known to Mabel, who wrote of it in a June 23, 1887, letter to her husband's father, Melville Bell. "It is strange what a hold Baddeck has already on Alec. The other day, night I mean, when Alec was in pain and fever, he bade me remember if anything happened that he would be buried nowhere else except at the top of Red Head."

Immediately following Bell's death Mabel threw herself into making arrangements for his funeral. Typical of her, it was meticulously planned— from the private gathering of family at The Point, to the funeral march and procession up the mountain to the foot of the tetrahedral tower where the inventor would be laid to rest in a coffin made in his own Laboratory.

More details of the event were to be gleaned from Daisy's August 6 letter to Elsie, still far removed from the scene.

No one ever saw Daddysan again. They dressed him in his grey corduroy knickerbockers and put the rosette of the Legion of Honor in his button-hole.

The day before [the funeral], Mabel [her daughter], representing you and I, went up to the top of the mountain and chose the place—under the Tower between the one big spruce tree and the stairway leg of the Tower. Mother wanted the Tower taken down. It has demonstrated the principle and having been only put up as an experiment, it doesn't seem fair to let it go to pieces and have people feel that it was meant to be permanent.

Casey climbed up and knocked off all the loose boards of the platform and stairs so it now looks like lace work against the sky. They will cover the tree and the grave and pull it down sometime—and mother wants a permanent one erected.

Jean MacDonald…came to the house and played Chopin's funeral march while Casey and five of the men carried him downstairs and placed him at the foot of the stairway. It was a thrilling sight—Casey and Graham walking at the head of twenty or thirty men, all bare-headed, then John and the buckboard with its fir-covered load. Graham and Bobby Baldwin raised the flags to the staff and we all went away.

Just now she [Mabel] wants to sell 1331 [the Washington house] without ever seeing it again. The Naval target must be made. If Casey can find his life work still here, mother can go on living here too— going away of course in the winter and keeping it the home for all of us in the summer. So far there seems no reason why this will not work out. Casey loves the place, the work, the life, and Mother, and he and Mr. Lash have $20,000 of their own money invested in the HD patents and the company.

Mabel had followed the express wishes of her husband, which he had given to her so many years earlier, and arranged for his burial on the mountain at Beinn Bhreagh. Still, it was a difficult decision for Mabel as she revealed in correspondence following the service. On August 12 she wrote to Elsie in Rio de Janeiro, "It was not quite easy for me to do as he had told me he wished, put him to rest on the mountain top. I wanted America to have him—the United States to whom he was so proud to belong. But, after all, this was the home of his love, and he came back here with such pleasure. I couldn't have carried him back to Washington, and now I am content."

Mabel more than anyone else knew how devastated Casey was by the loss of his mentor. She was quick to console and reassure him in his grief.

I'm getting all the sympathy, but I'm not sure but you need it the most. On you falls all the burden. I cannot do much but stand by you as he bade me.

I know you will justify his faith, but it's going to be a hard pull. I wish he could have stayed to see you triumph; it would have meant more to him than any further honour to him. He was always talking about that. This spring he was so anxious you should have it, and everything I can do I will because it's what I can do for him whom we both loved. He was so very, very fortunate in having you these last years of his life—it is you who made them so full of achievement.

Elsie and Daisy were well aware of their parents' devotion to Casey, Kathleen, and their little family. That love and affection had been nurtured and was something they themselves were part of from growing up with the Baldwin family on Beinn Bhreagh. They and their husbands, Bert and David, shared in that relationship. Mabel was not unaware of this but took the opportunity in the sad days following the death of Gipsy in January 1919 to write to her daughters spelling out what she expected of them in relation to the Baldwin family upon the demise of herself and their father. It was a very intimate writing, which, had there ever been any, left no doubt as to where the Baldwin family stood with Alec and Mabel Bell. The letter is lengthy; it is edited here for the sake of brevity.

The uncertainty of life is necessarily impressed upon one at this terrible time, and before it is too late I want to write this letter to commend to your love and consideration Casey and Kathleen Baldwin and their children.

It goes without saying that your Father has done a great deal for Casey. He has had the opportunity and the power. Casey will always be the first to insist on his indebtedness. What may not be so obvious is that Casey himself has done his best to hold up his end—and as he will always be the last to do that it is for me to insist on it.

He and Father worked together all these years in harmony and single mindedness—seeking but to increase our knowledge of things that will be of benefit to mankind—and with no thought of pecuniary benefit. Casey has some small independent means and so has Kathleen, but I believe he is poorer now than he was when he began work with Father. He certainly has not profited in a monetary way, and my great trouble now is what is to become of him and his family when Father and I go. I do not know what he and Kathleen will want to do. They have never talked of it. Gipsy talked to them about it and told me that Casey had apparently never faced the question. She tried to make him do so, but he feels his obligation to us so strongly that he does not want to.

What I have to ask of you my heirs is this: He has been like a son to us all these years. He has had opportunities of helping us which Bert and David have not—and he has used them as Bert and David would have as surely done. I love him very dearly, and Kathleen and the children, and I cannot bear to think that with Father's and my going he may be turned out of the home and place that has been his so long.

There has never been any formal contract between him and Father. We paid him $2,500 a year and he has the bungalow and ground around it free. He did not want us to give him so much. It was father's arrangement and insistence. There is no arrangement whatever about the Laboratory and boat building. Father wanted the laboratory made self-supporting and agreed with Casey that a small boat building plant would likely effect that purpose. And so Casey has put the best of himself into it all, and now if he wanted to he could hardly leave because so much of our money has gone into the necessary plant. He has not received one penny of profit from all his hard work. His one desire is if possible to relieve me of the heavy burden of the laboratory through the profit of the boat shop.

What I want is that you should now give him his choice: let him stay on occupying his house and developing the boat-building so that he will at least have something to show for his devotion to us, or if he prefers to go away, make some arrangements with him whereby he gets some benefit out of his work. In short, I do not want him [to] lose at once his friends, his home, and his work. He will never look out for himself. I want you to look out for him. While we are here I think he is happier here than anywhere else, so there is nothing I can do. While, if he and Kathleen left it would practically mean taking our home from us because we could not now live here without them.

Gipsy's death is a terrible loss to us at this time for this reason among many others—that she was able to see things from Casey's and my points of view. He talked to her as he could not to me, and Father and I talked to her as I could not to him. With her help we were approaching a better understanding of how things should be put on a business basis, but it was impossible to finish our work because the War was still on, and Casey's one idea was to get the HD-4 in such shape that he could go to the War. It was his feeling of his obligation to us that was part of the reason which held him back before—part, not all—and he has suffered terribly in consequence. This is part of our debt to him.

I who love him commend him to you as a younger brother. Let him and Kathleen feel that you remember all the happy years he has brought into your Father's life that you would have brought had your interests been along the same lines. I am not making any bequests to them, that's not what I mean in writing this letter, only that you give them fellowship in your love for us and remembrance of us, and help them readjust their lives so that they shall lose as little by our going as needs must. And I love and trust you my children and think Mother was never more blessed than I in my daughters and sons-in-law.

This was a powerful letter, estate planning in effect, which undoubtedly was in the minds of both Daisy and Elsie upon their father's death. Their mother, Mabel, was still with them, but sadly not for much longer. Mabel must have thought as much, for a main preoccupation following Dr. Bell's death was how best to give effect to Dr. Bell's last wishes—to carry on the HD work, to stand by Casey, and look after Kathleen and the children. Within a few short weeks Mabel had things in hand, as she wrote in Home Notes on September 6.

Mr. Baldwin and I have today signed a contract whereby we agree together that we will continue to carry on the work that Mr. Bell, Baldwin, and I have been carrying on—so far as it is possible to do so without Mr. Bell. This agreement is to last for ten years and calls for an expenditure of $10,000 a year for experimental work to be at Baldwin's sole discretion. This I believe to be along the lines of Mr. Bell's wish many times expressed. We hope it will be possible to make this experimental laboratory so successful that at the end of the ten year period it will be so well established that it will be permanent without further financial help from the family.

Life returned to some sort of normalcy at Beinn Bhreagh in the weeks following Bell's death. Mabel together with the Fairchild and eventually the

Grosvenor families remained at Beinn Bhreagh into the fall while Casey resumed his HD work. August 20 was an important day in the lives of both the Baldwins and the Bells. Mabel, who in all likelihood had played some role in orchestrating the event, wrote a short description, which belied its import. "On Wednesday, August 20th Patrick Alexander Graham Bell Baldwin was baptized by Mr. Godfry, student in theology at St. Peter's [Anglican] church here. Mr. Grosvenor was one of the godfathers and Mrs. Fairchild the godmother. The baby behaved beautifully."

It was a poignant moment. Both the name—after "Gampie" Bell—and the choice of godparents reflect the importance of the continued relationship between the Baldwin and Bell families.

In a letter to Elsie written August 30, just after the Grosvenors had arrived back from South America, Mabel wrote about her grandchildren and how they were helping to strengthen the bond with the Baldwins.

> The children call Casey and Kathleen "Uncle and Aunt" and I hope you will encourage them because it helps to bring us all nearer together and is in accordance with Papa's last dictation in which he said we were to "stand by Casey" and that he wanted "to consider Casey and Kathleen and their children as sort of children and grandchildren as far as it is possible with people not related to us by blood." Of course he didn't think of their giving them these titles, but the children did it and say now that it makes them seem so much nicer and nearer.

It was a time for focus on family and friends, particularly now with Mr. Bell gone. Mabel's diary mentions a milling frolic, a family picnic aboard the houseboat *Get-Away*, and a Halloween party at the courthouse in Baddeck. However, as time passed, Mabel's health deteriorated. In early November she wrote to Bert from Beinn Bhreagh (where she hoped to stay for Christmas) to acknowledge concern within the family over the state of her health.

> I am very sorry to have worried Elsie. Personally, I cannot see anything wrong with me, more than would be natural under the circumstances. It is hardly to be expected that a wife should take separation from her husband with perfect calmness, and it is simply that I am coming to the realization of things. When you were here I was too busy to realize

anything at all, and could do things impossible to me now. I only want to be let alone. I have my hands full of things I want to do for Father, and, as I do not have much energy, it takes a long time to get things done.

On Thursday, November 23, Mabel and Elsie left Beinn Bhreagh; for Mabel, it would be for the last time. They telegraphed from Shenacadie, saying that they expected to arrive that Sunday at Johns Hopkins Hospital in Baltimore via Boston. Following five days spent at Johns Hopkins, Mabel's diagnosis was not good. As Daisy said, "The worst we feared was true." Mabel had cancer and spent the following weeks with the Grosvenors at their home in Chevy Chase, Maryland.

Throughout December there was a barrage of correspondence between Kathleen, wondering about Mrs. Bell, and Daisy, reporting on her mother's condition. The news on the medical front was discouraging; the letters were intended to put on a brave face and hopefully cheer Mabel up. Most of Kathleen's letters contained news of happenings in Baddeck, school meetings and the like—one letter was twenty-five pages! Mabel was not up to writing and had Daisy respond to letters on her behalf, a sure sign that her days were numbered. Toward the end Mabel asked Daisy to look after things regarding Beinn Bhreagh as she did not have the energy to do so. Daisy wrote to Casey on December 12 to advise of this and offer her assistance in any way, although she knew very little about the estate management. "Having the contract arranged with you removes the only thing she was really worried about. Won't you please Casey, let me know if there is anything you want Mother to make definite statements about, and I will get her to make them when I can do it without worrying her."

Kathleen last wrote to Mabel on December 27, a letter describing Christmas at the bungalow. It is doubtful that Mabel received this last communication before she passed away on January 3, 1923, at the age of sixty-five, a mere five months after her husband's death.

Casey was on his way to Washington when Mabel died. He was one of the last things she spoke of before passing away. The very day she died Elsie and Daisy directed a letter to Kathleen. "Mother passed away peacefully in her sleep tonight. Towards last she recovered sufficiently to ask for Casey and was so pleased to hear he was on his way. We know your heart is here. Much love. Please telegraph when Casey left."

Mabel's burial was a simple affair attended by only the immediate family. On August 7, 1923, just one year after her husband was laid to rest, her ashes were placed in his grave atop the mountain where now she and Alec were together once again.

Upon Mabel's death, the informal agreement she had reached with Casey following Dr. Bell's death was deemed to be an obligation of her estate. Daughters Marian H. ("Daisy") Bell Fairchild and Elsie May Grosvenor were heirs of their mother's estate. On December 1, 1923, they and the executor, American Security and Trust Company, executed a formal agreement with Frederick W. ("Casey") Baldwin honouring that agreement and setting aside sufficient monies from the estate to cover the monetary requirements for the requisite term of ten years.

Mabel and Alec were gone. In a few short months Casey's world had been totally transformed. It was a dark time, yet Casey was not alone. The family would stand with him, and Beinn Bhreagh would remain home to the Baldwin family.

TOP: *Casey "flying" HD-3 hydrodome on Baddeck Bay.* BOTTOM: *HD-4 under construction beside Laboratory building on Baddeck Bay.*

TOP LEFT: *HD-4 speed trials at Baddeck, 1919.* TOP RIGHT: *Casey with son Robert sitting with Alexander Graham Bell in cockpit of HD-4.* BOTTOM: *Casey's grandson Sean Baldwin beside beached HD-4, Baddeck Bay.*

TOP: *Casey and William Nutting in bungalow discussing plans for ketch* Typhoon. BOTTOM: *Casey (bottom right) photographed with other members of "the family" just prior to Bell's death.*

TOP: *Casey in foreground attending funeral of Alexander Graham Bell.*
BOTTOM: *Bobby, Betty, and Patrick Baldwin "at play" on shore of Baddeck Bay.*

TOP: *Betty Baldwin (with cup), captain of Edgehill girls field hockey team.*
BOTTOM: *Casey and Kathleen fishing on Margaree River, Cape Breton.*

CHAPTER 17

Targets, Tuberculosis, and Tragedy

O N THE DAY MABEL LEFT BEINN BHREAGH FOR THE LAST TIME, Casey had been out on the water testing his latest target. Despite all of what had been going on with first Dr. Bell's and now Mrs. Bell's death, he still had a contract to honour with the United States Navy for the supply and delivery of hydrofoil targets.

Casey had begun work on the US Navy contract by constructing a ten-foot model target in July 1922. It tested satisfactorily and in August of that year a much larger forty-foot model was built. It was large enough to fulfill the contract requirements and was built of light materials in order to permit towing by the Beinn Bhreagh motorboats. Baddeck Bay was the scene of towing trials, with the *Sigpy* as tow vessel. Mabel Bell had been a frequent spectator, ever interested in observing Casey's ongoing efforts to perfect this art.

By May 1923 the forty-foot model target had been shipped, uncrated, and assembled at the Portsmouth navy yard. Walter Pinaud, with the aid of two men, assembled the structure in a mere five hours, providing conclusive evidence that the targets could be stored, shipped, and assembled with comparative ease.

Testing of various targets took place in May and June with tows initially by tugboats and for the larger targets, the destroyer USS *Reuben James*. The tests at Norfolk, Virginia, proved to be successful. The terms of the contract were met and in due course payment of $10,000 was made.

Daisy corresponded with Casey while he was in Norfolk. On May 27 she wrote from her home in Maryland expressing delight in how the trials were proceeding and to thank Casey for sending photographs. "As for the picture of her [the target] skimming on the water, well, she looks as tho she owned the place—and knew it. No wonder you are designing two hundred footers! I do so hope that some real people have seen these trials." In September back in Baddeck, Casey designed and constructed a 110-foot target for use in "firing trials." The HMCS *Patriot* returned to Baddeck and "declared war" on this target while under tow by *Dundee*. *Patriot* fired eighty-five rounds toward the target as it was towed by at a range of four hundred yards. On examination afterwards there were found to be multiple hits but little if any structural damage to the target itself. Captain Walter Hose was impressed enough with the results to suggest that such targets could be used effectively for gunnery training for ships of the Canadian navy.

On December 1, 1923, Casey signed a formal written agreement with Daisy Fairchild and Elsie Grosvenor as sole heirs of Mabel's estate that secured his own future and that of his family on Beinn Bhreagh—at least for the next ten years. It formalized details of the informal arrangement made by Mabel with Casey immediately after the death of Dr. Bell.

The agreement set up a trust, providing Casey with an annual income of $10,000 in equal quarterly installments of $2,500 for a period of ten years commencing December 1, 1923. The monies were to be provided to Casey for his use in carrying out "researches that have for their object the increasing of human knowledge, particularly in directions likely to benefit mankind." In other words, he would continue to do what he had been doing all his working life. There were no restrictions placed on the use of the funds. Casey was free to use them as he saw fit—as salary for himself as director of the Laboratory, as salaries for others, or for the purpose of obtaining patents. The agreement also provided that the Laboratory buildings, together with machinery and equipment and lands on which the buildings stood, would be leased to Casey at a rental of $1.00 per year, with an option to renew "upon terms to be mutually agreed upon by him and the heirs" at the end of the initial ten-year term.

There was no supervision or oversight of Casey's work written into the agreement. Casey had complete freedom, although the document did express a wish, which Dr. and Mabel Bell would have appreciated, by stating that "It is the confident hope of the heirs that the said Baldwin will keep them informed of the general outline of the uses to which he may, from time to time, put the sums paid to him, as aforesaid, but this is not obligatory upon him."

With his near future thus secured, Casey's mind was freer to focus on further target technology. His success with towed targets also led him to consider possibilities for remote-controlled self-propelled targets. He may have pursued this more vigorously, but the future of hydrofoil target technology and Casey's efforts, ostensibly in the hands of the British Admiralty, were given a setback. In February 1925 Casey was advised that the Admiralty had "decided not to adopt the hydrofoil design of the target." Alec and Mabel Bell would most certainly have shared in his disappointment.

It was time for Casey to take stock. The last few years had been a hectic time for him. He was deeply involved with hydrofoil target work when his own world was shattered with the death of Dr. Bell followed soon thereafter by Mabel's passing. They had both been entirely committed to his success with his work with hydrofoils, and out of respect for them he pursued that work relentlessly, despite having to deal with his grief over their passing. His hard work, and the Bells' unrelenting support, both in life and in death, went unrewarded. By the end of 1925 negotiations for the development of hydrodromes had collapsed, and now both the Admiralty and the US Navy had indicated they were no longer interested in hydrofoil targets. Casey was at a low ebb, and for the next few years he discontinued work on the HD series.

That interest revived again early in 1928 when Casey became involved in the design and development of hydrofoil boats for racing. This resulted in the creation of a number of new craft, HD numbers 7 to 12. They were produced from the Bell Laboratories in rapid succession, some with the collaboration of American naval architect Philip L. Rhodes. At this time Casey became associated with the Ollendorff boatbuilders—a family-owned business in Saugatuck, Connecticut. Casey corresponded using corporate letterhead that listed Sydney Ollendorff as President, Sydney Ollendorf Jr. as Secretary-Treasurer, and F. W. Baldwin as Vice-President of Ollendorff Inc. "Builders of Fine Boats."

Saugatuck is located on Long Island Sound, about fifty miles north of New York City. In 1928, while Casey was engaged at Saugatuck, Kathleen found work teaching at a high school in New York City. The two oldest children, Bobby and Betty, were each attending private school, in Ontario and Nova Scotia, respectively, while Patrick was at home in the capable care of a Miss Campbell from Baddeck. In 1929 Kathleen took a leave of absence from the school to go on a world tour with a friend. The trip was severely compromised by health issues for Kathleen who had been anemic since her late teens but never properly diagnosed. Seven hospitals, twenty doctors, and fourteen months of bedrest later, it was determined by Dr. William P. Murphy, a specialist in Boston, that Kathleen was suffering from acute pernicious anemia, which by then necessitated the use of a cane, rendering her "a cripple." Fortunately, under Dr. Murphy's care Kathleen made a good recovery, and in early 1930 she wrote, "Learning to walk was a slow and very difficult process and I still walk with a cane and my feet and legs are still painful; but for all that, I am not bedridden and at this moment I am studying in Europe and enjoying it."

By May of 1928 Casey had designed HD-11 with twin screws in an attempt to produce an entry for the Harmsworth Trophy Race, a British international trophy for motorboats, which he and William Nutting had first experienced when at Cowes with *Typhoon* a few years previously. Tragedy had befallen Casey's sailing friend in the intervening years. In July 1924 Nutting set out from Bergen, Norway, with two others in a small vessel in an attempt to follow the Viking course to Labrador. The craft was appropriately called the *Leif Ericson*. Neither the boat, Nutting, nor his sailing companions were ever seen or heard from again.

A much more serious attempt at creating a "speed boat" employing foils was the HD-12, a thirty-foot "runabout" designed by Casey and Rhodes and built in 1928 for Marion "Betty" Carstairs, a wealthy British motorboat racer who wished to challenge for the Harmsworth Trophy. She had already established a reputation as the fastest woman on the water but wanted to become the fastest, period. She had learned about the work of Bell and Baldwin with hydrofoils and contracted with Casey for a craft that, powered by a 650 h.p. engine, would produce a speed of 115 mph. Unfortunately this boat was never completed as designed; halfway through construction Carstairs announced that she had withdrawn from the race, stopping work on the boat.

Casey was attempting during this period to interest American financiers or well-heeled businessmen to buy into the hydrofoil business. Having recently met Vincent Bendix, an American inventor, Casey told Daisy in a letter on May 2, 1929, of further modifications required before he would be fully satisfied with the HD-12. "In the meantime and far more important—thanks to Mr. Kerkam who introduced me to Mr. Bendix, we have an opportunity to have someone else take over the whole hydrofoil business. Mr. Bendix as you probably know is the inventor of the Bendix Drive, the little gadget that goes between the electric starter and engages the flywheel on practically all motors."

Casey found Bendix to be quite interested in the history of hydrofoil even though "it did not seem much in his line of business which is one of the biggest mass production businesses there is." Nevertheless Bendix subsequently sent an executive and two engineers to Saugatuck to talk further with Casey, which filled him with hope.

> The upshot of the whole thing was that he has offered to form a company to take over the whole thing. I do not understand the stock business well enough to explain but we would all get a share of some sort and I would much prefer a small share of a concern that has the financial strength and necessary enterprise to make a success of it than a large share in a weak organization.
>
> Kerkam is going down to Miami [where the Fairchilds had a winter home] soon and I have asked him to explain the details and general situation to you. I will then try and explain it to Bert [Grosvenor] or Kerkam can on his return, but I don't think any time should be lost.

The reference to Bert Grosvenor and by inference to David Fairchild suggests that Casey was soliciting the help of the Bells' two sons-in-law in promoting his hydrofoils. Mabel would have been pleased, knowing that Casey was incapable of doing it on his own.

Work pressures kept Casey away from Baddeck that spring, leaving it to the Laboratory staff and Miss Campbell to orchestrate the commissioning of the Beinn Bhreagh "fleet" before the arrival of the summer residents. Casey wrote to Daisy from Saugatuck on May 10, 1929, to thank her for her support of "the Bendix scheme," which he felt "was the best bet" and also to describe arrangements to launch *Elsie*, *Scrapper*, and the houseboat. "The summer cruise of the Cruising Club [of America] is from New York to Baddeck, arriving there about end of July so I have to get up there somehow but 'how' does not appear any simpler than getting all the ships launched at one time. Wire Miss Campbell and trust to God."

The Bendix scheme never did materialize. A few more HD models followed HD-12, and other proposals to develop hydrofoil craft were cast about, but in the end Casey was never able to cement a deal. It was time to return home to Beinn Bhreagh.

THE BALDWIN CHILDREN WERE GROWING UP. BOBBY, THE ELDEST, WAS now sixteen and had left home to follow in his father's footsteps as a student at Ridley College. Closer to home, his sister Betty (or "Betts") at fourteen was a student at Edgehill, a private school located in Windsor on mainland Nova Scotia, about two hundred miles from Baddeck. Patrick was just eight years old and still at home. Until now, they had all grown up together on Beinn Bhreagh. It was their home and all they knew, and they loved it.

Like their parents the Baldwin children had all become part of the larger Bell family. Alec and Mabel had been their godparents and had treated Bobby, Betts, and Pat as grandchildren. The children's closest friends were the Bells' grandchildren. Growing up on Beinn Bhreagh was a great adventure, particularly for Bobby and Betts who were able to experience first-hand much of the experimental work carried on by their father and Dr. Bell before the inventor's death in 1922.

The Baldwin children all became accomplished sailors, which was no surprise given where they lived and their father's predisposition for the sport. A strong bond had developed between Bobby and Betts, who were only two years apart in age. Betts was a chip off her father's block, both in appearance and personality. She was a favourite around Beinn Bhreagh and later at Edgehill where she excelled in athletics and was captain of the ladies' field hockey team. Bob was a good athlete too, playing soccer, football, and other collegiate sports while attending Ridley. Even when separated from each other in schooling, Bobby and Betty kept in regular contact though correspondence, no doubt a trait acquired from their mother.

The beginning of the third decade of the twentieth century dawned at Beinn Bhreagh where the air was always fresh, and yet there was increasing concern in the Baldwin household over the prevalence of TB. Tuberculosis was very common in the late nineteenth and early twentieth centuries, and many families were devastated by it. "The Great White Plague" is an air-borne infectious disease that generally affects the lungs and, less frequently, other parts of the body. It is spread through coughing, sneezing, and even speaking, has been around for centuries, and persists even to this day. One of the most common symptoms other than coughing and high fever is weight loss, and thus the word "consumption" that was historically used to describe the disease.

Alexander Graham Bell lost both of his brothers and a nephew to tuberculosis. Bell's parents were so frantic that they might lose their only remaining son that they promptly moved with Alec to Canada (they settled in Tutelo Heights in Brampton, Ontario) where they hoped the promise of fresh air might keep the scourge of TB at bay.

Tuberculosis also struck Mabel's family. Her sister Gertrude, Gipsy's mother, died of tuberculosis shortly after her husband's death, leaving Gipsy to be raised by Mabel's parents.

In 1930 the Baldwins became concerned for the health of their children, two of whom were away at school. This concern soon became a constant preoccupation of Kathleen in letters to Bob and Betty. Inter-family correspondence now included frequent references to Patrick who had been ill for quite some time. Everyone was becoming increasingly concerned that he may have or develop TB. In February 1931 Betty wrote to "darling Mum" from Edgehill. She described a very social time she was enjoying at school—obviously "on top of her game." It is a letter mixed with compassion as well as irony.

> I am so sorry you haven't been feeling well Mum. I wish you'd take a rest and leave the household affairs alone. I still think you ought to go away for a little while. Oh, I forgot about poor old Pat. Well, couldn't you take him along too? I should think it would do him good. Or is he in bed and not well enough to travel? I certainly hope he gets better and that it isn't tubercular trouble he has.
>
> Last night we had our form party. We had a skating party. The KCS [Kings College School] boys have an open rink which they let us have. It was an awfully nice night but the ice wasn't very good but in spite of

it we had a good time. Afterwards we came back and had our refreshments in the kitchen.

What sort of weather have you been having? Today hasn't been very nice. It was half raining this morning and we had to go on a long walk after church! At present in the room I'm in I'm just about suffocating it is so hot. I think that the heat must be on full force. Six weeks today is Easter Sunday. That really doesn't seem so far away. Won't you be glad to see me again? We get out about April 2nd and get about ten days.

Betty was obviously looking forward to getting home for Easter. Within two weeks she wrote "Mum" again from "Same Place," having just received a letter from Kathleen. TB, or the threat of it, had found its way into the Baldwin family.

It certainly is a shame about poor old Pat. Do you mean that he really has TB? TB always sounds a terrible thing to me. I hope it isn't as bad as it's always seemed to me. But with good care and eating good food he should be able to build up a resistance. Once you've got the germ you can get rid of it, can't you? I hate to think how tired you must get, what with all the household affairs and looking after Pat. Do try not to get over tired Mum.

Well, only about four weeks till I'll be home again. It certainly will be great. I hope Pat will be up then and OK. Go out and get some fresh air sometime. Please do. I can just picture you in the stuffy house all the time.

Daughter looking out for mother. Soon the roles would be reversed.

Patrick, aged ten, was diagnosed with tuberculosis; an X-ray revealed that he had a shadow on his lungs. Casey and Kathleen provided care as best they could at home, even to the extent of building a small wooden structure, a convalescent dorm of sorts, that was located on the shore near the bungalow. The side facing the water had panels that when opened exposed Pat, the single occupant, to the fresh "airs" off the lake. The anxious parents could do little more than watch and wait.

Kathleen's extended family in Ontario was a constant support to her during this difficult time. She had been corresponding with her brother Reg about Pat and, more recently, Betty who had been feeling ill of late. On May 30 Reg wrote to Kathleen,

I have certainly been thinking a lot of you and Casey and your troubles and am of course in touch with Aunt Jessie who keeps me posted with the situation. There is nothing I can say except to express the hope that poor Betty will come through OK and that Pat will also get rid of his trouble before long. They are both so young that everything is in their favor and I certainly hope the next few weeks will bring us heartening news that, as the song goes, "Everything is going to be alright." You will have to be very careful with Bob too as he seems to have a bronchial weakness.

Things went from bad to worse for Betty who in May was admitted to the sanitorium at Kentville, Nova Scotia. Bob talked about her condition in a letter he sent to his mother from Ridley on June 3.

Got your letter yesterday and was very glad to hear that Betts is doing all right. It certainly was a shock hearing about it first from aunt Marion and when she first phoned I thought that maybe Pat had had a relapse, but never dreamed that anything would be wrong with Betts. It's certainly terribly tough luck both for you and Dad and also for poor Betts. I guess that means that her summer is practically wrecked.

Does this mean that we'll be in Kentville for the summer? I hope not. Won't Betts be out of the sanatorium in a month or so and fit to be looked after at B.B.? She'd be a lot happier there in Baddeck I mean.

The provincial sanatorium, "the San" at Kentville, was the only facility of its kind in Nova Scotia. It was located a short distance from Windsor where Betts attended school. Following Betts's admission, Kathleen remained in Kentville, initially taking a room at the Cornwallis Inn. It was the beginning of a long and gruelling ordeal. At one point Kathleen was spelled off by "Aunt Daisy." Betts's condition never did improve, and for the ensuing months Kathleen wrote to Bob, now attending Institut Le Rosey in Switzerland, to give him regular updates on his sister's health. A consistent theme in all her letters was that Bob must take every precaution to protect his own health.

In September Kathleen, becoming increasingly anxious over Betts's failure to show improvement, wrote despairingly to Bob, "She is about the same—never a murmur. She usually says more when her temperature is down, such as wondering what our plans for Christmas will be, what winter coat she'll have, etc. But whenever her temperature is up, she is very silent about everything like that. She is coughing much more again. I couldn't talk about her to you Bob dear and it's better not to write any more. I will get through it some way, I suppose."

By then Kathleen and Casey were taking turns at staying with Betts. They found different accommodations: the Cornwallis Inn, Oak Farm just outside Kentville, and by late September Casey was writing to Kathleen daily from a boarding house. She and Casey were by then considering taking Pat to Kentville from Beinn Bhreagh as there appeared to be no end in sight for Betts's treatment.

By late November 1931 Betts had been in the sanitorium for six months. Her temperature had risen and fallen, giving hope one minute and despair the next. Adhesions had now formed on her right lung, which made it difficult to collapse that lung (assuming the left lung was clear) as one means of treatment. She remained very brave but depressed by lack of improvement in her condition. The whole matter was particularly hard on her brother Bob who remained at school in Switzerland and relied on letters from his mother for updates on his sister's condition. As it worsened, Kathleen shared her growing despair in correspondence with her son. "It is all so complicated and I feel that they [the doctors] know nothing and are working in the dark."

Betts spent Christmas that year in her room in the sanitorium with her family, minus Bob. Kathleen described it as a happy Christmas. "She received oodles of presents and flowers. Her room was prettily decorated and she had a tree." It would be her last Christmas. The only good news was that Pat had been totally cleared of TB. Casey and Kathleen struggled to find some sort of normalcy in their lives. In a December 30 letter to Bob, Kathleen wrote, "Dad has finished an article for the *Halifax Herald* New Year Edition on Lake Ainslie Hydro. It's worried him a lot and he couldn't sleep. It has been terrible—turning night into day and vice versa and it's so difficult living in two rooms with one person trying to sleep in the other."

By January 1932 the entire Baldwin family, with the exception of Bob, was living in Kentville at the Cornwallis Inn. Pat was enrolled in a small private school in town where he was one of just six pupils. Betts's condition showed no improvement, prompting Kathleen to confess to Bob, "I can't make myself ask the doctors what they think of the outcome. I just go on from day to day, thankful that she appears to be about the same."

X-rays taken of Betts in mid-February were not encouraging. The doctors described the disease as "gradually progressive." A bit of a routine had by now been established. Casey had taken up curling at the local rink and on February 10 gave a talk at the San on "the early history of man's attempts to fly." Kathleen had assumed responsibility for taking care of the Fairchild and Grosvenor accounts, but always her main focus was on her daughter. Her letters to Bob became increasingly despairing. "She is what they call on a 'bland diet'; her temperatures the highest for some time; she is getting terribly thin. It nearly kills me and I have to be bright and talk to her as though everything were coming along all right. And Oh, the regrets and might have beens—it all could have been avoided."

On May 3 Kathleen wrote, "Bob, our darling is just skin and bone. She can only take liquid nourishment and very little of that. She isn't suffering to any extent. Her voice is weak and sometimes she just whispers. It is an effort for her to talk. Poor Dad can hardly control himself when with her. It's a terrible ordeal to go through. When I think of that glorious vitality that was always hers—her keen mind and beauty—going out—Why must it be?"

With the end near, Bob wrote to share his guilt and his parents' grief. "Now that there's no longer any hope I feel worse than ever at being over here and not with you and Dad to do what I can in the way of encouragement. I'm no good at expressing myself but there's no need for me to, you know how I feel. It's unbelievable. I hope this letter and the postcards will amuse her poor kid. She's been so brave and uncomplaining and such a thoroughbred. And so have you and Dad."

Kathleen's last letter to Bob from Kentville was postmarked May 8. She and Casey were on a deathwatch. "Darling, it can't be very much longer now. I think it is only her spirit that keeps her now. It doesn't seem possible that anyone can live and be as wasted as she is." Betts died just a few days later, on May 12, 1932. She was just seventeen years old.

Heartfelt letters of sympathy were quick to follow from both the Fairchild and the Grosvenor families. Elsie sent off a letter of sympathy to Casey and Kathleen noting that her daughter Carol "will be terribly upset when she hears about Betty; she loved her like a sister and Beinn Bhreagh without her will be desolate."

Betty Baldwin's funeral took place at Beinn Bhreagh on May 15, 1932. She was a very popular young lady, particularly among sailing enthusiasts around Cape Breton. An account of the event was published in the *Sydney Post* the following day.

The late Miss Baldwin of Baddeck was accorded a funeral with full yachtsmen's honors yesterday at Baddeck, one which was attended by a large number of friends from all sections of Cape Breton. Services both at home and at the gravesite were conducted by Reverend C. K. Whalley, Rector of St. George's Church, Sydney. The casket bearing the remains of Miss Baldwin, who was an ardent sailing enthusiast, rested on a platform covered with sails of her own yacht and following the service at the home, were conveyed by boat to the old cemetery on Beinn Bhreagh where interment took place.

The three yacht clubs in the Island, the Royal Cape Breton Yacht Club of Sydney, the Northern Yacht Club of North Sydney and the Bras d'Or Yacht Club of Baddeck were represented at the ceremony, and the wreaths sent by the two latter clubs, in club colours, were exceptionally beautiful and the profusion of flowers and wreaths which banked the platform testified to the esteem in which Miss Baldwin was held by her many friends.

Bob, still attending school in Switzerland, brought his own form of closure with his final communication.

The clipping from the Sydney Post was nice. That's the way she would have liked it, taken in a boat, wrapped in the red sails she loved so much. I know how you feel Mum, now that the end has come I feel sort of empty inside all the time, and though outwardly I try and seem just the same and carry on studying, it's awful hard. Things will never be the same again for me either; time may gradually make me feel less empty inside but I know that feeling will never leave me—one of loneliness and sadness and the sense of an irretrievable loss of one of the dearest things in my life, the dearest thing excepting you and Dad and Patiger. God grant that I do not lose any of you for a long, long time.

The final words were left to Casey when writing to Daisy and David Fairchild a month later. His thoughts, composed into words, were vintage Casey—simple and forthright.

In some ways it seems a thousand years ago that Betty died, in other ways but yesterday. But, for the most part, I cannot escape the conviction (deeper than all reason) that it never happened at all. Perhaps this feeling from which I cannot get away is really some pagan first cousin to a belief in a hereafter.

These things only come home to one after the loss of a dear friend. As for my part, I confess I have never cared much one way or another as to what lies beyond. In any case, assuming that we are on this earth for some purpose, Betty brought more beauty of character and personality into it than anyone I have ever known. Her life, short as it was, was like a beautiful opening in chess which never even got to the middle game before the board was knocked over and it could never be recovered.

With all of Kathleen's good points and none of my failings it is not surprising to me she was the ideal youngster. It is remarkable however that so many others felt so nearly as I do about her.

There is nothing to tell you about the service that you do not already know and you can picture it as well as if you had been here. It was fitting in its simplicity and beautiful in its sincerity. Pat thank God is well and Bob seems to be now although he had a most inconvenient attack of jaundice just before his exams.

Kass has gone through this bitterest of all ordeals true to form, but keeping up had undermined her nerves more than she herself realizes.

With much love and gratitude for your sympathy and all that you have done for Betty and the rest of us.

Elsie's prediction would prove to be true—life on Beinn Bhreagh was never the same again.

CHAPTER 18

"Heart's in the Highlands"

FREDERICK WALKER "CASEY" BALDWIN WAS NEVER INTERESTED IN politics despite the fact that politics ran in the family. In the mid nineteenth century his grandfather Robert Baldwin had risen to political prominence in Ontario; he is best remembered for sharing the premiership of the combined provinces of Upper and Lower Canada with the French Canadian Louis-Hippolyte LaFontaine. Until now Casey had never sought political office although he was very interested in local matters, pursuing ways in which to improve the lot of fellow citizens. Residents in and around Baddeck and Victoria County soon took notice of this genuine interest in their well-being.

One of Casey's early interests was roads, few of which were in Cape Breton at that time. Given that typically the person expressing the interest ends up with the task, Casey became Road Commissioner for Victoria County. In this role he came into contact with a lot of people. Roads were something that everyone, particularly in a rural setting, could relate to. Transportation around Cape Breton in the early twentieth century was predominantly by rail and water; the Trans-Canada Highway would not become a reality here until the 1960s. Meanwhile the only road of consequence was a single route from the Strait of Canso to Sydney via St. Peter's—the Sydney Road, as it was commonly known.

Baddeck in Casey's time had an active Board of Trade composed of enterprising local businessmen who were interested in opportunities to further the commercial aspirations of the village. A new road, if constructed through the centre of the Island to Sydney via Baddeck, was regarded as having great potential to boost the local economy. If built, however, it would necessitate the construction of a bridge over the Great Bras d'Or Channel to Boularderie Island. In 1931, as part of the study for such a venture, Casey dealt directly with the Dominion Bridge Company in Montreal to obtain estimates for the costs of spanning this waterway. Three potential sites were identified: Carey Point, Munro Point, and Seal Island, the latter being the least expensive and the ultimate location of the bridge.

On May 1, 1931, Casey wrote to the Nova Scotia Minister of Highways, Percy Black, with the estimates, saying, "We simply wanted to have the information as to the possible cost of a bridge to answer critics who will probably claim that a bridge will never be justified. Now that the Grand Narrows Route is definitely out of the picture, North Sydney, Sydney Mines and of course Inverness are all of one mind and are beginning to take interest in opposing the St. Peter's Route."

It was not, however, until thirty years later, in 1961, that a bridge structure was built—and at a considerably higher cost than the 1931 estimate of $1 million. Whether Casey stipulated it or not, in each case the estimates he obtained provided for bridges built with one swing span, giving a sixty-nine-foot channel to permit passage by ships. Later construction did not include a swing span, probably due to bureaucratic cost-cutting. Thus the Great Bras d'Or Channel—the primary access in from and out to the Atlantic—has restricted shipping traffic due to height limitations ever since the bridge was constructed.

Casey had evidently also been pushing for a road to Pleasant Bay in the northern part of Victoria County, which until now had been resisted by the highway department. Casey, having his hand on the pulse of the people, made the case. "It seems to me that it would be a great thing to make a showing in getting even a rough trail through as soon as possible. I have a number of letters from people up North who should be our friends and whose support we need, and I am simply handing on to you an expression of what the feeling was."

Casey had long harboured great hopes for the northern part of Victoria County, which he saw as having unlimited tourism potential. He was a constant proponent of building a road that would circle the northern part of Victoria County to join Pleasant Bay from the east, as had just a few years before been accomplished on the western side when a road was pushed through from Cheticamp. Casey was soon recognized as a champion of what would become the Cabot Trail. Part of his fascination with the northern sector stemmed from his interest in the outdoors and promoting "fish and game"; he was an active member of the Cape Breton Fish and Game Association. Most of the land in this area represented otherwise inaccessible wilderness, which Casey regarded as an outdoor paradise.

He also was deeply interested in energy and conservation, sometimes mutually exclusive concepts, at least in the eyes of critics. Such was the case with a proposal for the development of a hydro project in the Lake Ainslie area of Cape Breton. Casey became a spokesperson for such a development when he published an article, "Now is the time to Develop Lake Ainslie," in the January 18, 1932, edition of the *Chronicle Herald* newspaper (the one he was working on during his daughter's last months in the sanitorium). The long talked about project had received the support of the provincial Conservative government led by Premier Gordon Harrington. It was a sensitive topic about which Casey felt strongly enough to write his views in hopes of silencing critics worried about the environmental impact upon the pristine Lake Ainslie watershed.

Casey observed that "the only criticism of the project which does not emanate from selfish motives or financially interested sources" is whether the development would spoil Lake Ainslie or hurt the Margaree River salmon fishing. He was well prepared to answer that argument as a mechanical engineer, a representative of the Fish and Game Association, and as a plain speaker.

If we have to choose between fish and electric light, by all means, let us continue to put up oil lamps, tallow candles, even the agricultural equipment and industrial tools of the stone age, if necessary. Cape Breton is too lovely a country to spoil and the fishing too valuable and health-giving a sport to be endangered. Happily there is little or nothing to fear on this ground. The level of Lake Ainslie will not be materially changed and adequate fish ways will protect fishing. Less water will of course go down the southwest branch of the Margaree but there is very little salmon fishing on this branch anyway. Practically all of the fishing is on the northeast branch, which will not be effected in any way. Certainly one net at the mouth of the Margaree can do more damage by preventing the fish getting up to spawn than the proposed development at Lake Ainslie can ever do. Let those who are honestly apprehensive on this score apply themselves to having our present fishing laws properly enforced or better ones enacted.

Lake Ainslie is the answer to cheap power in Cape Breton, and nine out of ten impartial observers will agree that the government is doing a wise thing in developing it, especially at the present time when employment is so urgently needed. It has been well said that "to gather the streams from waste and draw from them energy, labour without brains, and to save mankind from toil that can be spared, is to supply what, next to intellect, is the very foundation of all our achievements and all our welfare."

It was a carefully worded and thoughtful presentation that all came to naught. The Conservative government shortly afterwards went down to defeat and with it, this project. Years later Cape Breton would source power from another initiative—the Wreck Cove Hydro Project. Nevertheless Casey had put himself out before the public and in doing so attracted the attention of many people, including the executive of the provincial Conservative party.

Casey had two loves of his life: his family, including his extended Bell family on Beinn Bhreagh, and his adopted home of Cape Breton. They were inseparable. Casey also had the good fortune of having travelled around the world and had crossed Canada from coast to coast. The days spent at Banff, Alberta, with the Bells as they began their world tour two decades earlier had made a lasting impression on him. The mountains of course were grand, but it was the concept of a national park that captured Casey's imagination. As the years passed and he became more infatuated with Cape Breton Island, Casey became convinced that the Highlands of Cape Breton, accessed by the soon to be completed Cabot Trail, would create a spectacular national park for Nova Scotia. He became an outspoken advocate for both the trail and the park and would live to see both become reality.

Cape Breton Island has long been considered one of the most beautiful islands in North America, due in no small measure to the Cabot Trail, heralded by twenty-first-century travel magazines as one of the most scenic drives in the world. Baddeck traditionally has been referred to as the beginning and end of the Cabot Trail, which forms a circuitous 185-mile route through the northernmost segments of Victoria and Inverness counties.

Building the Cabot Trail was a gargantuan task, particularly in a small province like Nova Scotia. The results of years of planning and construction culminated in an official opening of "the Trail" on October 16, 1932. Casey and Kathleen were among the dignitaries present that day at Cape North. The occasion was described in the *Halifax Herald* under the headline "Beautiful Country is Now Open."

On October 16, 1932, a beautiful fall day at Cape North, Victoria County, the Cabot Trail, circling Cape Breton and giving highway access to many villages and some of the most picturesque scenery in eastern America, was officially opened.

Hundreds of visitors who had come from all parts of the Island as well as the mainland were on hand for the event. The Rev. Father R. L. MacDonald, PP, of Inverness had the honor of being the first to cross the Trail, leaving Inverness shortly before noon that day and arriving on the scene just before ceremonies got underway.

Dignitaries present included Premier Harrington, Hon. P. C. Black, Provincial Minister of Highways, Commander Murray of HMCS Saguenay, Hon. Albert Parsons, D. R. Cameron, MLA Glace Bay, and Mr. and Mrs. F. W. Baldwin of Baddeck.

Following a luncheon appropriately served in a construction camp, the entourage proceeded to almost the top of the mountain where the actual opening ceremony took place. Premier Harrington touched off a blast which cleared away the last boulder—the quiet of the countryside was broken by a deafening roar; the Canadian Ensign was run up on a nearby flagstaff and the new Cabot Trail declared open to traffic.

Casey had a personality and a way with people that made him the ideal political candidate. The Nova Scotia Progressive Conservative Party recognized a potential winner in Casey and encouraged him to run for public office. There was a provincial election scheduled for August 1933. Casey allowed his name to stand, and on June 7, 1933, in Baddeck Casey won the nomination to represent the Conservative Party for the County of Victoria.

To say that Casey was a very popular choice was an understatement. The occasion was extensively covered by the press. More than 150 delegates ratified Casey's nomination at the Baddeck courthouse. Here is an account from the *Sydney Post*, June 8, 1933.

On June 7th a crowd of literally hundreds had gathered for the occasion, so many in fact that they could not all be accommodated at the Court House. Accordingly, following the formal nomination all hands adjourned outside to an open air meeting where principal addresses were given by ranking conservatives from within the district.

Veteran observers said it was the first time in recent years that the Court House had proved absolutely inadequate to handle the crowds wanting to view the proceedings and hear the candidate and other speakers. Baldwin was unanimously endorsed by the largest nominating convention ever held in the political history of Victoria County.

Mr. Baldwin in a modest address accepted the nomination, reviewed the record of the administration he will support and promised to work for the best interests of Nova Scotia and Victoria County. His speech was received with great enthusiasm and he was accorded an ovation at its close.

Immediately following Casey's nomination Archibald MacMechan, provincial archivist and a good friend of Casey's, wrote a short piece for the Halifax newspaper drawing attention to the Baldwin family tradition in politics and making specific reference to a certain statue on Parliament Hill in Ottawa of two men clasping hands. "One represents LaFontaine, the French-Canadian leader who joined with the English statesman to give Canada good government. That English statesman was Robert Baldwin, the ancestor of F. W. Baldwin who has worked long and unostentatiously for the betterment of Cape Breton, and is now entering public life as a candidate for Victoria. If there is anything in heredity and character 'Casey' Baldwin is the kind of man needed in our Legislature."

The MacMechan article gave rise to an editorial espousing the virtues of Casey the candidate.

"Casey" Baldwin is a modest man who for decades at Baddeck has been doing most remarkable work. He persisted in the "fooleries" of his university days and was a pioneer in aviation. Indeed, certain improvements to airplanes in the past few years were thought out by "Casey" Baldwin long ago; one in particular [the aileron], now in universal use originated in the brain of this engineering genius.

Nova Scotia is honoured in having this man as a citizen. Some day no doubt someone will write an adequate account of his career—and the facts will read like powerful fiction.

Casey had become a darling to the press long before Nova Scotians went to the polls.

The election that followed was a spirited affair. The campaign slogan for the incumbent Conservatives was "Keep Harrington at the Helm," the nautical theme perhaps having been inspired by Casey the yachtsman. Casey was running against a very tough opponent—the sitting Liberal, Donald B. MacLeod from Ingonish—and was not expected to win. He shared his thoughts about his prospects in a letter to Kathleen, who was in Europe at this time. The letter is erroneously dated June 31, 1933, suggesting a certain preoccupation at that moment. "Ever since nomination I have been on the jump although we have not started any meetings or regular campaign yet. My first job was to get all over the County and see about the road situation. 'D. B.' thinks he is going to win in a walk, but I don't think he can if we can hold Iona and Ingonish, the two key polls. Both are in hands of rabid RC priests, Rankin and Kyte, and they have great hopes of an RC Premier, Angus L. MacDonald [*sic*] being one." (Religion has historically been very much a part of politics in Cape Breton.)

When the votes were all counted, Casey had 2,216 and his opponent 2,031; MacLeod had lost by a mere 185 votes, which he later attributed to his lack of familiarity with Baddeck and area. Victoria County had been a Liberal stronghold until Casey appeared on the scene. Casey's win over the incumbent Liberal was a major upset; the circumstances were colourfully described in the *New Glasgow Eastern Chronicle* of May 31, 1934.

In the election of last August two very opposite persons presented themselves before the electorate. The Liberal candidate, Donald B. MacLeod was a typical Highlander. Big of stature and stalwart; one who speaks and sings the Gaelic; a true son of Cape Breton. He had carried Victoria in 1925, one of only three Liberals in all Nova Scotia to be elected. He had won again in 1928. But in 1933, when the going seemed more easy, the big, honest, loveable Scot, farmer and merchant, in his third essay, was not successful.

The Conservative standard-bearer was Frederick Walker Baldwin, M.E., suave, city-bred, college-educated, wealthy son of distant Toronto. A pioneer in the field of engineering and aeronautics, this was his pioneer election, and he won.

Only in one respect were these candidates strikingly similar: they are both very fine gentlemen and especially good fellows. Hail fellows, well met, we'd say, if you were participatin' in a wee Scotch night, or celebrating an '00 class reunion.

"Casey" (that's his name and you at once like him for it) Baldwin moved a long ways from his birth surroundings to enter the Legislative Halls. He is of historic lineage....

Even a brief acquaintance impresses one with the notion that Casey Baldwin is one of those fellows who knows what he wants and will keep a-hammering after it. He wants to do something worthwhile. In the centre of Northern Cape Breton, with its rugged scenery on the coastline, is a huge plateau. It is neither timber area or farming land. It could be a sportsman's paradise as it is absolutely uninhabited. It is dotted with lakes. Mr. "Casey" Baldwin conceives the idea that it should be converted into a National park, a Mecca for those who love the wild, open stretches and the wild things that roam thereon. The National Parks commission he submits should take it over, maintain the Cabot Trail that surrounds it and by stocking it with deer, moose and caribou, convert it into a place that annually thousands would visit. He divested himself of any political bias and presented his mind's picture to the House. The members listened attentively, met him half way and accorded him, from both sides, a round of applause that few members received.

You just naturally look on "Casey" Baldwin not as a politician, but as a new found friend. "Hang politics, Donald; let's get together on this thing!" You appreciate the sincerity of the fine little gentleman and hold the belief that he will work for the common good, and endeavor to be constructive in his public efforts.

Following Casey's victory in Victoria County, the *Halifax Herald*, professing itself to "Champion the Policy of Maritime Progress and Prosperity," printed yet another editorial, this one under the banner "Will Be Welcomed," referencing Casey's win in Victoria.

> Apart entirely from political considerations, one of the most useful results of the provincial contest just held is the election to the Legislature of F. W. Baldwin in Victoria County. The one regret is that Mr. Baldwin had to defeat that popular veteran and friendly man, D. B. MacLeod in order to secure a seat. More men of the type of "Casey" Baldwin are needed in legislatures and parliaments today. He is in no sense of the term a bitter partisan. He is a man of vision, broad experience, genius and very real ability; and it goes without saying that his welcome to the Legislature will be a genuine one from all parts of the House.

Casey may have won the battle, but his leader Harrington and the Conservative party lost the war. The Liberals led by Angus L. Macdonald swept the Conservatives from office. Casey's was but one of eight seats won by his party. This did not deter him. Before his four-year term was over Casey became a sitting member revered by MLAs on both sides of the House.

Early in 1934 Casey went on the offensive in promoting tourism as a major market for Nova Scotia in a country where revenues from tourism already exceeded that of any single export commodity. He continued his advocacy of establishing a national park in his adopted province. He introduced his topic in the legislature with a history of the national parks of Canada, declaring that they had been of great value in the development of the country as a tourist destination. Parks had first been established eighteen years earlier, and so far not one had been developed in Nova Scotia or any of the other Maritime provinces. He felt it was time that the province took concerted action in the matter, and he hoped that a resolution would be introduced and adopted by the legislature that would bring about their establishment.

Hon. Mr. Harrington, now leader of the Opposition, suggested that northern Cape Breton Island would be an ideal location for such a park. Premier MacDonald spoke out in favour of the scheme, proclaiming that the government was prepared to look into Casey's proposal for a national park "when full information had been obtained."

The Halifax media supported Baldwin's national park initiative. Here is an editorial that appeared in the *Halifax Herald* on April 10, 1934. "The question of national parks—and the desirability of the establishment of a national park or parks in Nova Scotia—has been discussed in the provincial legislature, the subject being introduced by F. W. Baldwin, member for Victoria County. Mr. Baldwin has pointed out that there is no national park…east of the Thousand Islands in the St. Lawrence River. Nova Scotia has many ideal locations for national parks; and the member for Victoria County has done the province a real service in raising the question in the legislature and focusing public attention on it at this time."

It wasn't long after that Casey went "on the stump," using speaking engagements around the province to inspire interest in a national park. First stop was his hometown of Baddeck where on June 12, 1934, the Baddeck Board of Trade hosted a meeting attended by a large audience to hear Casey speak on the subject of a national park for Cape Breton. Casey commended the Baddeck Board of Trade for being the first to take up the matter, noting that the government in Halifax was unanimously in favour of a national park in Nova Scotia. He produced a telegram from Premier MacDonald saying that an engineer would be sent from Ottawa to look over the park situation in Cape Breton with all expenses paid by the federal government.

Casey was able to garner support for a park from politicians regardless of party affiliation. Dr. M. E. McGarry, Liberal MPP for neighbouring Inverness County, was also present and invited to the podium where he was quick to state that he fully supported Casey's proposition. It was a rare evening of political unanimity in Cape Breton.

Soon the topic of a national park for Nova Scotia was everywhere in the news, with Casey right in the middle of it all. On June 13 an article in the *Chronicle Herald* engaged in the dialogue over three possible sites for a national park in Nova Scotia.

Ottawa: Establishment of a National Park in Nova Scotia is receiving serious consideration by the Dominion Government. Three proposed sites in that Province will be examined by R. W. Cautley, engineer of the National Parks Branch of the Department of the Interior, who leaves shortly for Halifax. He will join an official of the Nova Scotia government for a visit to Blomidon, Yarmouth County and north Cape Breton, the three sites suggested. When the Senate tourist committee was sitting last Spring under the chairmanship of Senator W. H. Dennis, it was repeatedly brought home to members that the Maritime Provinces had fared badly with respect to establishment of national parks.

Continuing his stump, on June 24 Casey addressed the Glace Bay Fish and Game Association, where he gave an account of his recent trip to Ottawa. He had met there with members of the Senate and the federal Parks Commission. His address received broad and favourable coverage in the *Glace Bay Gazette* the following day.

Speaking of his mission to Ottawa Casey said he was greatly encouraged by the attitude of the Federal authorities. They had given him every encouragement and he felt that if the proper push was put forth Cape Breton North would get one of the Nova Scotia parks. He congratulated the pioneers of the movement—the Glace Bay Fish and Game Association and commended the officers and members on their untiring efforts and urged them to continue bringing the question before the authorities. The NS government to a man was sympathetic and the matter had already been broached on the floors of parliament and received serious consideration of all the members, irrespective of politics.

In the fall of 1934 the federal government appeared to be vacillating on the park proposal. It had no immediate plans to create a national park in Nova Scotia but bowed to the provincial government's request that a suitable future site be found. Much of the credit for that decision was due to Casey Baldwin.

The chief surveyor appointed by the National Parks Branch to investigate the three potential sites in Nova Scotia, R. W. Cautley, was initially skeptical of the Cape Breton location. He reported, "It does not possess those high qualities of scenic attraction that are absolutely essential to the success of a National Park." Never having been there he formed this opinion based entirely upon maps and photographs. He changed his mind after spending five days exploring the Cabot Trail accompanied by two provincial representatives and then criss-crossing northern Cape Breton alone. In his official report to Commissioner James Harkin that December, Cautley, making a complete about-face, recommended a national park for Cape Breton stating that "the scenic values of the site are outstanding."

In 1935 the park plans stalled with some interdepartmental changes following the election of William Lyon Mackenzie King's Liberal government; however, by mid-June of 1936 Parliament was ready to pass a bill establishing Nova Scotia and PEI national parks. The unrelenting efforts of Casey Baldwin—his lobbying, speeches, letters to editors, even the sponsorship of an essay contest on "The Advantages of a National Park in Cape Breton"— were about to be rewarded. The devil was now in the details, determining the actual park boundaries (no one seemed to know) and expropriation. Local residents did not learn until 1937 that the new park would mean the expropriation of settled land, not just the reservation of the Highland plateau as Casey Baldwin had preached. Nor would anyone learn that the park boundaries had shifted to include Ingonish and omit Pleasant Bay and the northern tip of Inverness County until August of 1938, almost two years after the Province and the Parks Branch had agreed to this. Casey was of the belief that the park would be made even more attractive if it were enlarged by the addition of the northern portion of Inverness County from Pleasant Bay to the lowlands near Cape St. Lawrence. It didn't happen and the matter continued to be the subject of debate for years after the park became a reality.

In March 1938 as the park for Cape Breton neared reality, there was talk that the new national park might be named after Casey. An editorial in the *Halifax Star* acknowledged the suggestion but was more supportive of a name that was more descriptive of the park's character, like Nova Scotia Highlands or some such idea. It pointed out that although Baldwin was an ardent worker in the cause, its original proponent was the late Samuel P. Challoner of Sydney, formerly head of the Cape Breton Tourism Association, and the man who actually brought it about was Nova Scotia premier A. S. MacMillan. The paper did, however, support an initiative "for some suitable recognition in the nomenclature of the Province of Mr. Baldwin, J. A. D. McCurdy and the other pioneers who conducted the Baddeck adventures culminating in the first heavier than air flights in the British Empire. As time goes on this epoch event is looking steadily larger in the history of aviation development."

Cape Breton Highlands National Park was officially opened July 1, 1941. It was a typically great day for the politicians. Casey was no longer a sitting member; governments had come and gone since he took Victoria County for the Conservatives back in 1933. On this day, Baddeck MLA James M. Campbell, who had been active in promoting the park, presided over the opening held at Ingonish. Premier A. S. MacMillan, assisted by Hon T. A. Crerar, federal minister of Mines and Resources, cut the MacDonald plaid ribbon that stretched in front of the Ingonish entrance on the Cabot Trail to officially open Canada's new national park. Quietly standing in the background was F. W. "Casey" Baldwin who, according to the July 3 edition of the *Halifax Herald*, "saw in the park opening a dream of long years standing come true."

Casey's niece Joan Parmenter Radcliff, daughter of Kathleen's brother Reg, wrote an unpublished, poignant account of Casey, at home in nature and among his friends in Cape Breton.

On a July afternoon in 1935 the big Nash rolled to a halt on Cape Breton's Cabot Trail overlooking an island set in the sparkling Atlantic. Seabirds swooped by the thousands past island cliffs pocked with the nests of the young. It was one of those idyllic Nova Scotia days, daydream warm with the wash of salty air keeping it comfortable. Pointing from the front seat Casey Baldwin suggested to my father he buy the island. "It would be less than five hundred dollars," Casey cheerfully prompted. Reg Parmenter, a conservative Toronto lawyer, could not have been more astonished and asked why on earth he should buy a hunk of rock covered with birds. "If someone doesn't," said Baldwin seriously, "we are in danger of losing those nesting grounds." It was twenty years before Rachel Carson's *Silent Spring* awakened the spirit of conservation, and Parmenter thought the suggestion a joke. A small but illustrative anecdote about an unsung Canadian genius whose pioneer contributions to Canada and the world ranged from ecology to aviation.

The Trail had just opened in 1935 when Casey insisted on showing it to his Toronto guests with true Maritime flair. Before any personal effects were allowed in father's Nash, we loaded a keg of dark rum, a case of Scotch, and a case of beer. The Trail was pure terror for mother; the dirt track without guardrails at one point plunged 1,200 feet straight down to the Atlantic, and she refused to look out the car window.

Casey seemed to know every fisherman and farmer on the island, stopping frequently in coves and barnyards. Rum was offered Mr.

MacLeod or Mr. Fraser over drying nets or farm fence, and they inevitably went behind the barn or whatever to avoid the prying eyes of "the missus." As the dark demerara disappeared, talks ranged from crops to lobster traps. Among the greying frame houses of a fishing village signs outside the General Store proclaimed the monthly arrival of the dentist or a movie. Salt cod hung drying with nautical gear beside an obviously idle lobster cannery. Casey inquired of the storekeeper who sadly explained that the Depression had driven lobster below nine cents a pound, which made canning unprofitable. His concern for them and their response to Casey was heartwarming, even if nobody could cure Depression times single-handed.

Twenty-five years after he first introduced the subject of a national park in the Nova Scotia legislature, and eleven years after his death, Casey was acknowledged in the April 15, 1959, edition of the *Victoria-Inverness Bulletin* as the person to whom credit for Cape Breton Highlands National Park should be given.

The years have proven the wisdom of his introduction of this measure in the provincial legislature, and instead of the over-cautious reservation of Premier Angus L. MacDonald [*sic*], the national park became a reality with "no great monetary loss to the province." Although largely a Federal undertaking it became an asset to the province as a whole, and resulted in giving a great lift to the economy of Northern Victoria and transformed the Ingonish districts in up-and-coming modern villages.

The people of Victoria are daily becoming more conscious of the great benefits that have accrued to the county due to the vision and foresight of the late F. W. Baldwin and it is pleasing to note that the movement to name the Seal Island bridge, a part of the Trans-Canada Highway project, in his honour is gaining impetus and is being advocated in every district of the County.

The 1930s were a period of transition for Casey. As 1933 drew to an end, so did Casey's service contract at Beinn Bhreagh. The agreement entered into with the estate of Mabel Bell (i.e., Marion H. Bell Fairchild—Daisy—and Elsie May Grosvenor) back in 1923, providing annual remuneration for his continued experimentation, had a term of ten years. That time now passed, Casey was free to pursue other interests for the first time since he arrived at Beinn Bhreagh. His brief but spectacular foray into provincial politics "in service of the people" was his first such initiative. As with everything else he had accomplished in his life to that point, he left his mark during his four-year stint as an elected politician. During that time he came to be regarded by his peers as "a man of the people" and one of the most popular politicians ever to hold office in Nova Scotia.

The mid-1930s also brought Casey back into contact with his old friend Douglas McCurdy. The occasion was an event held in Baddeck to celebrate the twenty-fifth anniversary of the flight of Silver Dart, the first in a succession of such anniversaries. A lot of water had flowed under the bridge since February 23, 1909.

Then in 1935 Casey went back to sea—traversing the Atlantic again by sail, this time accompanied by his two sons, thus continuing the family tradition established by his father, "Robert the Sailor."

CHAPTER 19

National Aviation Day and "Barnstorming *Bluenose*"

T HE BALDWINS WERE NO STRANGERS TO DIGNITARIES AND royalty. While the Bells were still alive, Casey and Kathleen had helped to entertain at dinners and gatherings for princes, Governors General, and premiers visiting Beinn Bhreagh. Both Casey and Kathleen had an easy manner with people from all walks of life and were not intimidated by wealth or power.

In October 1930 the Baldwins entertained Lord Willingdon, Governor General of Canada, together with Lady Willingdon and staff for a weekend at Beinn Bhreagh. The Marquess of Willingdon, a titled Englishman, was appointed Governor General of Canada in October 1926. Soon after assuming office he travelled extensively throughout Canada and became the first Governor General to travel by airplane when he flew from Ottawa to Montreal and back.

Willingdon was an avid sportsman and enjoyed a good game of golf. Casey invited him to play a round on the Beinn Bhreagh course. Sometime during play the Governor General was struck by an errant golf ball, which was the sole focus of a newspaper account the next day. The Sydney newspaper reported, "happily the injury was of a minor nature and will not interfere with the programme drafted in connection with his visit here today." The incident no doubt was at first cause for some concern; Casey's son Bob speculated that his father's renowned slice may have been to blame.

In August 1934 Hon. J. Ramsay MacDonald was completing a pleasure trip throughout Nova Scotia that was intended to allow him to regain better health after a number of years without respite from his work as the British prime minister. While in Cape Breton he chose to visit both Baddeck and the Margaree. His time in Baddeck was short, but while there he was entertained over a luncheon by Casey and Kathleen. He was given a tour of Beinn Bhreagh, which included a look at the Laboratory and a visit to the top of the mountain and the final resting place of the Bells. The *Sydney Post Record* account noted that before departing Baddeck, the party proceeded to the courthouse to watch work underway on the construction of a stone monument that was to be unveiled the following week in a ceremony to commemorate the twenty-fifth anniversary of the first flight of a heavier-than-air machine in the British Empire by J. A. D. McCurdy on February 23, 1909.

The Baddeck Board of Trade was anxious to see this milestone celebrated in some tangible way. They had an ally in George Ross of Ottawa who was organizing secretary of the Associated Flying Clubs of Canada. That group had met in May at New Glasgow, Nova Scotia, where, as reported in the *Victoria News* of July 28, 1932, it was decided that this national club would hold a "Maritime Good Will Tour of Airships ending with Baddeck as its climax on August 16, 1934." This celebration would mark a significant event not only in the British Empire, but the entire world.

The Baddeck Board of Trade had applied to the Historic Sites and Monuments Board for a cairn to commemorate the first flight. George Ross pursued the matter before the board in Ottawa who approved the application, appointed a subcommittee to take charge of the matter, and, according to the *Victoria News*, decided to place a cairn at Baddeck "instead of some other place in Canada as had been on their program." The date for the unveiling of the cairn, August 16, 1934, was described as National Aviation Day by the Nova Scotia press. (According to Transport Canada, February 23, the date of Silver Dart's historic flight, is currently officially designated as National Aviation Day when Canadians "commemorate the past, celebrate the present, and advance the future of aviation in Canada." It would appear that since its inception, this special day has become neither well known nor celebrated.)

The Baddeck Board of Trade spent weeks making plans for the twenty-fifth anniversary event. They established an aviation committee with members of the Cape Breton Flying Club based in Sydney, the closest such club to Baddeck. There were two issues that needed to be resolved, one being a site for the cairn and the other being a suitable landing field in Baddeck; activities planned for the day included demonstration flying over Baddeck, necessitating a landing field. Work progressed on both those fronts, and a few days prior to the event a meeting was held at the courthouse in Baddeck to more thoroughly acquaint the general public with the plans for National Aviation Day. The occasion was written up at length in the *Victoria News* of July 28.

Appreciation was expressed...to Messrs. Ruttiven MacPherson and Hector MacNeil in offering their fields as a landing field for the air pageant to be staged here by planes of the various clubs that will participate in the goodwill air tour. In this regard the Board was able to avail itself of the most valuable services of J. A. D. McCurdy who entered into the spirit of the undertaking with the greatest enthusiasm and virtually superintended the whole work of preparing the landing field. It has now been graded and rolled and is larger than at first was intended.

Before the meeting adjourned the Warden of Victoria County, M. N. MacRae addressed the other issue, that of erecting a suitable monument to commemorate the first flight in the British Empire by McCurdy. He advised that municipal authorities would be glad to give the monument a place on the Court House Square if it was decided to put it there. A motion to that effect was quickly put on the floor, and the people present by almost a unanimous vote expressed a wish to have it on the Court House Square.

Casey wasn't one of those who voted in favour of the motion. He was adamant that the monument should be built as close to the actual site of the flight of Silver Dart as possible. This would have placed it "down the bay," about a mile beyond the village. An offer for such a site had already been received from a local resident but was dismissed in the rush to choose the courthouse as the preferred site. The meeting concluded with lip service given to the alternate proposal. "As Mrs. W. F. McCurdy of Crescent Grove had generously offered a free site for the monument on her property which is very near the origin of the first flight by Mr. McCurdy, a resolution was moved...expressing appreciation of her public spiritedness in this matter and extending to her the thanks of the Board of Trade for her gracious act."

The day before the event the entire fleet of planes from the Cape Breton Flying Club, several carrying passengers, landed at the new Baddeck Board of Trade landing field. The pilots expressed themselves to be well pleased with the condition of the "airport," one of the first in Nova Scotia. They were particularly happy that through the efforts of the Baddeck Board of Trade, the new field would provide a suitable landing place within a reasonable distance of their home field at Grand Lake and the next nearest field at New Glasgow.

National Aviation Day took place as planned on August 16, 1934. Every home and business in Baddeck was decked out in flags and bunting. Thousands of spectators gathered around the courthouse to watch Nova Scotia's lieutenant-governor, the Hon. Walter H. Covert, unveil a tablet honouring the event. It was built into a stone cairn some twelve feet in height, erected by the Canadian Flying Clubs Association with the following inscription: "Commemorating the work of the AEA which resulted in the first flight within the British Empire made by J. A. D. McCurdy at Baddeck, Nova Scotia, on February 23, 1909. The AEA was founded at Baddeck by Dr. Graham Bell. The other members were F. W. Baldwin whose first successful flight was made at Hammondsport, NY, on March 12, 1908, G. H. Curtiss, J. A. D. McCurdy and Thomas E. Selfridge. Their contributions to aeronautical science are gratefully acknowledged."

According to the report in the August 17, 1934, edition of the *Halifax Herald*, homage was paid by guest speakers to both McCurdy and Baldwin "who brought Canada to the forefront in Empire aviation and created a tradition signally fostered throughout Canada today." Most of the attention was focused on McCurdy "whose achievement had brought Canada to the forefront in aviation circles the Empire over. Amid thunderous applause McCurdy arose to reply to the eulogies voiced by the speakers. He was followed by Mr. Baldwin who also responded to the kind sentiments expressed."

It was an awkward moment for Casey, one that would be felt again on subsequent milestones marked to celebrate Silver Dart. Both Casey and Douglas knew that Silver Dart really represented the culmination of the work of the

AEA and not the accomplishments of one person or the success of one aerodrome. Casey was glad when this day was over; he didn't like to be in the limelight anyway. In an account of the celebration addressed to Daisy, he wrote, "The whole thing was pretty distasteful to me, for several reasons that I can tell you when I see you. One thing was that it was not done by the Historical Society of Canada (a really authoritative body) and the second, that the cairn was put up in front of the Court House instead of down the Bay where the flight took place. I did my best to have the cairn put down the Bay and did not approve of going ahead without the authorization of the Historical Society."

The monument still stands today on the steps of the Baddeck courthouse—a bleak and nondescript pillar of stone that would look less out of place in a cemetery. The tourist or casual passerby would not know of its significance without stopping for a close look. Even then the tablet is so weathered as to be almost illegible. The monument does little to enhance public awareness of the event it is intended to commemorate—National Aviation Day, largely unknown to Canadians. A more suitable monument to celebrate the day and the historic flight of Silver Dart, perhaps relocated on or near the alternate site, is worthy of consideration.

BY 1935, FOLLOWING THE EFFECTS OF THE GREAT DEPRESSION, THE iconic schooner *Bluenose* had established its career as a sailing ambassador for Nova Scotia. In the most recent International Fishermen's Cup Race, in 1931, *Bluenose* had retained the undisputed title of Queen of the North Atlantic by defeating its American challenger, *Gertrude L. Thebaud*. In the years that followed, *Bluenose* was on the tour circuit—attending the Chicago World's Fair in 1933 and visiting Toronto in 1934.

In what was perhaps the schooner's most significant role as an international ambassador, it was decided that *Bluenose* would sail to England to represent Canada at the Silver Jubilee of King George V and Queen Mary in 1935. In 1935 Casey, in addition to being an accomplished sailor, was a member of the Nova Scotia legislature with an abiding interest in tourism. He was of course well acquainted with Captain Angus Walters through his prior involvement with the first schooner races as an unofficial member of the race committee, and Walters was quite familiar with Casey's crossing of the Atlantic years earlier in *Typhoon*. Walters invited Casey to join *Bluenose* for this voyage, the iconic vessel's first transit of the Atlantic. It was to be a family affair; Casey's two sons—Robert, 21, and Patrick, 13, both good sailors—became part of the crew as well.

Casey was by now a favourite of the Halifax press, which quickly picked up on the story. Under the headline "Spirit of Adventure is Handed to Sons," the *Halifax Herald* of May 8, 1935, provided a full account of the saga.

> The spirit of adventure that led F. W. "Casey" Baldwin, MLA Victoria County to pioneer in skies that few dared traverse and won for him the glory of being the first man in the Empire to fly has been handed down from father to sons. At the age of 13 [*sic*], "Casey" Baldwin sailed for England in one of those Nova Scotian marine miracles, the square rigger. When the fleetest of North America fishing craft, Captain Angus Walter's Bluenose sails for the Old country Wednesday, Pat Baldwin, his 13 year old son will step down the same trail of romance and adventure. With him will stride his 21 year old brother Robert, King's University student. And "Casey" Baldwin himself sails too.

Plans were for the *Bluenose* to spend five months sailing the strait of Dover and the North and Irish Seas with perhaps some races with English yachts or American craft, notably the America's Cup yachts *Endeavour* and *Yankee* and the Royal Yacht *Britannia*. The original plan was to have the "mistress of the North Atlantic fishing fleets," hailed by the media as the "Barnstorming *Bluenose*," race across the Atlantic with a Gloucester fishing schooner, but that project fell through.

Bluenose arrived in Plymouth, England, on May 29, 1935, after a boisterous crossing just shy of twenty days. In commenting on the voyage, Casey remarked that "all were well during the entire passage and the speedy ship showed comfort under extraordinary conditions." The weather was variable, beginning with light but favourable winds as far as the Grand Banks. It was there they encountered icebergs, which then gave way to warmer weather and water in the Gulf Stream followed by continuous heavy headwinds, which slowed their progress. Captain Walters, the crusty Lunenburg skipper, was unimpressed with the twenty-day crossing, which he felt was slow for

Bluenose. When asked by an English reporter if he had had a good crossing his curt answer was, "Rotten, thanks."

The English press, already well-versed on Casey's background, interviewed him as well. If they had hoped to get a scoop on his prior accomplishments both in the air and on the water, Casey's unflappable modesty left them disappointed. The following is from the transcript of a radio interview for the "Empire Program" on June 6, 1935:

> "You've been a good many things besides a sailor, haven't you, Mr. Baldwin?"
> "Well, I've always been interested in experimental engineering."
> "Weren't you one of the earliest aviators?"
> "Yes I was, as a matter of fact."

Kathleen was understandably anxious while Casey and the boys were gone. *Bluenose* had departed Halifax on May 9 with her whole family aboard. It was still early in the year, with the threat of icebergs and fog making for a perilous passage. There was no communication with the schooner and only occasional sightings of it during the crossing. On May 23, while *Bluenose* was still en route, Kathleen wrote a letter to Casey, more to express her anxiety than anything else, as he would not be in receipt of it until *Bluenose* reached its destination. She hadn't appeared to be too concerned when Casey set off with William Nutting years earlier in *Typhoon*. This time, however, was different— her sons were aboard. "It's hard not to have any word of you," she wrote. "I'm beginning to get nervous about ice. I hope that you went far enough south. You were reported by a National Fish Company mother vessel twenty-four hours out and making good progress. Some other boat may have reported you but have not heard. Loads of love to all my dears."

She needn't have worried. Father and sons were in good hands on a stout ship. The boys were having the time of their lives. Pat sent his mother a couple of postcards, custom-made and featuring a picture of *Bluenose,* "Undefeated Champion of the North Atlantic Fishing fleet." The first, on which he wrote "At sea on Bluenose, latitude 49 degrees 00' North, Longitude 26 degrees 30 minutes West" on Sunday, May 18, was brief and to the point. "We are ten days out and having a great time. She is a fine ship and the grub is great. We will be back sometime in June. Love Pat." The second card was dated June 29,

1935, a full month after *Bluenose* arrived in Plymouth, England, and appears to have been posted upon the return of the boys to Canada. "Dear Mom, We are having a great time and all well. She is a fine ship and the grub is great. Hope to be back soon. Much love, Pat."

Casey and his two sons returned home via ocean liner. *Bluenose*, after surviving a vicious hurricane, the worst Walters had ever experienced and necessitating repairs in Plymouth, returned to a boisterous welcome in Lunenburg on November 4, 1935. By that time it was too late in the season to arrange any international fishing race off Gloucester.

Bluenose may not have been a square rigger, but for the Baldwin boys the crossing was a great adventure and replicated crossings made by both their father and grandfather in their youth. It was the only crossing of the Atlantic ever made by the Canadian sailing icon. *Bluenose*, Queen of the Atlantic, ended its days ignominiously after striking a reef in Haiti on January 28, 1946, resulting in a total loss.

Soon after his return to Cape Breton, Casey resumed his passion for sailing on his beloved Bras d'Or Lakes. Having served as commodore of the Bras d'Or Yacht Club for six consecutive years dating back to 1912, Casey had been elected again to that post in 1931 and still occupied the position. The club was seeking to lease more land to expand members' activities. Casey helped to obtain a lease from the Dominion government for a lot extending from the back of the clubhouse lot to the rear of the post office lot. The entertainment committee was appointed to lay out quoit pits, and another committee was struck to lay out a tennis court once a lease was obtained. Busy times at the BYC as a centre of activities in the Village of Baddeck.

The last year for Casey as commodore was 1935. At the annual meeting of the club on October 1, Casey presented his final report, recorded in the club minutes. "Commodore Baldwin made a very nice speech explaining the work done by the Yacht Club during the past year and appealing to the people of our town to support the Club which was our chief summer attraction for tourists." John D. MacNeil was elected commodore while Casey and J. A. D. McCurdy were appointed to serve on the race committee. Then, to the cheers of the members present, Casey was elected honorary commodore. Casey clearly was as popular then as he was nearly twenty years previously when he was made honorary commodore in 1918. Having twice been bestowed with this title, Casey must be considered the highest ranking honorary commodore in club history!

Casey always retained a strong belief in the importance of the Bras d'Or Yacht Club to the Village of Baddeck and spoke of it often. One of the last occasions he had to do so was at the BYC annual meeting of July 15, 1937—the year that son Bob was named fleet captain—when Casey was elected rear commodore and a member of the race committee along with Douglas McCurdy, who was now a regular summer resident. The minutes of that meeting recorded an address by Casey in his honorary role. "Honorary Commodore Baldwin spoke and congratulated the club on their progress during the past few years. He felt that sailing was coming back stronger every season. He also felt that the town should support the club more than it had done in the past, as we were really a community club for the benefit of the town generally. Honorary Commodore Baldwin was warmly applauded."

Casey only served a single four-year term as a sitting member of the Nova Scotia legislature; he did not re-offer in 1937. His party, the Conservatives, were in Opposition during this time. As a party they were only as effective as their eight seats allowed, but despite that, when Casey spoke he was a man to be listened to, regardless on which side of the House you sat. No other member received the attention and praise of the press like Casey. Just before his term ended, an editorial appeared in the *Halifax Herald* entitled "A Priceless Possession."

F. W. Baldwin, member for Victoria did a good day's work for the Province in the Legislature on Tuesday when he urged so ably the value of and need for forest conservation. Mr. Baldwin is no theorist on questions of this kind: he knows what he is talking about. And when he tells us of the ills that follow in the wake of forest depletion, he emphasizes one of the most serious matters which any public body could be concerned. For the loss of forest growth in terms of commercial value alone is a very small part of these ills and consequences.

"A land stripped of its forests is a poor land indeed.

A land of alternate flood and drought.

A land of violent fluctuations in weather.

A land in which wild-life cannot exist.

A land reduced to hard and forbidding conditions."

No one in this Province has made a closer study of what it all means than Casey Baldwin. The question is, the grave question—will men like

F. W. Baldwin be listened to? Will their advice be taken? Or will their warnings fall upon deaf ears?

Casey's message and altruistic spirit truly transcended party lines. Often his point of view, as in this case when speaking about conservation, remains as true today as it did back then.

Instead of re-offering for election, Casey chose to accept the position of president of the Nova Scotia Conservative Association at its annual meeting held in Halifax on November 19, 1937. His acceptance speech was considered one of the most remarkable ever given by a politician in Nova Scotia. It was in the nature of a manifesto—a blueprint for the revitalization of the economic life of the province. In it he made reference to the challenges facing all sectors of the Nova Scotian economy—fishing, farming, mining—and the plight of the youth, many of whom were unable to secure employment at home. Casey made it clear that he was not suggesting the Province should be looking for handouts, but rather how Nova Scotia might better itself. He was quoted in the November 20, 1937, edition of the *Halifax Herald*. "I would like this distinctly understood. I am not talking about 'Confederation' and the rest of Canada. I am talking about this Province and our own domestic affairs. We had, and have, disabilities of National significance. But in this case and at this time, I am discussing what we, as Nova Scotians, within our own Province, can do to help ourselves if we are to solve these urgent problems and make that progress Nova Scotia requires and deserves."

Casey concluded his address with the introduction of the following resolution, which was adopted by the audience of more than six hundred, with only one dissenting vote:

RESOLVED that the Nova Scotia Conservative Party do immediately undertake, as its foremost purpose, a study of the major economic problems which confront this Province, with a view to presenting the result of such study to a Provincial convention to be held at a time in the future when this committee will be prepared to report, and when there will be placed before the Convention for consideration and adoption policies based upon such report and designed to cope courageously, sincerely and effectively with the economic disabilities which confront the people of this Province....

AND FURTHER RESOLVED that ALL Nova Scotians, irrespective of party, be invited to assist this Committee in its investigation and study.

It was a powerful treatise and a crowning moment in Casey's political career. It was seized upon by the press and published in its entirety in the *Halifax Herald* the following day. A full-page article boldly entitled "Forward, Nova Scotia" contained an editorial note that "Mr. Baldwin's address is one that warrants the careful consideration of the people of this Province and for their information it is published in full herewith."

If there ever had been any doubt about where Casey's heart and soul lay, it was now put to rest. Casey, Toronto-born, had become a true blue Nova Scotian—a Bluenoser in every sense of the word. Few native Nova Scotians can claim to have given as much to their province.

CHAPTER 20

When All is Said and Done

On November 30, 1938, with Pat attending Ridley College and Bob at King's College in Halifax, Casey and Kathleen set off for Europe. It was to be a mixed business and pleasure trip with Casey hoping to study the co-operative movement in various countries. It was a dark and dangerous time as the clouds of war gathered. The Baldwins took every possible precaution in preparing for the trip. Casey even obtained an ingratiating "letter of introduction" from Nova Scotia's Liberal premier, Angus L. Macdonald: "Mr. Baldwin is a scion of one of the most distinguished Canadian families—a family that has been prominent in the public and professional life of this country for more than a century. During the years 1933–1937 he was a member of the Nova Scotia Legislature in which capacity he proved himself to be possessed of marked ability, high character and attractive personality."

By mid-December Casey and Kathleen had visited Germany and were then in Poland. On December 16 they sent Bob a letter from Krakow in which Casey described tensions in Poland over a move for independence in neighbouring Ukraine.

We called at the British Embassy to see the Secretary regarding Russian Visas. Dad wanted to get a card for the House [i.e., Parliament] in

Warsaw. It ended in the Secretary ringing up two days after to say that the House, though really in session was not sitting within a few days. The reason for this was because the Ukraine which is a large district on the Russian border were bringing in a Home Rule Bill. This Bill had the complete support of all the Ukrainians in Poland and demanded control of their own affairs, their own language etc. They wanted a referendum on the question, just like the Sudeten Germans, but the Speaker of the Polish house ruled it out of order as unconstitutional and the feeling is very intense because the Poles feel that this move was backed by the Germans. The Poles are, outside of this question, very friendly to the Germans and afraid of Russia. This question has raised very awkward angles to the whole international situation.

Casey and Kathleen were not able to get to Russia and took a train directly from Warsaw to Berlin. Kathleen wrote to Bob from there at the end of December. She told him that Germany was clearly a country preparing for war. Nazis sporting their swastika armbands were everywhere to be seen throughout the city. While in Berlin the Baldwins managed to take in an international hockey match. "One night we went to the Sports Palast to see Berlin-Kanada play hockey. Our boys call themselves 'The Trail Smoke Eaters.' We were away up on top and could hardly see. Couldn't get decent seats and bought standing places from a youth outside who apparently was willing to sell them for a consideration. But it was unsatisfactory: score 9–1, our favour."

By mid-February 1939 the Baldwins were in Stockholm. Casey described Sweden and the government in a letter to Pat.

Sweden is very up-to-date, most of the railways electric etc., and there seem to be no poor people or anything even remotely suggesting slums such as Water street in Halifax. The Government is one of the best in the world. All parties are properly represented as they have had proportional Representation since 1909 and the people take such a keen interest in Public Affairs that there is no graft or practically none and political patronage is Taboo—which shows that it is possible for a democratic government to be clean and effective.

Casey and Kathleen managed to return home just before Canada went to war with Germany. A few months later Kathleen received a letter in broken English from Frau Else Baumgarten, a lady she had met while in Berlin, which provides interesting insight into the mindset of some German people at that time. "The newspapers in the foreign countries didn't write in a nicely form from Germany. They tell falsehoods. We Germans are so glad to have such a wonderful man as our Fuhrer is."

The outbreak of the Second World War brought Casey back into production mode once again at the Beinn Bhreagh Laboratory. Although the military in Canada, United States, and Britain had rejected his hydrofoil targets in the years following the First World War, Casey remained of the belief that his targets, now more than ever, would prove useful to all armed services for training in gunnery and bombing. For the next three years, 1940–1943, he devoted himself to improving both design and construction of the earlier target models.

While in England in 1939 Casey had met with members of the Air Ministry in an attempt to interest them in use of his hydrofoil targets for bombing practice. This produced some positive results; by April 1940, approval was given for the purchase of a high-speed hydrofoil target, the cost to be shared by the RCAF, RCN, and Canadian Army. The two essential elements of tetrahedral construction and hydrofoils remained, but the entire target was constructed of aluminum. The finished product, a 42.5-foot target, was built at Montreal and shipped to Halifax for water trials mid-October 1940.

For days Halifax Harbour was the scene of target towing trials in which a number of different towing vessels were employed, culminating with sea trials using two destroyers: HMCS *Columbia* and HMCS *St. Louis.* The trials proved to be satisfactory and the RCAF placed an initial order for ten twenty-one-foot targets in 1941. They were subsequently lengthened to twenty-four feet. Two such targets were tested in Dartmouth in April 1942. The targets towed well and performed well in smoke bombing by Canso aircraft. Spirits were high and fourteen more targets were ordered with a large volume of spares.

Early optimism faded when it was found that the specifications required by the navy differed from those of the air force, which required something larger than the twenty-four-foot target. Despite the initial enthusiasm that developed during testing, the targets were proving to be unsatisfactory in service. Problems encountered with yawing, pitching, and nosing-in produced frequent parts failures, and then there was the problem of detection from the air. The hydrofoil worked so efficiently on the water that it created little if any wake, making it difficult to locate from an aircraft, particularly if the sea was stirred with whitecaps. About the time the RCAF lost interest in the targets the Royal Canadian Navy ordered eighteen fifty-foot targets, six for the East Coast, four for the West Coast, and eight to be held in stores to provide spares. Delivery began about mid-summer of 1944.

Casey's last initiative had been to spark interest in a remote-controlled hydrofoil target. He went through the same process of design, construction, and testing, but after showing initial interest, naval authorities decided against pursuing this opportunity, despite the fact that Casey, characteristically, had given his own resources to the project without any form of remuneration.

The naval board sent an officer to see Casey at Baddeck to discuss the navy's withdrawal of support for this project and any outstanding claim he might have arising from it. Casey, modest to a fault, was reluctant to discuss what he might have expended out of his own resources, perhaps on patriotic grounds. Instead he insisted on nothing for himself but would be happy to receive $1,000 to go toward wages of his staff; otherwise the simple thanks of the department would suffice for his efforts. Mabel would have winced. Once again Casey had demonstrated a clear lack of business acumen and the need for a business manager the likes of Gardiner Hubbard, Mabel's father.

The war ended the following year and with it, the interest of the military in targets. For Casey, history had repeated itself. As with his efforts to promote HD-4 following the First World War, now, twenty years and another war later, his efforts with hydrofoil targets had met a similar fate. He was tired, worn out from his efforts, and this was taking a toll on his health.

The Second World War reawakened in Casey the frustration and lingering guilt he had experienced as a result of his difficult decision not to enlist during the First World War. He was too old to do so this time around, but both he and Kathleen now shared anxious times and worry over sons Robert and Pat who had chosen to serve in the Royal Canadian Navy.

Robert was twenty-seven in September 1940 when he received his commission as Acting Lieutenant, assigned to HMCS *Stadacona* and sent overseas for service with the Royal Navy. While stationed in England Bob became romantically involved with an Irish lassie by the name of Maureen

Mahoney. For two years they maintained their relationship by meeting each other whenever possible at Bob's various postings and during his leave within the UK.

Patrick was just nineteen at this time but old enough to enlist. After taking basic training at Esquimalt, British Columbia, Pat was sent overseas in 1942 where he served on motor torpedo boats (MTBs) with the Royal Navy. He saw considerable action in the English Channel and survived the loss of at least two MTBs, which were shot out from beneath him. Unlike his brother, Pat was not much of a writer. Casey and Kathleen did, however, receive correspondence on a regular basis from Bob, who served on escort duty for convoys transiting the North Atlantic.

Bob had been courting "Snooks" throughout the summer of 1941. Maureen was working with the American Red Cross in London most of this time, and after considerable effort she managed to secure paperwork and passage to Canada, destination Baddeck. She arrived on the doorstep of the bungalow in July. Bob managed to get leave, and he and Maureen were married in Sydney, Cape Breton, early in August of 1942.

At the end of April 1943 Maureen, settled at Beinn Bhreagh, wrote to Bob who was then serving aboard HMCS *Griffin* that his mother was well and that they heard from Pat quite often. For her part, Maureen noted that "time goes by very quickly, surprisingly so, and I appear to have fallen into a very contented rut." She was pregnant and expecting a child in June. Casey added a postscript.

> The target trials [in Halifax] were almost monotonously successful, but as seems to be the rule, exactly nothing has happened since....
>
> We are overjoyed about Maureen and very happy to have her with us. She seems very well and is getting lots of fresh air and lately some sunshine. It is certainly much better for her here than being in some stuffy place in Halifax. She and Kass are busy making all sorts of things and this new interest in life is a great thing for Mums.

On June 2 Maureen wrote to Bob, then serving aboard HMCS *Ottawa*, to advise that she had made preparations for the baby to be delivered at St. Rita's Hospital in Sydney. On June 20 she wired Bob in Halifax: "Casey Robert born twentieth. Eight pounds. Both well. Love Maureen."

A few weeks later Kathleen was hospitalized in North Sydney. Casey, now the primary caregiver for his grandson and his daughter-in-law, wrote to his sister Bess to tell her of Kass's misfortune.

Perhaps you have by now heard that Kass had a bad motorcar accident July 9th from which she is now recovering wonderfully well. It all happened just a little way from our gate. Kass was driving by herself to a meeting in Baddeck. About three quarters of an hour after she left a boy came down and reported the car was in the ditch and Mrs. Baldwin hurt. By the time we got there she was conscious but dazed. Her ankle was badly broken and her face was bleeding from a cut lip. The break was a bad one requiring traction to pull the bones apart so she will be there [in hospital] for weeks. Of course Kass suffered greatly from the shock and the pain but as you would know she stood up to it wonderfully well. Kass has no idea how it all happened.

The new Baldwin is a splendid little fellow and is very well although some of the hot days have made him fretful. Maureen is well and makes a charming and efficient mother. She sends her love.

Casey sent a copy of this letter with a short note to Daisy who was anxious to learn about Kass's condition, the baby, and his work.

The baby has taken complete charge of the household. I am assured he is very well but whenever I hear him cry I am convinced something is terribly wrong with his insides. But if nobody pays any attention he soon eases up with a cross between a chortle and a sneeze—and once more, all's well with the world.

You will be glad to know that the big boat shop has been most useful. We store both materials and finished floats there before shipment. Navy, Air Force and Army are all starting to use them and I am busy on the self-propelled type and other uses of hydrofoils.

At times all such work is terribly discouraging; not because of any particular failure but just because it takes so long, and there are so many things to do. At such times I miss Mr. Bell more than ever and long for someone I could talk things over with. Of course I know the people in the National Research Council, but an institution, however good, lacks the human gift of sympathy and understanding.

Casey was lonely in his work. He was at his best, and had done his best work, when in the company of others—engaged with others as in the case of the AEA, or with the reassurance and encouragement of his mentor, Dr. Bell.

The end of November found Kass now back home on crutches. Maureen had left "Casey Bob" with his grandparents and gone to St. John's, Newfoundland, to be close to Bob upon his return from active patrol duty. Corresponding with Daisy continued to provide Casey with an outlet for sharing his loneliness, bordering on despair.

I have however been terribly busy and not a little worried at being unable to get along faster with various hydrofoil experiments which I think are important. The authorities do not seem to share my views and I cannot spend my life and limited resources on my knees in Ottawa or Washington. As Mr. Bell used to say, remember that large bodies move slowly, but I can detect no motion at all. However the work itself has gone very well. The baby is really a wonderful little lad as I suppose all grand children are. It will be good to have you all up here next summer.

Casey periodically visited with Douglas McCurdy at his summer home in Baddeck. McCurdy was working in Ottawa with the Department of Munitions and Supply. It is apparent from correspondence exchanged between them in November 1944 that McCurdy was aware of the difficulty Casey had encountered with bureaucrats in moving his experimental work forward and specifically the undertaking of government to provide the remote-control apparatus for his self-propelled hydrofoil target. On November 9, 1944, McCurdy wrote to Casey offering to assist if he could. He provided Casey with the name of a former classmate at U of T, Leslie Thompson, who was now Secretary of the Inventions Board. Douglas felt that if Casey were to write to Thompson he would give the matter his "very sympathetic consideration."

Casey did not respond, whereupon McCurdy wrote to him again on January 30, 1945, on what he felt was "this matter of extreme importance which had not yet been dealt with."

I wrote you on November 20th (and November 9th), suggesting that you communicate with Leslie Thompson, Secretary of the inventions Board with the idea in view of having radar and operating crew sent to Baddeck to facilitate your experiments. Leslie advised me the other day that he has not yet heard from you. I am wondering whether you have given up the idea of this for the present or whether pressure of business has caused you to refrain from writing. He is still interested to receive your communication. With the Spring approaching and the idea in view that the ice will soon be out of the lakes, it might be well to get this matter under way as soon as possible.

This letter provoked a response from Casey. On April 16, 1945, he wrote to McCurdy with details of what he had in mind in regard to having the RCN and RCAF interest themselves in further work connected with his experiments. Preparing such materials, particularly at this juncture, would have tested Casey's willpower, knowing as he did from past experience that such effort had seldom produced any tangible reward.

McCurdy did what he could and immediately sent Casey's brief off with a letter to the board, endorsing Casey's work and commending him to the navy and air force.

I myself have seen his experiments and have no hesitation in recommending that the Navy and the Air Force examine further into his work and that the additional experiments which would be necessary to complete the investigation be appraised in dollar value and if not considered excessive the funds be secured and the experiments proceeded with. Whether the Navy or the Air Force immediately avail themselves of these experiments is neither here nor there; they will have however a permanent record with drawings and designs which will enable them to carry on in peacetime for the increased efficiency in gunfire and bomb-dropping in respect of these two services.

McCurdy, in sharing this information with Casey, felt it important that Casey know just what McCurdy had said to the board on Casey's behalf. He then wished Casey luck and the hope that the navy and air force would "proceed to bring your experiments to a successful conclusion." They did not. As the war came to a close, so too did the board's file on Casey's self-propelled targets. Casey had only sporadic contact with the military and National Research Council in the months following the end of the war and, according to Kathleen, "was pretty well, but doing very little."

Bob left the navy at war's end and went to Vancouver where he eventually found a position with a local law firm. Pat Baldwin had used up some of his nine lives but managed to survive the war during which he acquitted himself well, making his parents proud of his acts of valour. By August 1947 he was reunited briefly with his parents in Halifax before being posted to British Columbia. He never married.

In 1946 the Technical College of Nova Scotia in Halifax, for the first time in its history, presented honorary degrees to "two well-known Canadians." At its thirty-seventh annual convocation, held May 16, 1946, the degree of Doctor of Engineering was conferred upon Frederick Walker Baldwin of Baddeck and John A. McCurdy of Ottawa, a native of Baddeck. The honour was accorded "in recognition of their basic pioneer work in the field of aviation and for other engineering achievements." A short editorial in the *Halifax Herald* on May 3 captioned "So Well Deserved" suggested that the honours were both modest and long overdue.

> The Nova Scotia Technical College is honoring itself by honoring F. W. Baldwin and J. A. D. McCurdy. These are men who deserve all the recognition that can be bestowed upon them—Casey Baldwin, first British subject to fly an airplane...Douglas McCurdy, first to fly a plane in the British Empire.
>
> And it was right here in this Province that their pioneering was motivated and conducted. Associates of Dr. Alexander Graham Bell himself, Baldwin and McCurdy, with all the zeal and enthusiasm of youth, wrote aeronautical history.
>
> The strange part of it is that greater distinction, more honors of this kind have not been given them. If they were natives of the United States about the smallest things to which their names would be attached would be mountains.

The honour, such as it was, would be the only recognition given to Casey during his lifetime. Rather belatedly, in 1974 Casey was inducted posthumously into the Canadian Aviation Hall of Fame, which in my opinion should have been named after him. Like many an artist, the substance and significance of his work went largely ignored and unappreciated until after his death.

By 1947, the year after Casey received his honorary degree, life was starting to slow down for the Baldwins, with some notable exceptions. Kathleen spoke about her "social activities" in an August 18 letter to her sister Marion.

Since the 17th nothing very much to report in the way of social activities. On that day however there were great doings at the Point when their Excellences [Governor General Viscount Harold Alexander and Lady Diana Alexander] motored down from Keltic Lodge in the Park to have lunch. They had been there ten days and were to stay three weeks in all. Elsie had a huge lunch—mostly those on Beinn Bhreagh and the JAD McCurdys, and another McCurdy, the town clerk. By the way, John has got himself appointed Lieutenant-Governor of Nova Scotia which news had come out a few days before the lunch. Extreme modesty and surprise on his part. We had heard earlier that he was pulling all kinds of wires to get it. That's OK if he wants it and better people do the same thing, but what I can't stand is the attitude of it coming as a bolt out of the blue.

Writing again to her sister on March 22, 1948, from Beinn Bhreagh Kathleen said, "Our social activities have been practically nil. The odd game of bridge with occasional meals with people in Baddeck and vice versa. At one stage there was a possibility of going to Victoria but Casey finally decided definitely against it and now we intend going out in the Autumn to spend the winter which will make the long and expensive trip more worthwhile. Pat is to be out there two years probably so it will be very nice to all be together for a decent length of time. We get good reports from Bob and Maureen… and Casey Bob."

Kathleen was in the writing mood and the following day sent a letter to Daisy recounting a similar theme. "Casey I believe wrote you before or after Christmas—his letters like mine are few and far between. Our Christmas was exceedingly dull and quiet and we missed several gay gatherings in the village.… [Pat] sailed on destroyer Cayuga February 4th on her southern cruise and on to Esquimalt where she is to be permanently based and Pat to remain two years."

Casey and Kathleen were in a funk, which impacted Casey's health. By spring of 1948, according to Kathleen, he was "pretty well on the whole. He is in bed most of the time. He only dresses when people come in or the spirit moves him to go to the village."

Casey missed old friends from around Beinn Bhreagh, many of whom were near death or had passed away. His malaise was evident in a May 24 letter addressed to "Maureen, Bob, Pat, not to mention Casey Bob." "You will all be sorry to hear that the Old Guard is breaking up. Long John has been miserable all winter and they can do nothing for him. Also, Poker Dan, and now it comes as a great shock that Malcolm Doherty is practically dying, at least the Doc does not hold out any hope and they have sent for his sons. Hannah's tough and spunky old father is also failing rapidly and that would clean up all the old Brigade."

About this time Casey and McCurdy flew together from Baddeck to Halifax to attend an engineers' function in the city. It seems that being lieutenant-governor had some perks. "John McCurdy who has a Canso [amphibious aircraft] at his disposal offered me a passage which I gladly accepted. It was a bit thick in approaching Halifax but the trip back was clear as a bell and I enjoyed spotting all the familiar harbors. However, there is no pleasure like sailing no matter how much longer it takes, or perhaps because it takes longer."

Early in June 1948 Casey wrote to Bob, who was turning thirty-five; he expressed disbelief at how fast the years had gone by. It is quite apparent from the tone of the letter that Casey was down. "I feel that the years don't matter so much and what we are most thankful for is that you and Pat have lived through V.E. Day. To you V.E. Day probably seems a hundred years ago but to me it is as yesterday. It all depends on how much has happened to one and nothing has happened to your mother and me except a slow decline in the ability to do things."

Nova Scotia has notoriously slow springs, and this one in particular didn't do anything to improve Casey's state of mind. "We had a very severe winter, the coldest and longest in many years, and there hasn't been any Spring yet— just steady drizzle and fog alternated by fog and drizzle. Beinn Bhreagh gets duller and duller as the years go by and the younger generation grows up and begets still another generation."

This would normally be the time of year that Casey looked forward to all winter—the launching of the Beinn Bhreagh fleet, and most importantly, his sailboat. However, with advancing years and failing health he now needed help in both launching and sailing. The few youngsters that were around now "had not the slightest interest in sailing, and if they were, would want an Admiral's pay." The knowledge that his sailing days might be over, for one who had such a passion for the sport, would have been demoralizing.

It was very uncharacteristic for Casey to spend so much time writing as he did at this time. On June 5 he penned a letter to his sister Grace Lash with a similar tone; it seems Casey was anxious to share his malaise with family. "Bob's birthday came round the other day (V. E. Day) and Kass and I greatly wished that we could have been with them. Pat however was there…Casey Bob has been taken out in Pat's snipe [sailboat] and took to it like a proper old salt.

"This country is too damn big and I fear they are not likely to reduce the cost of flying in the near future. You and John and Bess perhaps don't always realize how lucky you are to have your children and grandchildren right around the corner."

Both sons had been lost to Casey and Kathleen throughout the war, and now that it was over, both Pat and Bob were living on the opposite side of the country, in British Columbia. The empty nest, long winter, no spring, friends passing away, "dull times" at Beinn Bhreagh, separation from immediate family—all these factors were on Casey's mind. It played upon both him and Kathleen, but Casey felt it the most. He wrote to a friend on June 28, 1948, "I miss Bob, Betty and Pat very acutely."

Summer, when it finally did arrive that year, did nothing to improve Casey's well-being. He died at home in the bungalow on Beinn Bhreagh on Saturday, August 7, 1948, the final day of the annual regatta week in Baddeck. He was only sixty-six years old.

An August 17 letter from Kathleen to her sister-in-law Grace contains some insight into the circumstances around Casey's death. It is a rather clinical account, lacking the emotion so frequently found in her correspondence.

I had got the night nurse's report Saturday morning. At first it seemed good—Casey had a good breakfast for the first time. When I went in to see him and asked how he felt he said "fair." I said I heard you had a good breakfast—did you enjoy it? "No, I only thought I'd better eat something." I wasn't happy. I had a foreboding. Shortly after Dr. Mayers [*sic*] came (Carol Grosvenor Mayer's [*sic*] husband). Casey perked up and greeted him cheerily and said he felt fine. I knew better. We went into Casey's room where Dr. M. was explaining by sketch what had happened to Casey's heart. The nurse rushed in and in a few minutes he was gone—quietly.

Casey's obituary appeared in the *Chronicle Herald* on August 8, the very next day after his death. One is left to speculate on who prepared the obituary notice as it contains a number of factual errors, but is exacting in its praise for the man. Casey had suffered a stroke a few months previously and had been in failing health since. He was described as "a Toronto native who became one of Nova Scotia's most distinguished adopted sons." Casey had made his final public appearance just the day before his death at the tenth annual Gaelic Mod at nearby St. Anns.

> Kindly, gracious "Casey" Baldwin was a legendary figure, not only in the lands of his birth but in many far places. He had an unusual trait of winning friends and keeping them. People of all ages from many parts of the United States and Canada knew "Casey" Baldwin and many visited him each year. He counted his friends in the thousands, this gifted and beloved man of Beinn Bhreagh. It was typical of him that on his Gaelic Mod visit he posed for pictures with two Highland lassies, one of them a Scottish War Bride from Antigonish who knew of "Casey" Baldwin before she came to New Scotland. That day he was the same loveable "Casey," greeting old friends and making new ones.

The *Sydney Post-Record* of August 9 contained a lengthy account of Casey's passing under the banner "Air Pioneer Dies Suddenly at Baddeck." In it he is described as a man "who brought fame and renown to Nova Scotia." He would have been particularly pleased with the reference made to his contribution to the war effort.

> During World War 2, Mr. Baldwin again took up hydrofoil work and produced both self-propelled and towed high speed hydrofoil targets

for the RCAF and RCN. Many other important experiments were carried out by him on behalf of the Canadian and British governments during the war, and his initiative and scientific talent played a major part in the all-out war effort of 1939–1945.

The death of Mr. Baldwin will be widely mourned as he was known internationally and held in highest respect and esteem. His passing cast a gloom over Baddeck and the whole of Victoria County Saturday when word was sent to the village that its renowned citizen had passed on.

The day of his funeral, August 9, 1948, the *Sydney Post-Record* included an editorial devoted to Casey.

In his own adopted Cape Breton "Casey" Baldwin was a beloved figure who identified himself with many movements looking to the progress and development of this Island.

Born in Toronto, Mr. Baldwin came to Baddeck in his twenties and fitted into his environment so completely that it ultimately became his permanent home. He loved to roam the hills of Cape Breton and during the past several years rarely left his adopted country. At every public event in Northern Cape Breton he was a familiar figure and usually took a prominent part. Hundreds of residents of Victoria County called him by the name by which he is so universally known, and there were few residents of the County whom he did not know personally. A little bit of Cape Breton died with Casey Baldwin, but the contribution he made to science and the fame he brought to Baddeck in the process will live long after him. For years to come the name of "Casey" Baldwin will remain a legend in Cape Breton.

It is perhaps fitting that the last word by way of eulogy was published in the October 1948 issue of *Yachting Magazine*, which paid tribute to Casey as a great international sailing ambassador.

It seems impossible to write a formal obituary about the kindly, loveable Casey Baldwin…who attained fame in sport, aviation, hydrofoils, and politics as a public speaker of great charm. But it was as a sailing yachtsman, long a Commodore of the Bras d'Or Yacht Club and charter member of the Cruising Club of America that his yachting friends knew him. When a sailor wanted advice on cruising in the Bras d'Or Lakes in particular and Nova Scotia in general it was to Casey that he wrote. Though he didn't always receive a reply to his letter, it was to Casey's mooring at Baddeck that the cruising man inevitably moored when he got that far East.

Casey and his Scrappers 1, 2 and 3 were almost equally famous. In one or another of these little boats he cruised the Nova Scotia coast to race where the racing was keenest; and in the society of fellow sailors there was none whose love of the sport transcended his. If there were an international competition of large yachts in an American port, Casey's Yankee friends would look for a Nova Scotian cruising boat, and, having found her would come upon the comfortable object of their search, chocked off in the cockpit amiably arguing or discoursing contentedly on the strategy of the races, the design and construction of the competitors and the level of sportsmanship to which the regatta had risen or fallen.

Death has taken a friend whose spirit pervaded the waters in which he sailed. For as long as the present generation of yachtsmen survives his spirit will be evoked whenever Baddeck is visited or mentioned.

Casey was laid to rest in a simple service beside his beloved daughter Betty in the small pioneer graveyard at the foot of the mountain that is the final resting place of Alexander Graham and Mabel Bell. Home is where the heart is. Casey, who was all heart and whose heart had finally failed him, was at peace—at home.

Casey sailing Scrapper III.

TOP: *Motoring the Cabot Trail, Cape Breton, in 1930s.* BOTTOM: *"Rigwash" on Cabot Trail.*

TOP: *Author's family summering at "Driftwood" on Baddeck Bay in 1980s.*
BOTTOM: *Author's sons, Adam and Andrew, playing at The Point in 1980s.*

Casey behind the wheel of his motor vehicle at The Point.

TOP: *Celebration Fiftieth Anniversary flight of Silver Dart, Baddeck, 1959. From left: Daisy Fairchild, Kathleen Baldwin, J. A. D. McCurdy, and Mrs. McCurdy.* BOTTOM: *Author's wife Judith hosting members of AEA 2005 Team with Canadian Astronaut Bjarni Tryggvason (far left) at Duffus House, Baddeck, 2009.*

TOP: *Hugh Miller, great-grandson of Bell, visiting pioneer cemetery at Red Head with sculptor Peter Bustin.* BOTTOM: *HMCS Bras d'Or hydrofoil at Maritime Museum of Quebec, Islet-sur-Mer, PQ.*

CHAPTER 21

Honour to Whom Honour is Due

NEEDLESS TO SAY, BEINN BHREAGH BECAME EVEN QUIETER FOR Kathleen following Casey's death. By August 23 Bob and family and Pat had all headed back west. Bob was in the midst of securing a position in a Vancouver law firm when his father passed away, leaving those plans in abeyance. Pat had to return to service with the navy. With the approach of autumn, the remaining Bell family summer residents soon left for home, leaving Kathleen alone at Beinn Bhreagh. The silence that followed must have been deafening.

Bob, Maureen, and Casey Bob eventually settled in Vancouver. In 1951 Kathleen became a grandmother for a second time when Maureen gave birth to Patrick Sean. A third grandchild, Kathleen Deneen, arrived in 1955. The family spent some of the following summers visiting with Kathleen at Beinn Bhreagh, Pat joining when he could, with many fine days spent sailing again on the Bras d'Or. By 1957 Bob and family had relocated from Vancouver to Bedford, Nova Scotia; Bob had left private practice and took up a position with the Nova Scotia Attorney General's department in Halifax.

Daisy Fairchild maintained a regular correspondence with Kathleen in the years following Casey's death. Her husband David died at their home in

Coconut Grove, Florida, on August 6, 1954. In March 1955 Daisy wrote to Kathleen, who was recuperating from a broken leg. She mentions the newly established museum in Baddeck that was to house artifacts from the Bell Laboratory. "It's been a very busy winter for me; lots going on at the Garden and I have been going through David's files and have help in getting pamphlets and books in order. Many things are to go to the University of Florida in Gainesville into a David Fairchild Room in their new Agriculture Building. We don't get any idea of when the Bell Museum will be ready for things to be put in it. I want to be on hand when they take things out of our little old building."

And she was. The location chosen for the Alexander Graham Bell Museum was a twenty-five acre parcel on the northern extremity of the Village of Baddeck overlooking Baddeck Bay and Beinn Bhreagh. It was designated a national historic site in 1952. A dramatic tetrahedral-shaped building was constructed in 1954 and officially opened to the public in 1956 featuring artifacts donated in 1955 from the Bell family's personal museum located in the old Kite House on Beinn Bhreagh. Since then the museum has been expanded in size in order to accommodate part of the original hull of HD-4, a full-scale replica of HD-4, and a full-sized replica of Silver Dart.

February 23, 1959, was the fiftieth anniversary of the flight of Silver Dart and cause for a great celebration in Baddeck. Unfortunately it was also the fulcrum for considerable angst in the Baldwin family. On this day Baddeck and the country once again paid homage to J. A. D. McCurdy, the sole surviving member of the former AEA and pilot of Silver Dart. It was tantamount to a "JAD McCurdy Day" in Baddeck. Casey Baldwin, McCurdy's friend and associate, had died eleven years previously so it was not surprising that attention would focus on the living and the local boy, McCurdy, on this occasion. Casey, who as chief engineer of the AEA had been very much in the forefront of the design and test-flying of all four dromes, including Silver Dart, was relegated to the background once more.

The *Cape Breton Post* of February 23, 1959, was full of news regarding events surrounding Canada's golden anniversary of flight. In a strange irony McCurdy shared front-page headlines with the ill-fated Avro Arrow, Canada's attempt to build a supersonic jet aircraft: "McCurdy Honored at Baddeck, Fiftieth Anniversary of Flight" and "Fast Avro Developments—Arrow Is Dead." On this most historic occasion, history was repeating itself in Canada: fifty years after the Canadian government failed to support a fledgling new aircraft industry launched by Baldwin and McCurdy and their Canadian Aerodrome Company, it was now cancelling the Avro Arrow jet interceptor program, and in so doing, sounded the death knell to the world leadership role Canada had established in this field.

A dinner was held for McCurdy on February 21 at the Legion Hall in Baddeck. There were upwards of two hundred people in attendance, including Casey's widow, Kathleen Baldwin. Another six hundred people were unable to gain admittance due to space limitations. Norman Bethune introduced McCurdy, now seventy-three, and apologized for the length of time the town had waited to honour its most famous son. He is quoted in the February 23, 1959, edition of the *Cape Breton Post* as saying, "It is regrettable that we in Baddeck should wait for the 50th Anniversary of an event to express to you the feeling of our community. This recognition is long past due. All that Baddeck is or ever hopes to be we owe to men such as yourself, Alexander Graham Bell and Casey Baldwin."

Fisher Hudson, Baddeck lawyer, presented McCurdy with a framed scroll "In appreciation of John Alexander Douglas McCurdy," which was inscribed: "On the occasion of the Fiftieth Anniversary of the first flight of a heavier than air machine in the British Empire, whose efforts and achievements as the pilot of that first flight, as the Father of the Royal Canadian Air Force, as a valiant Public Servant of Canada and as Lieutenant-Governor of Nova Scotia has brought international fame and recognition to his native village and whose every effort and achievement has upheld and dignified that fame and distinction for which the citizens of Baddeck will be forever proud and grateful."

The *Cape Breton Post* also contained an editorial entitled "Hailing Aerial Pioneers" in which McCurdy was lauded "for his epochal flight in the valiant baby of the aeronautical age—the Silver Dart—above the ice-coated reach of Baddeck Bay." Tribute was also offered to "the inventive genius of Alexander Graham Bell without whom the pioneer Silver Dart might never have occurred." The editorial concluded with a general observation about Bell's contribution to Baddeck and to Canada, words that still ring true today.

The memory of Alexander Graham Bell rests upon the Baddeck scene with the mystic quality of a benediction. Only rarely is a community granted the distinction of being the environment of the workings of genius. This was gloriously true of Baddeck in relation to Dr. Bell. His distinction was not alone in having invented the telephone. Perhaps Dr. Bell's greatest distinction was in having been inventively a prophet, a great white-bearded patriarch, and a herald of achievements to come. It was a wonderful contribution to life, and the exhibits in the museum in Baddeck that bears his name testify to the truth of these words.

Sadly the memory of and contribution by Casey as an "aerial pioneer" were conspicuous in their absence from this editorial.

Monday, February 23, 1959, was a cold, blustery day on Baddeck Bay. Despite the weather, some three thousand people gathered on the ice to witness a reenactment of the original flight. A replica of Silver Dart, built by the RCAF and piloted by Wing Commander Paul A. Hartman, made a short flight before being caught by a gust of wind, making a hard landing, and flipping over on the ice, damaging the plane but not the pilot. The *Halifax Chronicle Herald* of February 24 made an astute observation about the event and Silver Dart.

> The mishap illustrated once again the desirability of placing a replica of the famous air machine in the Alexander Graham Bell Museum at Baddeck. RCAF personnel, who produced the Dart flown yesterday, had promised it to the National Aviation Museum in Ottawa after its demonstrations in connection with the Golden Anniversary of flight in Canada. However, a second Dart could be produced for fifteen hundred dollars they have said. This being the case, perhaps the Nova Scotia government should contract for it and at the same time persuade the Federal Government to construct an addition to the Bell Museum which would house this article of historic interest to Cape Breton and the entire nation.

This suggestion was eminently reasonable but fell on deaf ears. It would take another fifty years until finally, in 2009, following centenary celebrations around the flight of Silver Dart, that a replica was placed in the Bell Museum—fifty years during which tourists and visitors to the museum continually asked, "Where is the Silver Dart?"

The fiftieth anniversary event in Baddeck was McCurdy's last hurrah. He died in Montreal just two years later, on June 25, 1961. He was buried in

Knox Cemetery just outside Baddeck on a knoll overlooking Baddeck Bay to where Casey lies interred on Red Head. McCurdy had accomplished much during his lifetime and had left his mark as a pioneer of aviation in Canada. He was not one to heap praise on others, unlike the man who had once attempted to adopt him, Alexander Graham Bell. His best days as a "team player" were when he was associated with Baldwin, Selfridge, Curtiss, and Bell during the heyday of the incredibly successful AEA. That "experiment" and his close working relationship with the associates, and particularly Casey Baldwin, was what launched him on his career and ultimately brought him fame.

In an article narrated by McCurdy to his biographer H. Gordon Green titled "I Flew the Silver Dart" that appeared February 7, 1909, in the *Weekend Magazine* of the *Montreal Star*, McCurdy stated:

> It seems strange now that there should be so much importance attached as to who actually was the man to fly first. We were so dependent upon one another in our group that there was certainly no attempt for anyone to "get ahead" of anyone else in those days. And on this day of March 12, 1908 when we trundled the Red Wing out onto the ice of Keuka Lake near Hammondsport, it was the most natural thing in the world for Casey Baldwin to be the man in the cockpit. The rest of us had all taken the trouble to get on to skates for the occasion, but Casey, with characteristic good-natured indifference, had simply not got around to finding any, and when we got to the lake he was slipping all over the place. So he was no good anywhere else but in the plane itself. The rest of us needed firm footing to steady the wingtips and to wind up the motor.

Interestingly, photographs taken of this event don't show anyone working around Red Wing to be on skates.

To coincide with the fiftieth anniversary, a biography of J. A. D. McCurdy written by H. Gordon Green was published under the authority of the National Co-ordinating Council for the Golden Anniversary of Flight in Canada. Entitled *The Silver Dart*, it proved to be controversial and dismissive of Casey's role as a Canadian aviation pioneer.

On May 9, 1959, Daisy Fairchild penned a letter to J. H. Parkin (who later wrote the comprehensive book *Bell and Baldwin*) in which she came to the defence of Casey. Parkin had suggested that Casey had not been the inventor of the aileron, some now preferring to give that honour to Bell himself. This was but one of the many affronts to her late husband's memory that Kathleen had been subjected to. Daisy wrote the following to Parkin:

> I am very much distressed at all the feeling that has been stirred up over the book of The Silver Dart. It is too bad it had to happen. And I'm just a little bit sorry about you too—I am sorry you gave the credit for thinking of ailerons to my father. I know he suggested them. I have seen a copy of his letter suggesting them. But he was seven days by mail away from Baddeck where the other members were working together constantly and it seems to me that Casey might easily have suggested ailerons at the same time, or before father did. Mrs. Baldwin who was there at the time says that he did. The A.E.A. was such a wonderful, harmonious group that it is almost tragic to have this sort of unpleasant post-mortem.

Daisy immediately sent a copy of this letter to Kathleen with a note. "This is the best that I can do, but I want you to know what I said and what I know. And I do think that it is a darned shame that anyone should upset what was decided upon. Of course I know that there were other snags too, but I don't know what they were about and it is all in the past now anyway. I know how mother felt about Curtiss after the A.E.A. was disbanded. Douglas is the only one still living and he happened to be the one who flew the Silver Dart."

A strained relationship with McCurdy was later alluded to in a letter Kathleen received in November that year from Colonel D. H. C. "Doggie" Mason, a former Kappa Alpha fraternity brother of Casey's from college days. The recently released McCurdy biography was once again the subject, this time with specific reference to the McCurdy–Bell relationship. "John McCurdy seems to me like a man who introduces a friend to his best girl and when they fell in love with one another, bore a grudge against him for life and after. I refer to the Bells, not you, obviously.

"I have been co-operating a bit with Tony Loudon [a U of T classmate] and J. H. Parkin in correcting the damage that fool book The Silver Dart did. I hope more can be done."

Of particular concern was the subtitle of the book: "The Story of JAD McCurdy—Canada's First Pilot." This of course was completely untrue—Casey was the first Canadian to fly, almost a full year before the flight of Silver Dart in Baddeck.

Casey would never have said as much, but all the evidence, including Casey's life and life's work on Beinn Bhreagh, would seem to suggest that regarding the Bell relationship, it was Casey who became and remained the favoured son. One possible explanation might be that, in a way, they were mutually dependent. Casey needed the love and affection bestowed upon him and Kathleen by the Bells. As much as the Bells loved him as a son, so too Casey regarded Mabel and Alec as mother and father figures, *in loco parentis.*

Unlike McCurdy, Casey's relationship with the Bells had grown ever stronger in the years following the dissolution of the AEA. Casey never gave the Bells any reason to doubt his integrity and absolute devotion to them. Casey remained at Beinn Bhreagh to work alongside Dr. Bell while McCurdy ventured out on his own into the commercial world and never did return to Baddeck, except during summers later on in his life. He and Casey were similar in talent but very different in personality. Together they were a force that changed the world. As individuals they left their mark in ways that reflected their individual character traits. Both were lives well lived. McCurdy's story has become well known, attributable in part to self-aggrandizement. Casey's, due to his implacable modesty, has not.

NOT LONG AFTER CASEY'S DEATH CANADA SHOWED RENEWED INTEREST in hydrofoil technology through the auspices of a newly formed Defence Research Board. Hydrofoil research in Canada had stalled out with Casey's innovative Comox Torpedo (an expendable unmanned self-propelled smoke-laying hydrofoil craft) and the aborted self-propelled targets. Both had proven to be effective in trials, but the war ended before they were ever put into practical use.

Commander D. H. Hodgson, who had previously been involved with the Comox Torpedo development, and Philip Rhodes, who had designed some of Casey's late model hydrofoil craft, were brought together to design a hydrofoil "to reflect intended Naval demonstration purposes." The result was a forty-five-foot hydrofoil christened "Massawippi," from a lake of that name near North Hatley, Quebec, where it was built. It was then given the cryptic letters "KC-B" to honour the technology attributable to Casey (KC) Baldwin (B).

So began years of design, construction, and testing of many models with huge outlays of money, all of which ultimately gave rise to Canada's hydrofoil equivalent of the Avro Arrow—the HMCS *Bras d'Or*, named after that famed inland sea in Cape Breton that had been the testing ground for the Bell–Baldwin HD-4. The time, effort, and money spent on the building of the HMCS *Bras d'Or* (FHE 400) is a story in its own right; I will make no attempt to replicate it here. Between 1950 and 1970 residents of the Halifax, Dartmouth, and Bedford area, much the same as Baddeckers before, witnessed many different shapes and styles of hydrofoil craft roaring around Halifax Harbour, Bedford Basin, and off Chebucto Head. HMCS *Bras d'Or* was the crowning achievement of all that effort, integral to which was the foil technology developed by Casey Baldwin with the HD-4 more than a half-century earlier.

The HMCS *Bras d'Or* represented leading edge technology in hydrofoil design and construction. It was considerably more advanced in design and propulsion than HD-4, which was driven by propellers powered by two massive 350 h.p. Liberty engines. The *Bras d'Or* had two propulsion systems: one for foilborne operation and one for hullborne operation. The ship's helmsman had to be qualified as both a sea pilot and an aircraft pilot. Foilborne power was provided by a gas turbine that generated 25,500 horse power, sufficient to produce a speed of 72 mph during sea trials, which may have made it the fastest warship built to that time. The *Bras d'Or*'s speed was only slightly faster than the HD-4's 1919 world speed record of 70 mph; by comparison, HD-4 was largely self-financed and built at a fraction of the $50 million cost of the HMCS *Bras d'Or*.

During the early years in the development of what would become the HMCS *Bras d'Or*, there were occasions when liberties were taken with the history of hydrofoil development in Canada and with the dominant role Casey had played in it. On one such occasion, July 29, 1954, Casey's son Robert came to his father's defence. The *Montreal Star* newspaper had written an editorial entitled "Neither New Nor Secret," which debunked what Robert described as "the extraordinarily cheap, vulgar and inaccurate account" of hydrofoil boats that the Canadian Press put out datelined Halifax July 22, 1954, under the caption "New RCN sub-killer flies—does 70 knots." Robert, expressing his appreciation for the *Star* editorial, approached the paper offering further background information about the history of the hydrofoil, which he hoped the paper would share with the public.

> There are two aspects of this [Canadian Press article] which I would like to draw your attention to and which I respectfully suggest should be publicized:
> The hydrofoil boat was my father's invention and not Mr. Bell's. This can be supported by the following among other documents: (a) *Alexander Graham Bell* by Catherine Mackenzie published in 1928 by Houghton Mifflin—see particularly Mr. Bell's cartoon "Ye Great New Invention of F. W. B." and the context in the latter part of the book; (b) a letter written in 1915 by Mr. Bell to Admiral Dewey in which Mr. Bell states that the Hydrodome was designed and built by F. W. B. with his assistance.

Robert went on to credit Signor Enrico Forlanini for having "quite independently invented and developed a hydrofoil boat, with water propeller, with hydrofoils fixed on the horizontal…. Mr. Bell bought Forlanini's patent, and had commercial development of hydrofoils gone ahead, this would have been valuable. In a word, Mr. Bell fostered and encouraged the development of the hydrofoils but he was not the inventor."

Robert was adamant that the Canadian Press article had cheapened his father's work by referring to it as "Mighty Mouse and Buck Rogers stuff" and was misleading by suggesting that hydrofoil theory had been developed by the navy. He also felt it was unfair.

> It gives absolutely no credit to men like my father who, without reward of any kind gave their experience, knowledge and time to the development of the principle and its various applications, e.g. high speed targets as a wartime contribution (and before that). No mention is made for example of Mr. Duncan Hodgson of Montreal who worked very hard and contributed materially, both in refinement of design and financially, to the results which were ultimately achieved

with "K.C.-B," the hydrofoil boat pictured in the Press. Incidentally "K.C.-B" was Mr. Hodgson's cryptic way of getting my father's name on the boat—Casey Baldwin.

There have been so many inaccurate accounts in the press both of the early flying, the AEA and so on, and finally this last, that I am most anxious that anything you publish should be correct.

My father died in 1948. While he was alive he disdained public recognition of the fact that he was the first British subject to fly at Hammondsport, N.Y., March 12, 1908 and that he conceived and designed the ailerons which were put on White Wing, the second of the AEA machines. This as you probably know was the most important of the AEA patents. While he lived my father cared very little as to where the credit fell and while he lived that was his business, but now that he is gone I think in justice to him, all Canada should be made aware of his achievements.

Ultimately the HMCS *Bras d'Or*, like the Avro Arrow before it, was a victim of its own success—and politics. On November 2, 1971, Canada's minister of National Defence rose in the House of Commons and, in a hushed House, advised members that with the recent release of the Defence White Paper and a switch from anti-submarine warfare to sovereignty protection for Canada's armed forces, the high-speed hydrofoil ship would no longer be needed. The FHE 400 Project—and the HMCS *Bras d'Or*—was dead in the water. For the next twelve years the *Bras d'Or* languished, under cover in Halifax Harbour. As Thomas G. Lynch said in his book *The Flying 400: Canada's Hydrofoil Project*, it was "a reminder of another Canadian development chopped off before it could prove its real worth."

In a final chapter of its sad story, the HMCS *Bras d'Or* was decommissioned and stripped before being offered to various museums for retention and display. Perhaps the ship was felt to be a leper; both the Maritime Museum of the Atlantic in Halifax and the Alexander Graham Bell Museum in Baddeck declined the offer, the former evidently for lack of room, while the Bell Museum, rather incredulously, claimed that "it lay outside its mandate." In the end the Bernier Museum at Islet-sur-Mer east of Quebec City negotiated for its acquisition. On June 6, 1983, the *Bras d'Or* was unceremoniously towed on a salve barge to Islet-sur-Mer. There it sits to this day—high and dry overlooking the mighty St. Lawrence River, far removed from the province that gave birth to the technology and Casey's engineering genius, which is *Bras d'Or*'s very DNA.

IN THE LATE 1950S KATHLEEN STILL SPENT PART OF EACH YEAR AT THE bungalow at Beinn Bhreagh and winters with Robert and his family in Bedford. The summer of 1961 was the last for Daisy Fairchild at Beinn Bhreagh. She passed away the following year at her home in Florida (two years before her older sister Elsie, who died in 1964 at Bethesda, Maryland, at the age of eighty-six). Kathleen's last trip away was in March of 1963 when she spent some time visiting with her son Pat, accompanied by her sister Marion, at St. Thomas in the Virgin Islands. Her health was failing and by the fall of 1963 she was run down after what would be her last summer in the bungalow.

The following summer Bob made arrangements to put his mother up at the Telegraph House, coincidentally the very place that the Bells had forged their connection to Baddeck. She was having trouble communicating and Robert had decided against trying to find a housekeeper for her at the bungalow. At the Telegraph House she would, as Robert put it in a letter to a friend, "be well fed and comfortable." It seemed to work out well according to a July 1, 1964, letter to Bob from Keilor Bentley, superintendent of the Alexander Graham Bell Museum. "Your mother seems very well and I think the Telegraph House is working out very well. She seems quite contented. We have had her out to the house a couple of times and took her to Sydney for the film Tom Jones. I don't think she enjoyed it as much as we did....However I am sure she enjoyed the trip and dinner out....I hope during the summer we shall be able to get her out for a few drives, and being in town makes it easier for...others to see her."

One of the final communications between Robert and the Bell family was in the summer of 1965 when Gilbert Grosvenor, then in failing health, wrote to Bob while at Beinn Bhreagh. "I was delighted this morning to see you and shake your hand again at the boat landing. I was venturing on my first excursion on 'the Elsie' this summer and as it was an experiment for me, Mabel [his daughter, a pediatrician], my doctor thought we should limit the party to us two and Jim MacKillop. I hope soon to be strong enough to ask you to join us for a sail and that you will favor me with your company." The letter was signed "Uncle Bert." The family ties were still strong although the bodies were tired.

It was appropriate that their last interchange was over sailing on the Bras d'Or. Bert's sailing days were over. He died at Beinn Bhreagh on February 4, 1966, at the age of ninety. Robert only lived long enough to be present for his mother's death. Kathleen died at Bedford on Christmas Eve, December 24, 1965, at the age of eighty-one. Six months later Robert passed away at the Camp Hill Hospital in Halifax of pulmonary fibrosis. He was only fifty-three years of age.

Maureen carried on at Bedford after Bob's death. She was comforted by the three children—Casey, Sean, and Deneen. Life at Beinn Bhreagh had of course changed considerably. The family spent some time during the following summers at the bungalow and it was there that Maureen passed away on August 8, 1981, at the age of sixty-two. Within two years she was followed by Bob's brother, Patrick A. G. B. Baldwin, who died at Halifax on June 16, 1984. He was only sixty-three. Longevity was not a trait of the Baldwin family.

The year before, 1983, represented the seventy-fifth anniversary of Silver Dart. There were of course celebrations in Baddeck but lacking the fervour of the fiftieth now that J. A. D. McCurdy had passed on. Perhaps this put him on a more level playing field with his old friend Casey.

The talk of the town was less on Silver Dart than it was on the recently announced expansion of the Bell Museum in order to accommodate HD-4. The hulk of the original craft had lain neglected on the beach beside the Laboratory until the mid-1950s when, with the assistance of members of the Canadian navy, it was cut into three sections, dragged across the ice of Baddeck Bay, and stored in a temporary shelter below the museum. A new wing was added to the original building to house the original HD-4 and a full-size replica. At last, recognition was being given to Casey's hydrofoil masterpiece, and none too soon. Time and tides had taken their toll on the craft; it was testimony to the skill and workmanship of its builders at Beinn Bhreagh that it had survived the ravages of nature for so long.

Now there was but one outstanding matter—securing a full-scale replica of Silver Dart, representing the fourth "aerodrome" and the culmination of the work of the AEA. It took just over one hundred years, but following the centenary celebrations of Silver Dart held in Baddeck in 2009, a full-scale model crafted by a fine group of aviation enthusiasts in Ontario and flown on a cold winter day on Baddeck Bay was gifted to the Bell Museum. It hangs today in the museum above the original and replica of Casey's HD-4. It seems fitting that the two works in which Casey had given so much of his talent and life should be displayed together—at last.

IT WAS A BRIGHT, BRISK DAY WITH A SKIFF OF SNOW ON THE GROUND when I accompanied Casey's grandson Sean Baldwin and his wife, Deborah, to a small graveyard on Beinn Bhreagh. It is here that some of the original settlers of what Bell later bought and named Beinn Bhreagh are buried: the MacAulays and the MacRaes. It is here that the Baldwin family has come to rest. It is a beautiful slope overlooking Bras d'Or Lakes, lying at the foot of Red Head atop which rest Alexander Graham Bell, Mabel Bell, and other members of the immediate Bell family: "As close as we can be together and not related by blood." Here lie Casey, Kathleen, Betty, Robert, Maureen, and Patrick. The Baldwin family, eternally linked with the Bells and to the history Beinn Bhreagh, "beautiful mountain." It is a fitting, serene place. On a large granite stone perched just above the Baldwin headstones sits a bronze figure of a child, placed there by Casey and Kathleen following Betty's death. It is a plain but powerful symbol of the love the family had for each other and the peace they now have in their final repose.

A fitting tribute to Frederick Walker "Casey" Baldwin appeared in the August 13, 1955, edition of *Weekend Magazine*, aptly entitled "Casey Blazed the Trail—Canada's pioneer of motion, an unsung genius who split his talents between sky and water." In it writer David Willcock states,

> Casey Baldwin was an authentic Canadian genius. His years of max-imum effort were spent cheerfully and loyally in the shadow of a genius of a different type—Alexander Graham Bell, inventor of the telephone; but this fact, plus official slowness to take timely advantage of his inven-tions, plus his own dislike of self-advertisement, have prevented his name from becoming a household word.
>
> Today, in the U.S. and several European countries as well as Canada, hydrofoil boats in many shapes and sizes are being experimented with,

hailed as the greatest marine advance since steam superseded sail. Says E. L. Davies, vice-chairman of the Defence Research Board: "We are working on exactly the same principles as those laid down by Casey Baldwin." This appreciation, late though it may be, is fitting tribute to the work of a great Canadian pioneer.

The unassuming Casey would be just as gratified however if he could see the way in which Cape Breton eyes light up when his name is mentioned and how these plain folk, with their deep understanding of human qualities, speak his epitaph: "He was a real gentleman."

Frederick Walker "Casey" Baldwin—a gentleman and an authentic Canadian genius.

Acknowledgements

IT IS QUITE POSSIBLE THAT THIS BIOGRAPHY MIGHT NEVER HAVE BEEN written but for the fine gesture of Sean Baldwin in allowing me unfettered access to his grandfather's estate papers. Excerpts from these materials, particularly letters which Sean's grandmother had the foresight to retain, are woven throughout the fabric of this work. The extensive repository of Bell family papers at the Alexander Graham Bell National Historic Site in Baddeck provided a veritable treasure trove of information. My thanks to Madeline Harvey and Valerie Mason at the museum for their kind assistance and encouragement. Appreciation is extended to Hugh Muller, great-grandson of Alexander Graham Bell, for kindly permitting me access to the Fairchild Papers at the museum. Rick Leisenring, curator of the Glenn Curtiss Museum in Hammondsport, NY, kindly helped with my research during my visit to that site. While visiting Garrison Petawawa I was assisted by museologist Ainsley Christensen and given a guided tour of the garrison grounds, including the cavalry field, by Public Affairs Officer Captain Daniel Mazurek. A last word of thanks is reserved for Marianne Ward whose professionalism as my editor as well as her grasp of and interest in the subject has contributed substantially to making this an account worthy of Casey Baldwin.

Selected Bibliography

Bruce, Robert V. *Bell: Alexander Graham Bell and the Conquest of Solitude*. Ithaca, NY: Cornell University Press, 1973.

Casey, Louis S. *Curtiss: The Hammondsport Era 1907–1915*. New York: Crown Publishers Inc., 2003.

Cole, Percy T. "Canada's First Airmen." *Maclean's*, September 15, 1931.

Cross, Michael S. *Robert Baldwin: The Morning-Star of Memory*. Don Mills, ON: Oxford University Press, 2012.

Eber, Dorothy Harley. *Genius At Work: Images of Alexander Graham Bell*. Toronto: McClelland and Stewart Limited, 1982.

Ellis, Frank H. *Canada's Flying Heritage*. Toronto: University of Toronto Press, 1954.

Gray, Charlotte. *Reluctant Genius: The Passionate and Inventive Mind of Alexander Graham Bell*. Toronto: Harper Collins Publishers Ltd., 2006.

Grosvenor, Gilbert H. "The Tetrahedral Kites of Dr. Alexander Graham Bell." Pamphlet reprinted from *The Popular Science Monthly*, December, 1903.

Lynch, Thomas G. *The Flying 400: Canada's Hydrofoil Project*. Halifax: Nimbus Publishing Limited, 1983.

MacKenzie, Catherine. *Alexander Graham Bell: The Man Who Contracted Space*. Boston: Houghton Mifflin Company, 1928.

———. "How the Airplane Made Its Public Bow." *New York Times Magazine*, March 18, 1928.

McCurdy, J. A. D. "I Flew the Silver Dart." *The Telegram Weekend Magazine*, vol. 9, no. 6, February 7, 1959.

———. "The Early Days of Aviation." *Dalhousie Review*, 109–16.

Nutting, William Washburn. *Track of Typhoon*. New York: The Motor Boat Publishing Company, 1922.

———. "The HD-4, a 70- Miler with Remarkable Possibilities Developed at Dr. Graham Bell's Laboratories on the Bras d'Or Lakes." *Smithsonian Report for 1919*, 205–10.

Parkin, J. H. *Bell and Baldwin: Their Developments of Aerodromes and Hydrodromes at Baddeck, Nova Scotia*. Toronto: University of Toronto Press, 1964.

———. "Wallace Rupert Turnbull 1870–1954: Canadian Pioneer of Scientific Aviation." *Canadian Aeronautical Journal* vol. 2, nos. 1 and 2 (January and February 1956).

Roseberry, C. R. *Glenn Curtiss: Pioneer of Flight*. New York: Doubleday, 1972.

Toward, Lilias M. *Mabel Bell: Alexander's Silent Partner*. Agincourt, ON: Methuen Publications, 1984.

Warner, Charles Dudley. *Baddeck and That Sort of Thing*. Boston: James R. Osgood and Company, 1874.

Willcock, David. "Casey Blazed the Trail." *The Telegram Weekend Magazine*, vol. 5, no. 33, August 13, 1955.

Willmot, Ross. "The Day They Flew the Silver Dart." *Imperial Oil Review*, February 1959.

Image Credits

Courtesy Alexander Graham Bell Museum, Baddeck, Cape Breton:
138, 139 (top), 141 (top), 205, 206 (top left), 207 (bottom), 208 (top)

Courtesy of author:
139 (bottom), 265, 266, 268 (bottom), 269

Courtesy of Baldwin Family:
140, 142, 206 (bottom), 207 (top) 208 (bottom), 209, 264, 267, 268 (top)

Nova Scotia Archives:
141

Index